A CONVERSATION
English in Everyday Life
Third Edition

Tina Kasloff Carver

Sandra Douglas Fotinos

Longman

Publisher: *Louisa B. Hellegers*
Development Editors: *Gino Mastascusa, Barbara Barysh, Janet Johnston*
Director of Production and Manufacturing: *Aliza Greenblatt*
Executive Managing Editor: *Dominick Mosco*

Electronic Production Editors: *Janice Sivertsen, Ken Liao,*
Christine Mann
Production Assistant: *Christine Lauricella*
Electronic Art Production Supervisor: *Ken Liao*
Electronic Publishing Specialist: *Steven Greydanus*
Art Director: *Merle Krumper*
Manufacturing Manager: *Ray Keating*

Illustrator: *Andrew Lange*

CONTENTS

UNIT 1: SOCIAL COMMUNICATION 1

UNIT 2: PERSONAL LIFE　　23

UNIT 3: FAMILY LIFE

UNIT 4: COMMUNITY AND CONSUMER LIFE 63

UNIT 5: STAYING HEALTHY 87

UNIT 6: HOUSING

UNIT 7: TRANSPORTATION AND TRAVEL 127

UNIT 8: FINDING A JOB

UNIT 9: LIFE AT WORK   161

UNIT 10: IN THE NEWS 179

FOREWORD

Almost immediately after the Third Edition of **A CONVERSATION BOOK 1**—featuring a picture dictionary format with a variety of student-centered material—was published in 1994, we started receiving requests for a split edition which would spread the material in **Books 1** and **2** over a four-semester sequence with the addition of sample conversations and a grammar-for-conversation reference section. **A CONVERSATION BOOK 1** is now available in both full and split editions (1A and 1B). This new edition of **A CONVERSATION BOOK 2** is the second half of our response to the many teachers who wrote or talked to us. It is designed to cover the third and fourth semesters of the four-semester sequence and to complete the series started with **A CONVERSATION BOOK 1**, providing flexibility while sacrificing none of the content or spirit of the original.

This Third Edition of **A CONVERSATION BOOK 2** is therefore available in both full and split editions. Both editions have Conversation Springboards and Grammar for Conversation sections in the Appendix, and the Conversation Springboards as well as the discrete vocabulary are also available on audiotape cassettes. A page-for-page spiral-bound Teacher's Guide with teaching suggestions and additional activities for each lesson, plus tests for each unit, is available for each book.

The new edition remains true to the original concept of **A CONVERSATION BOOK**: that students acquire conversation skills best when their own experiences and interests are part of the conversation, and that student-centered, cross-cultural materials with extensive vocabulary and engaging illustrations focused on everyday life and the community they live in can help make the learning process a pleasure. We hope that **A CONVERSATION BOOK 2, THIRD EDITION** will help to make your conversation class a meaningful, enjoyable, and memorable learning experience for you and your students.

ACKNOWLEDGMENTS

No book is written in isolation. We could never begin to cite all the teachers we have spoken with, the programs we have observed, and the authors who have influenced the writing of this book. They all have been part of our education and developing expertise as authors. We are indebted to them all, as well as to those teachers and students who have used the last two editions of the **CONVERSATION BOOK.**

The process of getting a book from first concept to press and out to the classroom involves many people. We were fortunate to have dedicated, competent support during this time. For the Third Edition, which is the basis of the Revised Edition, our sincere appreciation goes to Nancy Baxer, our editor, who encouraged us to recreate the **CONVERSATION BOOKS** in a new way and whose vision and tenacity supported the process. Andrew Lange, our artist and the designer of the book, has continually surprised and delighted us with the creativity and humor of his work. For examples of Andrew's imagination unleashed, look at the title page of each unit. We asked Andrew to draw whatever he wanted for those pages, and every unit surpassed the ones that came before! The result is a new artistic pedagogy—a major focus of change in the Third Edition.

For the long process of shaping our pages into a complex and complete finished product, our sincere thanks and great appreciation must go first to Gino Mastascusa, our development editor, who became our partner in every way. Gino's dedication, creativity, attention to detail, diplomacy, and long hours and unflagging hard work can be seen in every page. No words of thanks are really adequate. Kudos to you, Gino. Barbara Barysh, who helped in so many ways in the Third Edition, lent a superb editorial eye to this revision by catching so many inconsistencies and suggesting ways to make the materials more easily taught. And to Janet Johnston we owe a great debt of thanks for her expertise on the Grammar for Conversation sections.

In a text such as this, production qualities are of utmost importance. The appeal to the student, the "look" as well as the accessibility, contribute to its pedagogy almost as much as the content itself. We'd like to thank the production team that worked so professionally on the book: Ken Liao and Jan Sivertsen for the beautiful interior pages, Christine Mann for her wonderful design of the Grammar for Conversation pages as well as the rest of the front and back matter, Carey Davies for his additional technical support and extraordinary revisions of the maps, Steven Greydanus for his finely tuned "tweaks" to the art, and Christine Lauricella for her excellent preparation of the tapescripts.

Our appreciation goes to Ki Chul Kang, who for years gathered information and suggestions from teachers in Asia and who helped mold this new revision. Also, Steven Golden, Stephen Troth, Gunawan Hadi, Jerene Tan—thanks for your support both now and over the years, and for your thoughtful recommendations on the Conversation Springboards. Without you, this edition would never have been created!

Our sincere thanks to Louisa Hellegers, our publisher, who responded to the requests from the field and helped mold them into reality. Because of Louisa's belief in this project, these texts have been published with the values and the timeliness they need.

Our thanks to Professor H. Douglas Brown, who guided us through the Learning Strategies for every unit and wrote the To the Student.

The list could go on and on—and fearful that we have omitted someone, we thank also Tom Dare, Mike Bennett, Gordon Johnson, Susan Fesler, Rob Walters, and Maria Angione. Also, thanks to Andy Martin and Gil Muller, as well as to H.T. Jennings, Karen Chiang, and Norman Harris, for their professional contributions and personal support.

Our own personal experiences as ESL teachers and foreign language learners underlie every page of **A CONVERSATION BOOK 2.** As learners living and working in other countries, we were reminded daily that learning a new culture and a new language is very hard work! To the many people who afforded us friendship when we were far from home, helped us deal with the complexity of everyday life in a new place, and patiently shared perceptions and languages with us, thank you. Without those experiences and without those people to guide us, **CONVERSATION BOOKS** 1 and 2 would never have been written.

A Personal Word from Tina Carver

It is rare that an *editor* is afforded the opportunity to thank *authors*, but this time the role reversal is appropriate. I have the good fortune to have been the colleague and editor for authors who professionally exhibit the highest level of excellence to which I aspire, and who, through the years, have also become very good friends. I will always value that friendship. So, to Betty Azar, Bill Bliss, Doug Brown, and Steve Molinsky, thank you—much of the improvement in this revision is the result of the many years of our professional conversations and work together.

A special note of appreciation goes to Sandra Fotinos, my master teacher of so many years ago, whose expert teaching and instincts toward students' needs have set an example to me throughout my career. Through all these years and experiences, both personal and professional, we have remained friends and colleagues.

I would like to express my appreciation to my three children, Jeffrey, Brian, and Daniel, who grew up with the **CONVERSATION BOOKS** as youngsters. Now that they are young adults, their daily help and understanding—from reading the manuscript and offering suggestions to doing the cooking, laundry, shopping, and walking the dogs—made my work easier and, indeed, possible. My mother and father, Ruth and George Kasloff, influenced my early decision-making. My mother has continued to guide and to support me in all my endeavors. Finally, I would like to express my appreciation to Gene Podhurst for his support through the long process of this revision.

A Personal Word from Sandra Fotinos-Riggs

I would like to thank my colleagues at Cochise College, Northern Essex Community College, and Harvard University for the many good years of stories and teaching techniques that we have shared, and for the constant, gentle reminder that what works once does not necessarily work again in another class or for another teacher.

For whatever I have really learned of living across cultures and languages through the delights and the hard times of everyday life, I want to say thank you to my Fotinos family-by-marriage and especially to my mother-in-law, Kleopatra Fotinou, of Kallitsaina, Messinias, who for more than thirty years was my Greek teacher and a loving, understanding friend.

Finally, thank you again to my children, Christina, Elizabeth, and Paul, who, like Tina's children, grew up with the **CONVERSATION BOOKS** and whose cross-cultural life experiences are imbedded in so many of the conversations of the books. And for the personal support without which this revision would have been impossible, thank you to Gene Riggs, my incredibly patient husband, and to Tina Carver, for twenty-five years my co-author and friend.

New York/Arizona
October 1997

TO THE TEACHER

These notes are provided as springboards for your own creativity and initiative. We have revised **A CONVERSATION BOOK 2** to incorporate new English teaching methods with those that have worked successfully through the years. Our intention is to provide a wide variety of vocabulary and student-centered learning activities for you to use within your own style and that of your intermediate ESL/EFL students.

Equally important to these activities is creating an atmosphere of shared learning in which students' differences are valued and their life experiences are appreciated. We have endeavored to create materials that will foster the idea that the class is a partnership between teacher and student and between student and student.

LEARNING STRATEGIES

The Learning Strategies box on the first page of every unit suggests three or four ways to facilitate learning for the unit. These are meant as springboards to get students thinking about the best ways for them to learn. This small section is designed to guide students to understand, appreciate, develop, and broaden their own learning styles. The learning strategies encourage critical thinking and discovery of personal learning styles, both of which are essential to becoming a self-aware and independent learner.

Read the introduction from Professor H. Douglas Brown with the class and discuss the advantages of understanding how each individual has his or her own way to learn most effectively. Then, as you begin each unit, discuss the learning strategies for that unit. Have students concentrate on the strategies throughout the unit, and have them continue to practice the strategies from previous units. Add strategies as everyone in the class becomes aware of his or her unique learning style.

Integrate the teaching of independent learning skills throughout the course. To help students organize their learning tasks, have each student bring a notebook to class and divide it into four tabbed sections: Vocabulary, Dialog Journal, Community Information, and Activities. When new words are generated in the classroom from discussion or from activities, students should record the words and information about them in the Vocabulary section of their notebooks. Write new words and sentences on the board so that students can record them accurately. The Dialog Journal section should be set aside for journal entries, both those suggested in the text and other topics you—or the students—may choose. The Community Information section should be a place to note valuable information about the students' communities and could be used as a handy reference tool outside the classroom. The Activities section should be used for any activities the students do in class or at home. There are specific suggestions in the Teacher's Edition and the student text as to how and when to use the notebook.

ILLUSTRATIONS AND ACTIVITIES

Our "mascot" appears again in **A CONVERSATION BOOK 2**. Use him as a whimsical thread throughout the course. Giving the mascot a name has proven a valuable activity at the beginning of **A CONVERSATION BOOK 1**; it should be continued in Book 2.

The illustrations serve as a visual entrance into each lesson, presenting the vocabulary and concept of the lesson in the context of real-life situations. Some of these situations are presented as problems, others as stories—with and without endings. All are designed to stimulate discussion through the first activity of each lesson: Picture Discussion.

Subsequent activities tie the lessons' illustrations to the students' lives and interests in a variety of ways, such as through role plays, story telling, problem solving, brainstorming, and memory games.

There are many kinds of activities in this book. Step-by-step instructions for leading students through each kind of activity are included on pages 262 through 272 in the Appendix.

CONVERSATION SPRINGBOARDS

Here are dialogs for teachers who hate dialogs! We have developed these springboards as conversation starters, to serve as models and inspirations for students to talk about their life experiences. These conversations are NOT listen/repeat dialogs! They are NOT designed to be used for pattern practice. They are intentionally longer and more difficult than traditional dialogs because they are meant for listening to and understanding real, whole conversations about everyday life in English. They are designed as samples of native-speaker conversations, above the level of conversation that the students could be expected to produce themselves. In fact, they replicate the situation that ESL and EFL students most often find themselves in with native speakers of English, where the conversation is fast and full of idioms, and the students have to cope with understanding and participating at their own level.

An accompanying Audio Program is available that includes all of these Conversation Springboards. Cassette icons [icon] on student-text pages signal where to use the audiotape. Each icon is footnoted with a cross-reference to the Appendix page with the corresponding Conversation Springboards; each type has a specific purpose.

- *What's the process?* Conversation Springboards are to be used before specified activities, and are intended to help students understand and talk about the purpose and process of the activity, as well as possible complications and their solutions.
- *What's happening?* Conversation Springboards tell a story happening in the present. These dialogs are intended to help students listen to conversational narratives in present time, and to retell stories chronologically, using present and present progressive tenses.
- *What happened?* Conversation Springboards relate a story that happened in the past and give students practice listening to past-time narratives and retelling the events in order, using past tenses.
- *What's next?* Conversation Springboards tell a story without an ending, or with a next step implied but not stated. They give students practice in drawing conclusions from indirect information, as well as opportunities to create their own endings in future time.
- *What's your opinion?* Conversation Springboards present a situation where preferences and opinions are expressed, and give students opportunities to agree or disagree with others' opinions, express their own opinions, and participate in a class discussion of a topic.
- *Picture Springboards* are incomplete conversations between two or more characters in one of the pictures in the lesson. At the end of each conversation are blank lines for students to complete the conversation. There is one Picture Springboard for each lesson in this book.

We suggest the following method of using the Conversation Springboards and accompanying Audio Program:

1. Listen to the entire conversation once with books open or closed, depending on the class level and your preference. (Students with very limited vocabulary may find it reassuring to preread the conversation at home before class.)

2. Listen again, breaking up the conversation by stopping the tape after every two lines. Check for understanding. Define any words or phrases that are unclear. Whenever possible, have students write down unclear words and try to guess the meaning from context.

3. Listen to the entire dialog again. (If you have listened with books closed until now, listen this time with books open.)

4. Follow up by having students either explain the process, situation, or problem, tell the story, or finish the conversation, depending on which type of Conversation Springboard you are using.

5. You may wish to have students read the conversations out loud. If you do, go slowly!

VOCABULARY

Every lesson has a vocabulary box listing some of the basic vocabulary for the lesson, plus spaces for students to add words. Following the picture dictionary format of **A CONVERSATION BOOK 1**, each word in the vocabulary box is related to the art of the lesson, and is also included for practice on the audiotape for that lesson. Words already presented in **A CONVERSATION BOOK 1** Third Edition are not repeated in Book 2. Also, as in Book 1, each new word is listed only the first time it is used in the book. Keep this in mind if you are not using the book from beginning to end. Use the Index to find the words and their original page references. Take the opportunity to teach students how and when an index can be used in their studies.

To present the vocabulary, either have students look at the picture and call out the individual words they know, or begin by having students describe the scene. Then repeat the individual words and have students follow your cue.

Modeling the words for pronunciation is useful for students so they can hear how to say the word in English in conjunction with seeing the illustration and the written word. Although it may be difficult for you to hear all the pronunciations, choral repetition will give students an opportunity to verbalize the words they are learning. Be sure students understand all the words. Sometimes native language translation is appropriate; that is your judgment call!

Have students add to the vocabulary box with words they contribute to the class discussions. By adding the students' suggested words to the list, you are reinforcing their retention and recall of introductory-level vocabulary, encouraging them to explore new vocabulary, and validating their contributions to the class. The words may be ones that students already know or ones you provide as their "living dictionary." Or they may be words that students find in their bilingual dictionaries and then look up in their English/English dictionaries. At this level, students should begin to use an English-only dictionary to understand new vocabulary, rather than relying solely on their bilingual dictionaries. Help them ease into this important study skill by actively using English/English dictionaries in class.

A vocabulary problem common to intermediate-level English language students is predicting abstract noun and adjective forms and uses of a word from its basic verb form (permit/permission/permissive/permissible; resist/resistance/resistant; succeed/success/successful.) To begin to address this problem, we have included in some of the vocabulary lists varying word forms that are difficult to predict. Discuss and explore word families with your class as you expand the vocabulary lists together. It is always important to provide a meaningful context for each variant of a word (They want to succeed./Success in this course is important to them./They are successful students.) Have students experiment with uses of word variants themselves. Although the students will make mistakes, such guesses are essential to true vocabulary acquisition. This provides a good opportunity to encourage "risk-taking" tolerance.

The Word Families charts in the Grammar for Conversation section can be helpful in clarifying the idea of word families. Encourage students to keep their own "Word Families" lists in the Vocabulary section of their notebooks. In the Teacher's Edition, we have included additional activities for vocabulary expansion, retention, and recall.

GRAMMAR FOR CONVERSATION

In the Appendix, there are grammar paradigms for each unit, charted to illustrate useful patterns, phrases, and vocabulary from the unit. The grammar charts avoid complicated terminology and are meant to be quick references and springboards for incorporating grammar into conversation so that students can say what they really mean.

The conversations in this book are not grammar-based. On the contrary, the grammar emerges from the conversations. The practical needs of conversation in everyday life form the basis of the grammar included in this text. As a result, some of the grammar is out of sequence for a standard grammar-based approach, but is in sequence for real-life conversations. Any grammar that is "above" a student's grammar level can still be accessible as a usable set phrase, and all of the charts and lists are expandable for use in classes that are interested in talking about grammar.

CONVERSATION MONITOR

Some group activities call for a conversation monitor. The first time your class uses a conversation monitor, discuss what his/her functions will be and list those functions on the board (keeping the conversation going, covering the topics, being sure everyone gets a chance to contribute to the activity, organizing the "reporting back," etc.). Make sure that all students, not just the more outspoken students, take turns being conversation monitors. Practice with a demonstration group. Take the role of the monitor with the group. Narrate the role of the monitor as you are going through the activity.

RECORDER

While the conversation monitor's role is to keep the conversation going and to allow everyone to have a turn, the recorder is charged with taking notes on the various activities so there will be concrete written notes when it comes time to "report back to the class." It may help the class for you to play the recorder role at first and write the notes on the chalkboard as a model.

PRONUNCIATION

Encourage students to try to pronounce clearly but not to worry about trying to sound like native speakers of English. The students' emphasis should always be on communication and fluency in conversation. However, when pronunciation difficulty impedes communication, it is well worth focusing on a discrete point (e.g., can vs. can't). Role plays can also help improve pronunciation: often when students are pretending to be someone else, they are less inhibited about making "foreign" sounds. Pronunciation can be improved by repeating vocabulary words at the beginning of the lesson.

CORRECTIONS

Too much correction inhibits students' ability to think coherently and works contrary to developing integrated conversation skills. Teachers should aim to strike a balance, teaching syntax as well as pronunciation at opportune times. Make a note of the errors students are making. It is usually not helpful to interrupt the flow of students' conversations, but to correct errors at the appropriate time later in class, without referring to any specific student. Use your own judgment according to the individual student and the moment.

GROUPING

All activities require some type of grouping—pairs, triads, or groups of four, five, etc. As students get to know each other, informal methods of grouping usually work best. Occasionally, let students choose a partner or set up their own groups. For other activities, depending upon the subject, deliberately mix genders, age, language groups, occupations, or opinions. Try to avoid cliques sitting together. Remind students that the only way to develop conversational fluency in English is to practice in English!

CHALKBOARD

Because many students are visual learners, use the chalkboard as much as possible to encourage students to both see and hear the vocabulary, phrases, and sentences associated with the conversation topic. Write unfamiliar words on the board for students to copy in the Vocabulary section of their notebooks.

Use the board to expand the charts or grids in the text. Construct the chart or grid while students are engaged in the activity. Utilize the board so that all students' or all groups' information can be included. Also, use the board to write all the information generated from survey activities. Encourage students to come to the board and write also. Have students be "recorders" and write words on the board from time to time. This will build confidence and self-esteem.

WRITING

For follow-up activities that will give students a chance to write about many of the conversation topics, we suggest using the black line masters in **A WRITING BOOK**, a collection of one hundred complete writing lessons for using English in everyday life. Each lesson includes individual and/or cooperative writing tasks, such as writing letters, journals, notes, invitations, and shopping lists, and filling out forms. There is a cross-reference in the back of both **A WRITING BOOK** and **A CONVERSATION BOOK 2 TEACHER'S GUIDE** that correlates lessons in the two books.

TEACHER'S GUIDE

The page-for-page **TEACHER'S GUIDE** gives Warm-up and Expansion activities for each lesson, plus step-by-step suggestions for all the activities. It also includes a conversation test and a vocabulary test for each unit, as well as suggestions for administering the tests and for using them as teaching/learning tools. In addition, it provides a checklist of topics and skills covered in A **CONVERSATION BOOK 2** and correlations to writing activities in **A WRITING BOOK**.

TO THE STUDENT

In **A CONVERSATION BOOK 2**, your teacher will help you to learn English by using it in conversations with English speakers. Your work in the classroom is very important. It will help you to practice English, to speak more clearly and fluently, and to listen to others carefully and understand what they are saying. But it is also very important for you to practice English *outside* of the classroom.

To help you to be a better learner of English, I have ten "rules" for successful language learning that I encourage you to follow. These rules suggest ways to help you become a successful learner. If you can follow this advice, you too will learn English more successfully. Here are the ten rules.

1. Don't be afraid!

Sometimes we are afraid to speak a foreign language because we think we are going to make terrible mistakes and people will laugh at us. Well, the best learners of foreign languages try not to be afraid. They make a game of learning. They are not anxious about making mistakes. And they sometimes share their fears with friends. You can do that, too, and you will then feel better about yourself.

2. Dive in!

Try to speak out! Try to say things in English! The best way to learn English is to speak it yourself. Don't worry about perfect pronunciation or grammar; other people usually will not criticize you.

3. Believe in yourself.

You have lots of strengths. You have already learned some English. You must believe that you *can* do it! Compliment your fellow learners on their efforts. Then maybe they will return the favor!

4. Develop motivation.

Why are you learning English? Make a list of your reasons for studying English. Those reasons can be your individual goals for this course. If you have your own reasons for learning English, you will have better success.

5. Cooperate with your classmates.

You are learning language in order to communicate with other people. So, practice with other people and you will be more successful. Create your own conversation group outside of class. Try out new ways to communicate in that group. And, in class, remember your classmates are your "team" members, not your opponents.

6. Get the "big" picture!

Sometimes learners look too closely at all the details of language (words, pronunciation, grammar, usage). It's OK to pay attention to those details, but it is also important to understand general meanings (the "big" picture). Maybe you don't know all the right words or grammar, but you can say things anyway. See movies in English. Read books and magazines for pleasure.

7. Don't worry if you're confused.

Learning English is a big task! Sometimes you will feel confused about all the things you have to learn in a foreign language. Try not to worry about everything all at once. Don't try to learn *all* the rules right now. Ask your teacher questions about English. And try to learn a little every day.

8. Trust your "hunches."

Sometimes people think they should analyze everything (grammar rules, word definitions) in their new language. The best learners do some analyzing, but they follow their hunches (their best guesses, their intuitions) about the new language. If they have an intuition that something sounds right, they will try it. So, the next time you feel that something is right, say it. You'll probably be right, and, if you aren't, someone will give you some feedback.

9. Make your mistakes work FOR you.

A mistake is not always "bad." We all make mistakes learning anything new. Successful learners don't worry about mistakes; they learn from them. They take note of their errors and try to correct them the next time. Some things you can do:
- Make a list of your most common mistakes.
- Select grammar points to watch for.
- Tape-record yourself and listen for errors.

10. Set your own goals.

Teachers usually set goals (assignments, homework, classwork) for you. But *you* need to set your own goals, too. You can do that by doing the following:
- Set aside a certain number of hours a week for extra study.
- Learn a certain number of words a day/week.
- Read a certain number of extra pages a day/week.

Take charge of your own learning!

Try to follow at least some of these rules for successful language learning as you work with **A CONVERSATION BOOK 2**. I am sure that you will be a more efficient learner of English, and you will feel proud of your accomplishments. Good luck!

H. Douglas Brown, Ph.D.
American Language Institute
San Francisco State University
San Francisco, CA
May 1997

UNIT 1
SOCIAL COMMUNICATION

LEARNING STRATEGIES

As you study this unit, try to develop your own ways of learning. Here are some study tips:

➤ In your notebook, make a separate section: IMPORTANT VOCABULARY. List new words you see outside the classroom. Look up the words in your dictionary. If you don't understand their meanings, ask your teacher for help.

➤ Make another section: NEW CUSTOMS. Keep a list of all the new customs you observe. Make a list of customs that confuse you. Discuss the list in class.

➤ Make another section in your notebook: JOURNAL. Write in this **Journal** section whenever you can.

➤ Listen to conversations in English and in your language outside the classroom. What do you notice? Write your observations and impressions in your **Journal**.

INTRODUCTIONS AND GREETINGS

1. formal
2. Good afternoon.
3. Goodbye./Bye.
4. Good evening.
5. Good morning.
6. Good night.
7. greet
8. Have a nice day.
9. Have you met . . . ?

10. Hello./Hi.
11. How are you?
12. I believe you've already met . . .
13. I'd like you to meet . . .
14. I'm fine, thanks.
15. informal
16. It's my pleasure to introduce . . .

17. It was nice to meet you.
18. Nice meeting you.
19. Nice to see you again.
20. See you soon.
21. So long.
22. This is . . .
23. Yes, we've met.

See Conversation Springboards on page 202.

Picture Discussion

With your class, answer the questions about the scenes.• Use the vocabulary list. • Add more words.

1. Where are the people in each scene?
2. Who are the people?
3. What are they doing?
4. What are they saying?

5. Which introductions are formal? Which are informal?
6. Have you ever been in any of these situations? What did you do? What did you say?

Group Role Play

In groups of three, choose one of the scenes. • Create a role play. • Present your role play to the class. • Have the class guess which scene you are role-playing.

Class Game: *Nice to Meet You!*

On a slip of paper, write your name. • Make a pile. • Pick a paper. • Read the name and introduce yourself to that student.

Group Brainstorm

In groups of four, choose a recorder. • Add to this list of conversation topics. • Read your list to the class. • Make a class list on the board.

the weather   _____   _____

your school   _____   _____

your family   _____   _____

your work   _____   _____

your country   _____   _____

Group Conversation

In the same groups, choose one or more topics from the list. • Have a conversation with your group using the topics. • Include everyone in the conversation.

Class List

With your class, make a list on the board of all the students' names in alphabetical order. • Alphabetize by last name. • Copy the list in your notebook.

Find Someone Who

Review the vocabulary with your teacher. • Add to this list. • Then interview your classmates and fill in the name of someone who . . .

1. has a very short name.

    _____

2. has a very long name.

    _____

3. has a nickname.

    _____

4. is named after a relative.

    _____

5. is named after a famous person.

    _____

6. has the same name in English and in his or her language.

    _____

7. _____   _____

8. _____   _____

Cross-Cultural Exchange

In groups of four, choose a conversation monitor and a recorder. • Discuss these questions. • Compare cultures when possible. • Report the results of your discussion to the class.

1. Where do you think these people are from? What are the differences in the ways they greet each other?

2. In some cultures, people shake hands when introduced. What do people do in your culture?

3. When do you make formal introductions in your culture? Demonstrate a formal introduction.

4. When do you introduce people informally? Demonstrate an informal introduction.

5. What are common ways to say goodbye in your language? Are they similar to English?

6. What are common names and nicknames in your country?

7. What are some customs in naming babies and giving nicknames in your culture?

8. What words and customs for introductions or greetings in your culture are similar to those in English?

MORE ABOUT YOU

1. career advancement
2. classmate
3. communicate
4. communication
5. converse
6. educated
7. education
8. employment
9. explain
10. explanation
11. get acquainted
12. medical condition
13. medical consultation
14. purpose
15. qualification
16. qualified
17. qualify
18. reason
19. small talk
20. sociable
21. socialize
22. telephone skills
_____
_____
_____
_____
_____
_____
_____

Picture Discussion

With your class, answer the questions about the scenes. • Use the vocabulary list. • Add more words.

1. How does this classroom look like your classroom?
2. Where do you think these students are from?
3. What languages do you think they speak?
4. What reasons do these students have for studying English?
5. What are some other reasons?
6. Draw two more reasons in the empty bubbles.

See Conversation Springboards on page 202.

Class Survey

With your class, add to this list of reasons for studying English. • Write the list on the board. • Check your three most important reasons for studying English. • Compare your reasons with your classmates. • Circle the most common reason in your class.

Reasons for Studying English

- ☐ to talk with neighbors
- ☐ to study in more classes
- ☐ to get a job
- ☐ to talk with the doctor
- ☐ to talk on the telephone
- ☐ to order in a restaurant
- ☐ to travel
- ☐ to help my family
- ☐ to go to college

- ☐ _____
- ☐ _____
- ☐ _____
- ☐ _____
- ☐ _____
- ☐ _____
- ☐ _____
- ☐ _____

Partner Interview

Partner's Name _____

Ask a partner these questions. • Then report your partner's responses to the class.

1. What is your name?
2. Where are you from?
3. Where do you live?
4. What was the first language you learned?
5. Do you speak any other languages? Which ones?

6. What are the most important reasons you are studying English?
7. Where did you study English before?
8. Where do you work?
9. How do you come to class?

Group Conversation

In groups of four, fill in the chart. • Then discuss your responses.

Student's Name	Hometown	Languages	Reasons for Studying English
1.			
2.			
3.			
4.			

Class Game: *Guess Who!*

On a slip of paper, write where you are from, what languages you speak, and why you are studying English. • Make a pile. • Pick a paper. • Read it to the class. • Guess who wrote it!

8

Conversation Squares

In groups of three, fill in the chart. • First write your own information. • Then ask your partners for their information and write their answers. • Compare information with another group.

	You	**Partner 1**	**Partner 2**
Student's Name			

Address:
    Street
    City
    State
    ZIP Code			

Telephone Number			

Group Brainstorm

In the same groups, choose a recorder. • List situations where people have to give their name, address, and telephone number. • Read your list to the class. • Make a class list on the board.

Find Someone Who

Review the vocabulary with your teacher. • Add to this list. • Then interview your classmates and fill in the name of someone who . . .

1. lives near you.   _____

2. lives far away from your school.   _____

3. comes to class with a friend.   _____

4. speaks three languages.   _____

5. is studying English for work.   _____

6. _____   _____

7. _____   _____

Group Vocabulary Challenge

In groups of six, list everyone's name in the class. • Write something you know about each person. • Work fast! • Read your list to the class. • Which group has the longest list? • Make a class list on the board.

CONGRATULATIONS

1. All the best!
2. congratulate
3. deserve
4. event
5. Good luck!
6. graduate
7. graduation
8. Lots of luck!
9. lucky
10. marvelous
11. move in
12. new apartment
13. new baby
14. occasion
15. promotion
16. raise
17. special
18. twins
19. unpack
20. winning ticket
21. wonderful

_____

_____

_____

_____

_____

Picture Discussion

With your class, answer the questions about the scenes. • Use the vocabulary list. • Add more words.

1. What is happening in each scene?
2. How many different reasons for congratulations are in these scenes?
3. How will each event change these people's lives?
4. What did the man and woman buy for their friends' new apartment?
5. On what other occasions would you give congratulations? Make a list on the board.

Group Role Play

In groups of four, choose one of the scenes. • Create a role play. • Present your role play to the class.

See Conversation Springboards on pages 202 and 203.

Partner Activity: *Ask Aunt Betty*

Partner's Name _____

With a partner, read and discuss this letter. • Together, write a response from Aunt Betty, giving advice to Perplexed in Pittsburgh. • Read your letter to the class.

ASK AUNT BETTY

Dear Aunt Betty:

Last week, my next-door neighbors had a baby boy—their first child. They are very nice people, and they have always been very kind to me and my family.

I would like to visit them and offer my congratulations, but, in my culture, a mother and baby cannot have any visitors for thirty days. I don't know what the custom is here in the U.S. What should I do?

Perplexed in Pittsburgh

Cross-Cultural Exchange

In groups of four, choose a conversation monitor and a recorder. • Discuss these questions. • Compare cultures when possible. • Report the results of your discussion to the class.

1. How do you say "congratulations" in your language? Teach your group to say it.

2. On what special occasions do people congratulate each other in your culture?

3. On what occasions do people give presents to each other in your culture? What do they give?

APOLOGIES

1. apologize
2. Are you all right?
3. Are you OK?
4. bump into
5. by accident
6. Don't worry.
7. Excuse me.
8. Excuse me for . . .
9. I'm sorry.
10. I'm sorry I'm late.
11. intentional
12. mean to
13. No problem.
14. nuisance
15. on purpose
16. packed
17. Pardon me.
18. push
19. shove
20. tardiness
21. tardy
22. That's all right.
23. That's OK.
24. unintentional
_____
_____
_____
_____
_____
_____

Picture Discussion

With your class, answer the questions about the scenes. • Use the vocabulary list. • Add more words.

1. What is happening in each scene?
2. What apologies are necessary for each situation? Why?

3. Have you ever been in a situation like any of these? What did you do?
4. What other situations require an apology? Make a list on the board.

Partner Problem Solving

Partner's Name _____

With a partner, decide what problems are in the scenes. • Then decide on solutions. • Compare your solutions with another pair. • Choose the best ones. • Report your results to the class.

See Conversation Springboards on page 203.

Partner Role Play

Partner's Name _____

With a partner, choose one of the scenes. • Create a role play. • Present your role play to the class.

Group Vocabulary Challenge

In groups of four, list as many occasions to apologize as you can. • Work fast! • Read your list to the class. • Which group has the longest list? • Make a class list on the board.

Find Someone Who

Review the vocabulary with your teacher. • Add to this list. • Then interview your classmates and fill in the name of someone who . . .

1. has apologized for being late.

    _____

2. has apologized for bumping into someone.

    _____

3. has apologized to a classmate.

    _____

4. has apologized to a neighbor.

    _____

5. _____

    _____

6. _____

    _____

Partner Game: *What Do You Remember?* Partner's Name _____

With a partner, look at one of the scenes. • Remember as much as you can. • Then close your books. • Describe the scene with your partner. • List everything. • Open your books and look at the scene. • What did you forget?

GOOD AND BAD MANNERS

1. block
2. considerate
3. consideration
4. cut in line
5. delay
6. disrupt
7. double-park
8. get away with
9. impatient
10. impolite
11. inconsiderate
12. interrupt
13. loud
14. oblivious
15. offer
16. patient
17. pay attention
18. polite
19. quiet
20. share
21. thank
22. Thanks.
23. thoughtful
24. thoughtless

14

See Conversation Springboards on page 203.

Picture Discussion

With your class, answer the questions about the scenes. • Use the vocabulary list. • Add more words.

1. Which students should offer to share their food? When is it polite to share?

2. What will the people say to the woman cutting in line? Will she get away with it?

3. Why is it inconsiderate to double-park? What should the woman do?

4. Why is the man holding the door open? How is the girl being thoughtless?

5. Why is it bad manners to be late?

6. Why aren't the students paying attention to the teacher? What are they doing?

Class Game: *What Can I Say?*

Choose one of these situations. • Decide what to say. • Write it on a slip of paper. • Make a pile. • Pick a paper. • Guess what the situation is.

1. You are watching a movie, and the person sitting next to you is talking to a friend. You cannot hear the movie.

2. You are on a crowded train, and your stop is next. You need to get to the door before it closes.

3. You are waiting in line at the bank during your lunch hour. Someone cuts in line in front of you.

4. A salesperson calls your home during dinner time. This is the third call from the same company this evening.

Group Role Play

In groups of four, choose one of the situations above. • Create a role play. • Present your role play to the class.

Speech

Make a speech about good and bad manners in your culture.

HELPING EACH OTHER

1. assist
2. assistance
3. Can I help?
4. correct change
5. Could you change a . . . ?
6. Could you please . . . ?
7. Could you please help me?

8. decline
9. gratitude
10. hitchhike
11. hitchhiker
12. in distress
13. invitation
14. invite
15. lend/give a hand
16. May I have . . . ?

17. May I help you? _____
18. Need help? _____
19. Please help me. _____
20. Please pass the . . . _____
21. refuse a ride _____
22. uncomfortable _____
23. Would you like . . . ? _____
24. Would you mind . . . ? _____
_____

16

See Conversation Springboards on page 203.

Picture Discussion

With your class, answer the questions about the scenes. • Use the vocabulary list. • Add more words.

1. What is happening in each scene?
2. Which people need help? What are they thinking? What are they doing?
3. Which people are offering help? What are they thinking? What are they doing?
4. What would you do in each of these situations?

Partner Role Play   Partner's Name _____

With a partner, choose one of the scenes. • Create a role play. • Present your role play to the class. • Have the class guess which scene you are role-playing.

Group Brainstorm

In groups of four, choose a recorder. • List situations where people ask for help and offer help. • Read your list to the class. • Make a class list on the board.

Cross-Cultural Exchange

In the same groups, choose a conversation monitor and a recorder. • Discuss these questions. • Compare cultures when possible. • Report the results of your discussion to the class.

1. When do people use "please" and "thank you" in your language?

2. Have you had any problems with polite expressions in English? Tell the class.

3. When would people in your culture be uncomfortable asking for help?

Class List

With your class, say "please" and "thank you" in as many different languages as you can. • Make a class list on the board.

Please	Thank you

School Survey

Ask three people in your school these questions. • *Fill in the chart and report their answers to the class.*

Would you...	Yes	No	Maybe, if...
pick up a hitchhiker?			
help a stranger in distress?			
give work to someone who knocks at your door?			
contribute to a charity by telephone?			
help a classmate with English homework?			
give money to a friend in need?			

EXPRESSING SYMPATHY

1. burglarize	9. extend sympathy	17. saddened
2. burglary	10. funeral	18. sadness
3. car theft	11. graveside	19. sorrow
4. comfort	12. grief	20. state of shock
5. condolences	13. in mourning	21. stolen
6. console	14. in time of need	22. sympathize
7. crisis	15. loss	23. unhappy
8. death	16. mourn	24. upset

Picture Discussion

With your class, answer the questions about the scenes. • Use the vocabulary list. • Add more words.

1. What is happening in each scene?

2. How do the people feel?

3. What are they saying? What are they doing?

4. How would you extend sympathy at each occasion?

5. On what other occasions would you express your sympathy? Draw one example in the blank box.

See Conversation Springboards on page 204.

Partner Role Play

Partner's Name _____

With a partner, choose one of the situations or create your own. • Role-play a telephone call to express your sympathy. • Present your role play to the class.

Partner Activity: Ask Aunt Betty

Partner's Name _____

With a partner, read and discuss this letter. • Together, write a response from Aunt Betty, giving advice to Mixed-up in Minneapolis. • Read your letter to the class.

ASK AUNT BETTY

Dear Aunt Betty:

Last week my teacher's mother died. The substitute teacher brought in a "sympathy" card for the class to sign. I sent the same card to an American friend several weeks ago because I appreciated her friendship. Since "simpático" in Spanish means "nice" and "friendly," I thought it was appropriate. But the substitute teacher told us that people send sympathy cards to say they are sorry when someone has died!!! What should I do?

Mixed-up in Minneapolis

Cross-Cultural Exchange

In groups of four, choose a conversation monitor and a recorder. • Discuss these questions. • Compare cultures when possible. • Report the results of your discussion to the class.

1. What are the customs of expressing sympathy in your culture?

2. What are the mourning customs?

3. What are the customs to express your friendship in time of need?

4. How do customs of sympathy and mourning in the U.S. compare to those in your country?

REVIEW

Group Brainstorm

In groups of four, choose a recorder. • Decide when you would use these expressions. • Read your ideas to the class. • Make a class list on the board.

◆ **Thanks.**   ◆ **Congratulations!**   ◆ **I'm sorry.**   ◆ **Excuse me.**   ◆ **Good luck!**

Partner Role Play   Partner's Name _____

With a partner, create a conversation between two new students. • They are getting acquainted at a party. • Present your role play to the class.

Find Someone Who

Add to this list. • Then interview your classmates and fill in the name of someone who . . .

1. knows how to say "thank you" in three languages.   _____

2. has made a new friend.   _____

3. had to apologize this week.   _____

4. has picked up a hitchhiker recently.   _____

5. _____   _____

6. _____   _____

Dialog Journal   Partner's Name _____

*Write a **Journal** entry about your feelings on the first day of class. • Then read your entry to a partner. • Ask questions about your partner's entry.*

UNIT 2
PERSONAL LIFE

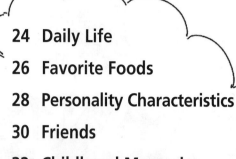

LEARNING STRATEGIES

Every day during this unit, write a THINGS TO DO list for yourself. At the end of each day, check all the things you actually did that day.

Among the "things to do," write down some *strategies* you will practice. For example, choose two of these learning strategies to practice every day.

➤ Watch English-language TV one hour each day.

➤ Learn five new English words each day.

➤ Talk with one person in English each day *outside* of class.

➤ Ask my teacher about anything I don't understand.

DAILY LIFE

1. asleep
2. awake
3. clean-shaven
4. cram
5. difference
6. disorganized
7. frantic
8. groggy
9. hurry

10. last minute
11. mess
12. messy
13. neat
14. organized
15. prepared
16. procrastinate
17. procrastination
18. put off

19. ready
20. roommate
21. rush
22. self-control
23. self-discipline
24. sloppy
25. unprepared
26. unshaven
27. untidy

_____
_____
_____
_____
_____
_____
_____
_____

See Conversation Springboards on page 204.

Picture Discussion

With your class, answer the questions about the picture story. • Use the vocabulary list. • Add more words.

1. What is happening in the story?
2. Which roommate seems to have more fun?
3. Which roommate gets to class on time? Why?
4. Which roommate is more prepared in class? Why?
5. Which student is sometimes in a rush? Why?
6. Which student is more like you? How?

Dialog Journal

Partner's Name _____

*Write a **Journal** entry about your daily life. • Then read and explain your entry to a partner. • Ask questions about your partner's entry.*

Superlatives

In groups of five, choose a recorder. • Answer these questions. • Then report your answers to the class. • Decide which students in the class fit the questions best.

1. Who went to bed latest last night? How late?
2. Who got up earliest this morning? How early?
3. Who ate the biggest breakfast today? How big?
4. Who procrastinated the most yesterday? What happened?
5. Who lives the farthest away from school? How far?
6. Who had the worst day yesterday? How bad? What happened?
7. Who had the best day yesterday? How good? What happened?

Find Someone Who

Review the vocabulary with your teacher. • Add to this list. • Then interview your classmates and fill in the name of someone who . . .

1. is usually well organized. _____
2. puts off difficult work. _____
3. wakes up to an alarm clock. _____
4. crams for tests. _____
5. _____ _____
6. _____ _____

Group Vocabulary Challenge

In groups of three, list your daily activities. • Work fast! • Read your list to the class. • Which group has the longest list? • Make a class list on the board.

FAVORITE FOODS

1. appetizer/starter
2. appetizing
3. bitter
4. bland
5. crisp
6. crunchy
7. delicious
8. filling
9. finger food
10. juicy
11. light
12. rich
13. salty
14. smooth
15. sour
16. spicy
17. sweet
18. tangy
19. taste
20. tasty
21. unappetizing

_____
_____
_____
_____
_____

Picture Discussion

With your class, answer the questions about the scenes. • Use the vocabulary list. • Add more words.

1. What do these people like to eat and drink?
2. What are they talking about?
3. Which foods are spicy? sour? sweet? salty?
4. Which foods are crunchy? crisp? smooth? juicy?
5. Which foods are filling? light? rich?
6. Which foods look appetizing to you? Why?

See Conversation Springboards on page 204.

Group Vocabulary Challenge

In groups of four, list all the foods you know. • Work fast! • Which group has the longest list? • Make a class list on the board.

Partner Interview

Partner's Name _____

Ask a partner these questions. • Then report your partner's responses to another pair of students.

1. Do you ever eat in a restaurant? What is your favorite restaurant? Where is it? What do you usually order?

2. Do you like to cook? What do you cook best?

3. Do you ever eat junk food or fast food? What kinds?

4. What kinds of food don't you ever eat? Why?

5. What are your favorite foods and beverages?

6. Are they good for you or bad for you?

Class Game: *Guess Who!*

On a slip of paper, write your favorite food. • Make a pile. • Pick a paper. • Read it to the class. • Guess who wrote it!

Group Role Play

In groups of three, create a "Favorite Foods Menu." • Include everyone's favorite food and beverage. • Create a role play, ordering food at a restaurant. • Present your role play to another group.

Favorite Foods Menu

Breakfast
_____
_____
_____

Appetizers
_____
_____
_____

Lunch
_____
_____
_____

Desserts
_____
_____
_____

Dinner
_____
_____
_____

Beverages
_____
_____
_____

PERSONALITY CHARACTERISTICS

1. affectionate
2. aggressive
3. cheerful
4. coy
5. determined
6. energetic
7. extroverted
8. flirtatious

9. fun-loving
10. gentle
11. inquisitive
12. introverted
13. lively
14. meditative
15. melancholy
16. moody

17. optimistic
18. outgoing
19. pessimistic
20. physical
21. serious
22. shy
23. talkative
24. withdrawn

_____
_____
_____
_____
_____

See Conversation Springboards on pages 204 and 205.

Picture Discussion

With your class, answer the questions about the scene. • Use the vocabulary list. • Add more words.

1. What are the people in this scene doing?
2. What personality characteristics do you see in each person?
3. What other personality characteristics can you think of? Make a list on the board.
4. Which person in this scene is most like you?

Group Questions

In groups of three, write as many questions as you can about the scene. • Ask another group your questions. • Then answer their questions.

Partner Game: *What Do You Remember?* Partner's Name _____

With a partner, look at the scene again. • Remember as much as you can. • Close your books. • Describe the scene with your partner. • List everything you can remember. • Open your books and look at the scene. • What did you forget?

Who Else?

List four personality characteristics that fit you. • Then find classmates who fit at least one of these characteristics. • Write their names in the chart and report your findings to the class.

	Personality Characteristic	**Student's Name**
1.		1. _____ 2. _____ 3. _____
2.		1. _____ 2. _____ 3. _____
3.		1. _____ 2. _____ 3. _____
4.		1. _____ 2. _____ 3. _____

Class Game: *Guess Who!*

Draw a picture of yourself. • On the back of the paper, describe your personality. • Do not include your name. • Make a pile. • Pick a paper. • Read the description to the class. • Guess who it is! • Now show the picture to the class.

FRIENDS

1. best friend	9. irresponsible	17. selfish *egoista* _____
2. carefree *sincarida*	10. jealous	18. sensitive _____
3. disloyal *desleal*	11. kind	19. sincere _____
4. envious	12. loyal	20. supportive _____
5. friendship	13. phony *no-autentico*	21. true friend _____
6. generous	14. reliable	22. trustworthy _____
7. insensitive	15. responsible	23. two-faced _____
8. insincere	16. self-centered	24. unreliable _____

Picture Discussion

With your class, answer the questions about the three picture stories. • Use the vocabulary list. • Add more words.

1. What is happening in these stories?

2. What is a true friend? Which of these stories shows a true friend?

3. What kinds of friends do the other stories show?

4. Do you think the man with the car will lend it to his friend again? Will they remain friends? Why or why not?

30

See Conversation Springboards on page 205.

Partner Activity: *Ask Aunt Betty*

Partner's Name _____

With a partner, read and discuss this letter. • Together, write a reply from Aunt Betty, giving advice to Troubled in Toronto. • Read your letter to the class.

Group Role Play

In groups of four, choose one of the picture stories. • Make up an ending for the story. • Create a role play. • Present your role play to the class.

ASK AUNT BETTY

Dear Aunt Betty:

I am a single mother with two small children. I work full time, and my neighbor Linda baby-sits for my daughters. Linda is a single mother like me. Lately, I have been feeling frustrated because every day when I pick up my girls at Linda's apartment, Linda comes over to my place with her two sons. She stays so long that I end up feeding everybody supper. How can I get time alone with my daughters without hurting Linda's feelings?

Troubled in Toronto

CHILDHOOD MEMORIES

1. adventure
2. adventurous
3. curiosity
4. curious
5. dangerous
6. experiment
7. fairy tale
8. fearless
9. imaginary
10. imagination
11. light/strike a match
12. memorable
13. nostalgia
14. nostalgic
15. play with dolls
16. play with fire
17. pretend
18. read aloud
19. remember
20. reminisce
21. rocking chair
22. sword fight
23. tea party
24. used to

Picture Discussion

With your class, answer the questions about the scenes. • Use the vocabulary list. • Add more words.

1. What are these students doing?
2. What is happening in each childhood memory?
3. Which of these childhood activities are dangerous?
4. Did you do any of these things in your childhood? Which ones?

What's the Story?

In groups of three, choose a conversation monitor and a recorder. • Then choose one of the students in the scenes. • Write a story about the student's childhood memory. • Everyone in the group should contribute at least two sentences. • Read your story to the class.

See Conversation Springboards on page 205.

Group Brainstorm

In the same groups, choose a recorder. • List as many childhood fears as you can. • Read your list to the class. • Make a class list on the board.

Speech

Tell the class about your favorite childhood possession. • Your speech should include:

◆ what it looked like

◆ what you did with it

◆ why it was so important to you

◆ how old you were at the time

Dialog Journal   Partner's Name _____

*Write a **Journal** entry about either your best, your worst, or your earliest childhood memory. • Then read your entry to a partner. • Ask questions about your partner's entry.*

CULTURAL IDENTITY

1. architecture	9. custom	17. religious	_____
2. belief	10. fur coat	18. reserved	_____
3. believe in	11. heritage	19. show affection	_____
4. body language	12. history	20. tradition	_____
5. cathedral	13. palm tree	21. traditional	_____
6. chopsticks	14. physical contact	22. tropical	_____
7. climate	15. plaza/square	23. tropics	
8. culture	16. religion	24. wintry	_____

See Conversation Springboards on page 206.

Picture Discussion

With your class, answer the questions about the scenes. • Use the vocabulary list. • Add more words.

1. Where do you think each student is from?
2. Describe their memories of home.
3. What differences are there in climate? in clothing? in architecture?
4. What traditional religion, food, music, and games could be part of each student's heritage?

Find Someone Who

Review the vocabulary with your teacher. • Add to this list. • Then interview your classmates and fill in the name of someone who . . .

1. enjoys meeting people from different cultures. _____

2. likes to travel to foreign countries. _____

3. loves to speak foreign languages. _____

4. is embarrassed speaking a foreign language. _____

_____

5. has had an unusual experience in a foreign country. _____

6. _____ _____

7. _____ _____

Cross Cultural Exchange

In groups of four, choose a conversation monitor and a recorder. • Discuss these questions. • Compare cultures when possible. • Report the results of your discussion to the class.

1. What traditions are part of your cultural heritage?
2. What climate is part of your cultural heritage? What clothing? food? music? games? architecture? religion?
3. How do people show affection in your culture?
4. When do people make a lot of noise in your culture? When are they quiet?
5. If you have been in a foreign country, which differences did you enjoy the most?
6. Which differences made you uncomfortable?

Speech

Bring something from your own cultural heritage to class and tell the class about it.

LIFE STORY

1. amazing
2. amusing
3. awful *terrible*
4. bizarre
5. delightful
6. dramatic
7. dreadful
8. embarrassing
9. fantastic
10. frightening
11. heart-rending
12. heartwarming
13. hysterical
14. incredible
15. painful
16. react
17. reaction
18. strange
19. suspenseful
20. terrible
21. true story
22. unbelievable
23. unusual
24. wild

_____
_____
_____
_____
_____
_____

Picture Discussion

With your class, answer the questions about the scene. • Use the vocabulary list. • Add more words.

1. How are the students reacting to each of their classmates' stories?

2. From the students' reactions, what can you guess about each story?

3. What are some possible subjects of each story? Make lists on the board.

4. What are the students thinking in each group?

See Conversation Springboards on page 206.

What's the Story?

In groups of three, choose a conversation monitor and a recorder. • Tell one of the stories from this scene. • Everyone in the group should contribute at least two sentences. • Read your story to another group.

Conversation Squares

In the same groups, fill in the chart. • First write your own answers. • Then ask your partners the questions and write their answers. • Compare answers with another group.

	You	Partner 1	Partner 2
Student's Name			
Where were you one year ago?			
Where were you five years ago?			
Where were you ten years ago?			

Partner Interview   Partner's Name _____

Tell a partner about good and bad experiences from your life. • Ask questions about your partner's stories.

FUTURE PLANS, HOPES, AND DREAMS

1. accomplish	9. dreamer	17. plan
2. accomplishment	10. fantasize	18. realistic
3. ambition	11. fantasy	19. succeed
4. ambitious	12. goal in life	20. success
5. daydream	13. hope	21. successful
6. daydreamer	14. imagine	22. unrealistic
7. determination	15. objective	23. visualize
8. dream	16. persevere	24. wonder

See Conversation Springboards on page 206.

Picture Discussion

With your class, look at the scenes. • Then answer the questions. • Use the vocabulary list. • Add more words.

1. What is each student daydreaming about?
2. Which daydreams are realistic? Are any unrealistic? Why?
3. What do the students need to do to make their dreams come true?
4. Will their dreams come true? Why or why not?

Class Game: *Guess Who!*

On a slip of paper, write your favorite daydream. • Make a pile. • Pick a paper. • Read it to the class. • Guess who wrote it!

Partner Interview

Partner's Name _____

Ask a partner these questions. • Then report your partner's responses to another pair of students.

1. What are your goals for this year?
2. What do you plan to accomplish next year?
3. What do you hope to accomplish in the next five years?
4. What do you dream of accomplishing sometime in the future?

Who Else?

Partner's Name _____

List four things you would like to do in the future. • Then find classmates who would like to do the same things. • Write their names in the chart and report your findings to the class.

	Things You Would Like to Do	Student's Name
1.		1. _____ 2. _____ 3. _____
2.		1. _____ 2. _____ 3. _____
3.		1. _____ 2. _____ 3. _____
4.		1. _____ 2. _____ 3. _____

LEARNING STYLES

1. CD-ROM
2. collaborate
3. discuss
4. discussion
5. field trip
6. group work
7. headset
8. independent study
9. instruct
10. instruction
11. Internet
12. memorize
13. method
14. multimedia
15. oral
16. practice
17. prefer
18. print out
19. research
20. review
21. take notes
22. technology
23. tutor
24. tutorial
25. visual
26. visual aid
27. word processor

Picture Discussion

With your class, answer the questions about the scenes. • Use the vocabulary list. • Add more words.

1. What methods of learning are the students using in these scenes?

2. What are the advantages of each different way of studying?

3. Which methods involve new technologies? How are these technologies helpful?

4. What other ways of studying and learning are there? Make a list on the board.

5. Which of these learning methods have you used? Which do you prefer?

See Conversation Springboards on pages 206 and 207.

Partner Interview

Partner's Name _____

Ask a partner these questions. • Then report your partner's responses to another pair of students.

1. What subjects do you enjoy studying most?
2. When do you prefer to study?
3. Where is your favorite place to study?
4. What problems do you have studying?

Conversation Squares

In groups of three, fill in the chart. • First write your own answers. • Then ask your partners the question and write their answers. • Discuss your answers with the class.

Which language learning skills are easier or harder for you? Number each skill from 1 (easiest) to 8 (hardest).			
	You	**Partner 1**	**Partner 2**
Student's Name			
Grammar			
Vocabulary			
Listening			
Speaking			
Pronunciation			
Reading			
Writing			
Non-verbal (Gestures)			

REVIEW

Group Review

In groups of three, review what you remember about each other from this unit. • Fill in the chart.

	Partner 1	Partner 2	Partner 3
1. Student's Name			
2. Favorite Food			
3. Personality Profile			
4. Childhood Memory			
5. Best or Worst Life Experience			
6. Future Plans			
7. Favorite Place to Study			

Group Questions

In the same groups, write as many personal information questions as you can. • Combine your questions with another group. • Read your combined list to the class. • How many different questions did your class write? • Make a class list on the board.

Partner Interview   Partner's Name _____

With a partner, practice asking and answering all the questions from your class list.

Partner Vocabulary Challenge   Partner's Name _____

With a partner, list all the qualities you like and don't like in a friend. • Work fast! • Read your list to the class. • Which pair has the longest list? • Make a class list on the board.

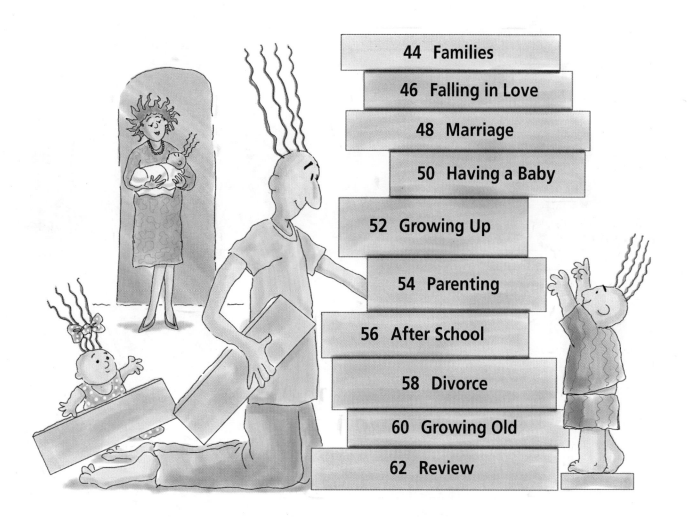

LEARNING STRATEGIES

➤ In the **Activities** section of your notebook, write everything you can about your family.

➤ In the **Journal** section of your notebook, write about a member of your family. Write about a different family member every day.

➤ In the **Activities** section of your notebook, list questions to ask about someone's family. Ask two classmates a different question every day.

FAMILIES

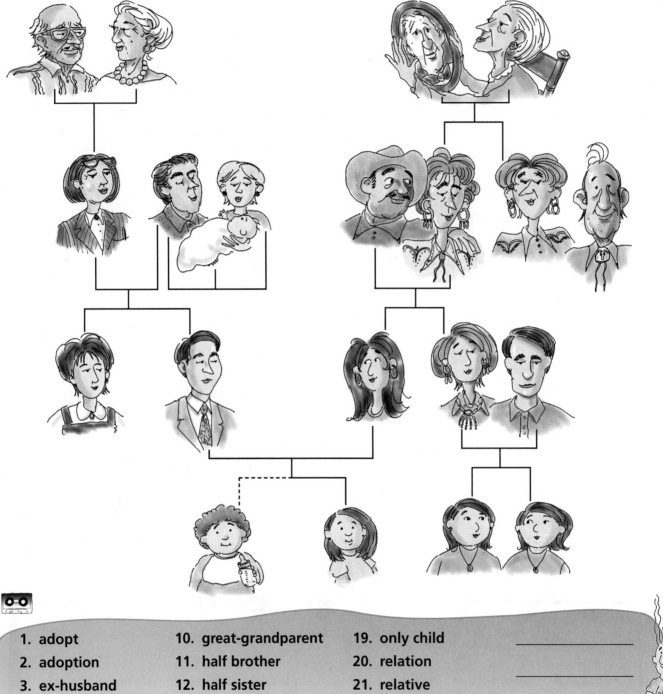

1. adopt	10. great-grandparent	19. only child
2. adoption	11. half brother	20. relation
3. ex-husband	12. half sister	21. relative
4. extended family	13. identical	22. remarry
5. ex-wife	14. in common	23. resemblance
6. family trait	15. look like	24. resemble
7. family tree	16. marriage	25. second marriage
8. generation	17. member	26. similar
9. great-grandchild	18. nuclear family	27. similarity

See Conversation Springboards on page 207.

Picture Discussion

With your class, answer the questions about the family tree. • Use the vocabulary list. • Add more words.

1. What are good names for all the members of these families? Give everyone a name.

2. Which people are married? remarried? widowed? divorced? single?

3. Which ones are twins? half brother? half sister? adopted?

4. Which family members resemble each other? What do they have in common?

5. What are the nuclear families in the family tree? What are the extended families?

6. What are all the different relationships in this family tree? Make a list on the board.

What's the Story?

In groups of three, choose a recorder. • Take turns telling the story of one of the people in the family tree. • Report your group's best stories to the class.

Find Someone Who

Review the vocabulary with your teacher. • Add to this list. • Then interview your classmates and fill in the name of someone who . . .

1. comes from a large family.   _____

2. has twins in the family.   _____

3. has lived with a grandparent.   _____

4. remembers a great-grandparent.   _____

5. is an only child.   _____

6. _____   _____

7. _____   _____

Partner Interview   Partner's Name _____

Ask a partner these questions. • Then tell another pair of students about your partner.

1. Who is the oldest person in your family? The youngest?
2. Whom do you have the closest relationship with in your family?
3. Whom do you resemble in your family? Describe him or her.
4. What important things did you learn from your parents?
5. Describe your family. What is special about it?
6. What is your best family memory?

FALLING IN LOVE

1. attract	10. engagement	19. infatuation
2. attraction	11. fiancé	20. in love
3. boyfriend	12. fiancée	21. newlyweds
4. bride	13. get engaged	22. proposal
5. ceremony	14. get married	23. propose
6. compatible	15. girlfriend	24. relationship
7. couple	16. go out	25. romantic
8. courtship	17. groom	26. true love
9. date	18. honeymoon	27. wedding

Picture Discussion

With your class, answer the questions about the picture story. • Use the vocabulary list. • Add more words.

1. What is happening in each scene?
2. What makes this couple's first date very romantic? What is your idea of a romantic first date?
3. What does the young woman's family think of her boyfriend? Is that important? Why or why not?

4. Is this a long or a short courtship? Which do you prefer? Why?
5. Is this romantic infatuation or true love? Will this couple have a compatible relationship?

46

See Conversation Springboards on page 207.

5

6

7

8

What's the Story?

Partner's Name _____

With a partner, give names to the people in the story. • Decide where they live, and why they fell in love with each other. • Then decide how to finish the story. • Draw pictures in the two blank boxes to illustrate your conclusion. • Tell the story to another pair.

Group Vocabulary Challenge

In groups of four, list places where people might meet "the love of their life." • Work fast! • Read your list to the class. • Which group has the longest list? • Make a class list on the board.

Cross-Cultural Exchange

In the same groups, choose a conversation monitor and a recorder. • Discuss these questions. • Compare cultures when possible. • Report the results of your discussion to the class.

1. How do single people meet in your country?

2. How are families involved in choosing marriage partners?

3. What ages are most common for men and women to get married?

4. Which are more common: long or short courtships?

5. What do the bride and groom wear for the wedding ceremony? Who marries them?

6. Where do the newlyweds live?

MARRIAGE

1. anniversary
2. celebration
3. close-knit family
4. commitment
5. committed
6. companion
7. companionship
8. cooperate
9. cooperation
10. cooperative
11. good times
12. hard times
13. pay bills
14. solution
15. solve
16. spouse
17. support
18. together
19. tolerate
20. trouble
21. work together

See Conversation Springboards on page 208.

Picture Discussion

With your class, answer the questions about the picture story. • Use the vocabulary list. • Add more words.

1. What is happening in each scene?
2. What are the good times in this couple's marriage? How did they celebrate?
3. What are the bad times?
4. How did they solve each problem?
5. What other problems are common in a marriage? Make a list on the board.
6. Is this a good marriage? If so, why? What makes a good marriage?

Partner Activity: Ask Aunt Betty   Partner's Name _____

With a partner, write to Aunt Betty, asking for advice about a marriage problem. • Exchange the letter with another pair. • Write a response to their letter. • Read their letter and your response to the class.

Community Activity: Marriage Survey

Ask a married person—a relative, friend, or classmate—the questions on this survey. • In groups of four, compare your results. • What is similar? • What is different? • Report your group's results to the class.

MARRIAGE SURVEY

1. How long have you been married? _____

2. In your marriage, who does more of these things:

   cooking _____   child care _____   making money _____

   cleaning _____   car care _____   spending money _____

   laundry _____   home repairs _____   driving _____

   shopping _____   paying bills _____   relaxing _____

3. What do you and your spouse like to do together?

   _____

   _____

4. How do you celebrate happy occasions?

   _____

   _____

5. What is the best thing about being married?

   _____

   _____

HAVING A BABY

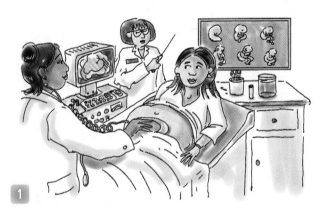

1. amniocentesis
2. baby bottle
3. baby shower
4. bottle-feed
5. breathing exercises
6. car seat
7. change a diaper
8. crib
9. deliver
10. delivery room
11. expectant parents
12. father-to-be
13. fetus
14. give birth
15. infant
16. in labor
17. midwife
18. mother-to-be
19. natural childbirth
20. obstetrician
21. pacifier
22. playpen
23. pregnant
24. stroller
25. ultrasound
26. walker

_____
_____
_____
_____
_____
_____

Picture Discussion

With your class, answer the questions about the picture story. • Use the vocabulary list. • Add more words.

1. What is happening in each scene?
2. Why do some pregnant women have an ultrasound or amniocentesis?
3. Does this woman prefer to know her baby's sex before birth? Why or why not?
4. What gifts is the mother-to-be receiving at the baby shower? What are other baby gifts?
5. How are the husband and wife preparing for the birth?
6. How does life change for this family after the baby is born?

50

See Conversation Springboards on page 208.

Cross-Cultural Exchange

In groups of three, choose a conversation monitor and a recorder. • Discuss these questions. • Compare cultures when possible. • Report the results of your discussion to the class.

1. In your country, where are babies usually born? Who delivers them?

2. What is a father's role during pregnancy? during birth?

3. Who helps take care of the new baby?

4. Do many women have natural childbirth?

5. Do most women bottle-feed their babies or breast-feed them?

Group Problem Posing/Problem Solving

In the same groups, list common problems associated with having a baby. • Read your list to the class. • Make a class list on the board. • With your class, discuss ways to handle or prevent these problems.

Group Brainstorm

In the same groups, choose a recorder. • List as many first names in English as you can. • Read your list to the class. • Make a class list on the board. • Write nicknames next to the names.

Speech

Tell the class about your name. • How did you get your first name? • Who chose it? • Why? • Do you like your name? • Do you know the history of your family name?

GROWING UP

1. absence	8. attendance	15. rebellion
2. absent	9. behavior	16. rebellious
3. acceptable	10. cut class	17. rules
4. acne	11. freedom	18. skip school
5. adolescence	12. home assignment	19. studious
6. adolescent	13. peer pressure	20. teenager
7. attend	14. rebel	21. unacceptable

52   *See Conversation Springboards on page 208.*

Picture Discussion

With your class, answer the questions about the two picture stories. • Use the vocabulary list. • Add more words.

1. What differences are there between the two sisters?
2. Describe the older sister's behavior.
3. Describe the younger sister's behavior.
4. How would you feel if these two girls were your daughters?
5. What would you do if you were their parent?
6. Describe the daily activities of both girls.

What's the Story?

Partner's Name _____

With a partner, tell the stories of the two teenage sisters. • Answer the questions. • Tell your story to another pair of students.

1. What are their names?
2. How do they feel about each other? Why?
3. How do they feel about themselves? Why?
4. How do they feel about their friends? about their parents?
5. Why do they behave differently?

Group Problem Posing

In groups of four, list problems that adolescents have. • Compare the list with other groups. • How many problems are the same? • Make a class list on the board. • Survey the class. • How many students have had each problem? • Which problems of adolescence are most common in your class?

Group Role Play

In the same groups, discuss these two situations. • Are these young people testing their independence or rebelling against their parents? • Or both? • Can you find a good solution? • Choose one situation to role-play for the class.

Dialog Journal

*Write a **Journal** entry about your experience growing up. • Then read your entry to a partner. • Ask questions about your partner's entry.*

PARENTING

1. behave
2. bicker
3. blame
4. dishonest
5. disobedient
6. disobey
7. disrespect
8. fault
9. get caught

10. get in trouble
11. honest
12. lie
13. misbehave
14. mischief
15. mischievous
16. naughty
17. obedient
18. obey

19. obstinate
20. refuse
21. respect
22. scold
23. shoplift
24. stubborn
25. tease
26. tell a lie
27. tell the truth

_____
_____
_____
_____
_____
_____
_____

Picture Discussion

With your class, answer the questions about the scenes. • Use the vocabulary list. • Add more words.

1. What is happening in each scene?
2. What parenting problem does each parent have? Make a list on the board.
3. What are the expectant parents thinking?
4. Should these parents punish their children? How?

5. What other problems do parents have with young children? Add to the list on the board.
6. Did your parents have any of these problems with you? What did you do?

54   *See Conversation Springboards on pages 208 and 209.*

Group Problem-Solving Role Play

In groups of four, choose one parenting problem from the scenes shown. • Create a role play. • Include the problem and the solution. • Present your role play to the class.

Group Vocabulary Challenge

In the same groups, list the kinds of help parents give their children. • Work fast! • Read your list to the class. • Which group has the longest list? • Make a class list on the board.

Partner Interview

Partner's Name _____

Ask a partner these questions. • Then report your partner's responses to another pair of students.

1. Have you ever taken care of small children? Who were they?

2. What did you do for the children?

3. What do you think is the most wonderful thing about taking care of small children?

4. What do you think is the most difficult?

Group Discussion

In groups of four, choose a conversation monitor and a recorder. • Discuss these questions. • Share your information with another group. • Does everyone agree?

1. When is it necessary to discipline your child?

2. What kinds of discipline would you use?

3. What kinds of discipline would you not use?

4. Who else besides a parent has the right to discipline a child? When? How?

AFTER SCHOOL

1. attitude	9. distraction	17. orderly
2. chaos	10. educational	18. report card
3. chaotic	11. encourage	19. role model
4. constructive	12. encouragement	20. supervise
5. destructive	13. grade	21. supervision
6. disciplined	14. guidance	22. undisciplined
7. disorderly	15. influence	23. unsupervised
8. distract	16. mayhem	24. waste time

Picture Discussion

With your class, answer the questions about the scenes. • Use the vocabulary list. • Add more words.

1. What is happening in each scene?
2. What are possible reasons for the differences?
3. How is this mother helping with her children's schooling? What more could these parents do to help? Make a list on the board.

4. Why are the unsupervised children creating mayhem?
5. What kinds of role models are the older children in each scene?
6. Which of these after-school activities are constructive? are destructive? waste time?

See Conversation Springboards on page 209.

Group Discussion

In groups of four, choose a conversation monitor and a recorder. • Discuss these questions. • Share your information with another group. • Report the most interesting information to the class.

1. Should parents control what TV shows their children watch? Why?

2. What kinds of shows do you think children should watch?

3. Should parents control how much TV their children watch? How?

Group Brainstorm

In the same groups, choose a recorder. • List reasons to stay home from school, be late for school, or leave school early. • Read your list to the class. • With your class, decide which reasons are good excuses, and which are bad excuses. • Make a class list of "Good Excuses" and "Bad Excuses" on the board.

Group Problem-Solving Role Play

In groups of three, discuss these two scenes. • Who are the people? • Why are they unhappy? • What are they saying? • What is their problem? • What will their solution be? • Create a role play. • Include the problem and solution in the role play. • Present your role play to the class.

Community Activity

In the same groups, research these questions. • Report your findings to the class. • Then plan a class trip to visit an interesting program.

1. What "after-school programs" are there in your community?

2. What special programs for children and families does your public library offer?

3. In your community, where are programs available for families to study English?

4. What help is available for special learning problems?

DIVORCE

1. abandon
2. abandonment
3. adultery
4. agree
5. agreement
6. alimony
7. child custody
8. child support
9. court
10. decision
11. disagree
12. disagreement
13. divorce lawyer
14. extramarital affair
15. file for divorce
16. fulfilled
17. happiness
18. incompatible
19. irreconcilable differences
20. joint custody
21. judge
22. marriage counselor
23. unfulfilled
24. unhappiness
25. visitation rights

See Conversation Springboards on page 209.

Picture Discussion

With your class, answer the questions about the picture story. • Use the vocabulary list. • Add more words.

1. What is happening in each scene?
2. How does each member of the family feel about what is happening?
3. What are the husband and wife arguing about?
4. What are their lawyers arguing about?
5. What are the causes of this divorce?
6. What are some other causes of divorce? Make a list on the board.

What's the Story?

Partner's Name _____

With a partner, answer these questions about the story.

◆ What happens to this couple after their divorce: What do they do? Are they happy? Why or why not?

◆ What happens to their children: Which parent do they live with? Are they happy? Why or why not?

Fill in the two blank boxes. • Show the new life of the ex-husband in one box. • Show the new life of the ex-wife in the other. • Tell your story ending to another pair and show them your picture endings. • Choose the best story endings to tell the class.

Group Role Play

In groups of three, decide what problems the couple in this picture could be having in their marriage. • How can a marriage counselor help them? • Create a role play of a marriage counselor and this couple. • Present your role play to the class.

Cross-Cultural Exchange

In groups of four, choose a conversation monitor and a recorder. • Discuss these questions. • Compare cultures when possible. • Report the results of your discussion to the class.

1. Is divorce common in your culture? Why or why not?
2. What are acceptable reasons for divorce in your culture?
3. Are there marriage counselors in your country? Do many people go to them?
4. What is the legal process for divorce? How long does it usually take?
5. Who usually gets custody of the children?
6. Who pays alimony? child support?
7. Do people usually remarry after a divorce in your culture? Why or why not?
8. If divorce is not an acceptable solution in your country, what do incompatible married couples do?

GROWING OLD

1. alone
2. arthritis
3. casket
4. cemetery
5. cope with
6. dead
7. die
8. elderly
9. fixed income
10. fond memories
11. free time
12. get old
13. hearing loss
14. lifetime
15. lonely
16. long life
17. lose a loved one
18. medication
19. memory loss
20. mobility
21. pass away
22. reaction time
23. retired
24. senior citizen
25. spare time
26. vision loss

_____
_____
_____
_____
_____
_____

Picture Discussion

With your class, answer the questions about the scenes. • Use the vocabulary list. • Add more words.

1. Describe the life of this elderly couple.
2. What pleasures do they have? How do they spend their free time in retirement?
3. What other activities might this elderly couple enjoy?
4. What problems do they have?
5. How can they cope with their problems?
6. What are other problems of growing old?

See Conversation Springboards on page 210.

Partner Interview

Ask a partner these questions. • Then report your partner's responses to another pair of students.

1. Do you have any elderly relatives, friends, or neighbors?
2. Tell about them: Where do they live? What do they do? How is their health?
3. Did you ever live with an elderly relative? Tell about the experience.
4. If your grandparents are not living, how did they die?
5. How do you feel about growing old?

Group Problem-Posing Role Play

In groups of four, discuss these two scenes and decide what problem each family has. • Choose one scene and create a role play of the problem. • Present your role play to the class.

Cross-Cultural Exchange

In the same groups, choose a conversation monitor and a recorder. • Discuss these questions. • Compare cultures when possible. • Report the results of your discussion to the class.

1. How are elderly people treated in your culture?
2. Who takes care of elderly people in your culture?
3. What happens to elderly parents when young family members move to a different country?

Dialog Journal

*Write a **Journal** entry about yourself in old age. • What will you be like? • What will you do? • What will you look like? • Then read and explain your entry to a partner. • Ask questions about your partner's entry.*

REVIEW

Group Questions

In groups of three, fill in the chart with two questions about each of these aspects of family life. • Don't look back in the unit! • Read your questions to the class. • Make a class list on the board.

1. Falling in Love		
2. Marriage		
3. Having a Baby		
4. Growing Up		
5. Parenting		
6. Divorce		
7. Growing Old		

Partner Interview   Partner's Name _____

Ask a partner the questions from the class list. • Then report your partner's responses to another pair of students.

Group Brainstorm

In groups of four, choose a recorder. • List the qualities of a perfect marriage partner. • Read your list to the class. • Make a class list on the board.

Partner Vocabulary Challenge   Partner's Name _____

With a partner, list some problems of growing up, marriage, parenting, and growing old. • Work fast! • Read your list to the class. • Which pair has the longest list? • Make a class list on the board.

UNIT 4
COMMUNITY AND CONSUMER LIFE

WELCOME

LEARNING STRATEGIES

➤ Notice the different services in your community. Make a list of them in the **Community Information** section of your notebook. Compare lists in class.

➤ Find people to talk to in English. Ask questions about services and stores in your community.

➤ Buy the Sunday newspaper. Save the advertising supplements. Look for good sales. Find something you would like to buy. Bring the ad to class and tell the class about it.

➤ Is there any information in other languages about your community? Ask at the local chamber of commerce, government office, or library. Show the information to your class. Explain it in English.

AROUND TOWN

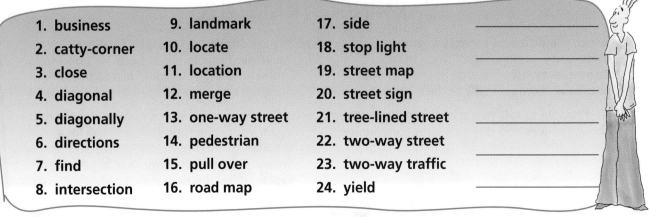

1. business	9. landmark	17. side	_____
2. catty-corner	10. locate	18. stop light	_____
3. close	11. location	19. street map	_____
4. diagonal	12. merge	20. street sign	_____
5. diagonally	13. one-way street	21. tree-lined street	_____
6. directions	14. pedestrian	22. two-way street	_____
7. find	15. pull over	23. two-way traffic	_____
8. intersection	16. road map	24. yield	_____

See Conversation Springboards on page 210.

Picture Discussion

With your class, answer the questions about the picture map. • Use the vocabulary list. • Add more words.

1. What businesses are on this picture map?
2. What landmarks are on Maple Lane?
3. What landmarks are on Central Avenue?
4. What landmarks are on Main Street?
5. What landmarks are on Pine Terrace?
6. What is the couple in the car doing?
7. What is the man saying? What will the women say?

Group Role Play

In groups of four, create a role play from the scene. • Give the people names and decide how to help. • Give directions to one of the places on the map. • Present your role play to the class.

Partner Vocabulary Challenge   Partner's Name _____

With a partner, list what you can buy or do in each of the places on the map. • Work fast! • Compare your list with another pair. • Combine lists. • Read your combined list to the class. • Make a class list on the board.

Place	What can you buy?	What can you do?

Draw with a Partner   Partner's Name _____

Tell a partner how to get to your home from your school. • Then have your partner draw a map as you describe the route. • Check the map and make corrections. • Reverse roles.

Share Your Story

In groups of four, tell about an experience in a new place. • Use these questions as a guide. • Decide which story to tell the class.

1. Have you ever been lost in a new city? How did you feel? What did you do? What did you say?
2. When you ask for help, are people always helpful? Do you always understand them? If you don't understand, what do you say?

COMMUNITY SERVICES

1. after-school program
2. community center
3. community program
4. contribute
5. contribution
6. day care
7. emergency care

8. fire department
9. free meal
10. handicapped services
11. homeless shelter
12. instructor
13. municipal pool
14. police department
15. provide
16. recreation

17. recreational
18. serve
19. service organization
20. soup kitchen
21. summer program
22. swimming lessons
23. volunteer

_____
_____
_____
_____
_____
_____
_____

See Conversation Springboards on page 210.

Picture Discussion

With your class, answer the questions about the scenes. • Use the vocabulary list. • Add more words.

1. What is happening in each scene? Describe the people.
2. What are the community services in each scene?
3. Who does each community service help?
4. Which of these services use volunteer help?

What's the Story?

In groups of five, choose a recorder. • Then tell a story about one of the scenes. • Everyone in the group should contribute at least two sentences. • Read your story to the class.

Cross Cultural Exchange

In the same groups, choose a conversation monitor and a recorder. • Discuss these questions. • Compare cultures when possible. • Report the results of your discussion to your class.

1. In your country, what community services does the government provide?
2. What volunteer organizations are there?
3. What services do they provide?
4. What services are provided for the homeless? the handicapped? the elderly?

Share Your Story

In groups of three, tell about your experiences as a volunteer. • Decide which story to tell the class.

Community Activity

With a partner, add to this list of community resources. • Use a telephone directory to find the telephone number and address of each resource. • Combine your information with the class to make a class list of community resources.

Resource	Telephone Number	Address
Fire Department		
Police Department		
Ambulance		
Senior Citizen Center		
Recreation Program		
Day Care Center		

UTILITY SERVICES

1. cable wire	10. gas company	19. reception
2. dump	11. gas leak	20. repairperson
3. electrical storm	12. hard hat	21. service technician
4. electricity	13. manhole	22. service truck
5. electric wires	14. odor	23. telephone pole
6. environment	15. out of service	24. trash
7. faulty	16. pollution	25. trash collection
8. garbage	17. power	26. trash compactor
9. garbage disposal	18. power lines	27. water pressure

See Conversation Springboards on pages 210 and 211.

Picture Discussion

With your class, answer the questions about the scenes. • Use the vocabulary list. • Add more words.

1. What is happening in each scene?
2. What kinds of recycling do you see?
3. How are the service technicians making their repairs?
4. What dangers are there with faulty electric wires? with gas leaks?

Find Someone Who

Review the vocabulary with your teacher. • Add to this list. • Then interview your classmates and fill in the name of someone who . . .

1. has cable TV.   _____

2. cooks with electricity.   _____

3. heats with gas.   _____

4. recycles.   _____

5. _____   _____

6. _____   _____

What Do You Say? What Do You Do?

In groups of four, decide what to say and do in each situation. • Compare your decisions with the class.

1. A fire hydrant is open, and the water pressure in your home is low.
2. Your neighbor throws trash in the street outside.
3. You have just come home. As you open the door, you smell a very strong gas odor.
4. You have ordered cable TV. You are supposed to get 50 channels. However, you get only three channels, and the reception is poor.

Community Activity

In your local telephone directory, find the addresses and telephone numbers of your local utility companies. • Report your findings to the class.

MAILING SERVICES

1. bulk mail
2. cardboard box
3. copy
4. copy machine/copier
5. dolly
6. efficient
7. electronic mail (e-mail)
8. face down
9. fax (facsimile)
10. home delivery
11. keyboard
12. next-day delivery
13. on-line
14. overnight delivery
15. packaging tape
16. postage supplies
17. receipt
18. receive
19. send
20. timesaver
21. transmission
22. transmit

_____
_____
_____
_____
_____
_____
_____

Picture Discussion

With your class, answer the questions about the picture story. • Use the vocabulary list. • Add more words.

1. Who are the two women in the story? What are they communicating about?

2. What services are the people using at the mailing services store?

3. What kind of mailing service does the older woman use for her package? How quickly does her package arrive?

4. Tell this picture story.

See Conversation Springboards on page 211.

Advantages/Disadvantages

In groups of three, list the advantages and disadvantages of faxes, e-mail, regular mail, and private mailing services. • Compare your answers with the class. • Make a class list on the board.

What Do You Say? What Do You Do?

In the same groups, decide what to say and do in each situation. • Share your answers with the class.

1. You want to mail a package to be delivered the next day.
2. You want to make a copy of a picture.
3. You want to mail a book as cheaply as possible.
4. You want to fax a letter.
5. You want to send money to another country.
6. You receive too much junk mail.

Cross-Cultural Exchange

In the same groups, choose a conversation monitor and a recorder. • Discuss these questions. • Compare cultures when possible. • Report the results of your discussion to the class.

1. In your country, when do people use the post office?
2. When do they use private mailing services? Why?
3. What is the most efficient method of sending mail?
4. What problems are there with sending international mail?

71

TELEPHONE SERVICES

1. business call
2. calling card
3. call waiting
4. car phone
5. cellular (cell) phone
6. conference call
7. extension phone
8. hang on

9. hard of hearing/ hearing impaired
10. hearing aid
11. in-flight call
12. on the line
13. personal call
14. prepaid telephone card
15. put on hold

16. speaker phone
17. telephone line
18. teletypewriter/ text phone
19. three-way calling
20. toll call
21. touch-tone phone
22. wall phone

See Conversation Springboards on page 211.

Picture Discussion

With your class, answer the questions about the scenes. • Use the vocabulary list. • Add more words.

1. What is happening in each scene?
2. Which are business calls? personal calls?
3. What are the people saying on the telephone?
4. Who is using a speaker phone? a text phone? call waiting?
5. Who is making a conference call? an in-flight call?
6. What other telephone services are these people using?

Who Else?

List four telephone services that you have never used. • Then find classmates who haven't used these services either. • Write their names in the chart and report your findings to the class.

	Telephone Service	Student's Name
1.		1. _____ 2. _____ 3. _____
2.		1. _____ 2. _____ 3. _____
3.		1. _____ 2. _____ 3. _____
4.		1. _____ 2. _____ 3. _____

Partner Role Play

Partner's Name _____

With a partner, choose one of these situations. • Create a role play. • Present your role play to another pair of students.

1. You are the only one home. A friend calls for your brother. Take a message.
2. You have a fever and sore throat and can't go to work. Call in sick.
3. Call a movie theater to find out what time a film begins.
4. You are on an airplane and your arrival time is delayed. Make an in-flight phone call to your office to explain the delay.

Advantages/Disadvantages

In groups of five, list all the advantages and disadvantages of having a car phone. • Compare your answers with the class. • Make a class list on the board.

Share Your Story

In groups of three, tell about a problem you have had using the telephone. • Decide which story to tell the class.

SHOPPING IN TODAY'S WORLD

1. boutique	8. item number	15. sales tax	_____
2. catalog sales	9. merchandise	16. shipping and handling	_____
3. charge	10. money-back guarantee	17. specialty shop	_____
4. ease of shopping	11. on-line shopping	18. telephone order	_____
5. exclusive	12. place an order	19. toll-free number	_____
6. home shopping channel	13. purchase	20. upscale	_____
7. introductory offer	14. retail	21. value	_____

Picture Discussion

With your class, answer the questions about the scenes. • Use the vocabulary list. • Add more words.

1. What different kinds of shopping do these scenes show?
2. What are the people buying in each scene?
3. What different ways can these people pay for their purchases?
4. How is the woman making a purchase using the TV? What is she saying?
5. What information does the catalog shopper have to give to place a telephone order?
6. Who will have to pay shipping and handling?
7. What are the advantages and disadvantages of each method of shopping?

74   See *Conversation Springboards* on page 212.

Find Someone Who

Review the vocabulary with your teacher. • Add to this list. • Then interview your classmates and fill in the name of someone who . . .

1. always pays with cash. _____

2. has bought something at a mall recently. _____

3. has paid for a purchase with a credit card. _____

4. has ordered something by mail. _____

5. has ordered an item on the phone. _____

6. has ordered something from a catalog. _____

7. has watched a home shopping channel. _____

8. has purchased an item on-line. _____

9. _____ _____

10. _____ _____

Partner Role Play   Partner's Name _____

With a partner, choose one of these situations, or make up your own. • Create a role play with a customer and a salesclerk or telephone salesperson. • Present your role play to the class.

◆ having a duplicate made of your house key
◆ buying a Mother's Day present for your mother

◆ buying a gift for your nephew who is graduating from high school
◆ buying a chair for yourself

Community Activity

Bring shop-at-home catalogs to class. • Look through them together. • What would you like to buy? • What are the advantages and disadvantages of shopping by catalog?

75

SHOPPING FOR CLOTHES

1. article of clothing
2. conservative
3. conventional
4. discount store
5. durable
6. fashion
7. fashionable
8. fashion conscious

9. garment
10. impractical
11. piece of clothing
12. practical
13. reasonable
14. seasonal
15. sporty
16. style

17. stylish
18. taste
19. tasteful
20. thrifty
21. trend
22. trendy
23. well made

_____

_____

_____

_____

_____

_____

_____

See Conversation Springboards on page 212.

Picture Discussion

With your class, answer the questions about the picture story. • Use the vocabulary list. • Add more words.

1. Who are the people in this story?
2. Why are they shopping for clothes?
3. How does the parents' taste in clothing differ from their children's? Why?
4. Why are the parents shopping at the bargain outlet?
5. How much are the parents spending on clothes today?

What's the Story?

In groups of three, choose a recorder. • Tell the story of this family's shopping trip. • Everyone in the group should contribute at least two sentences. • Read your story to the class.

What Do You Say? What Do You Do?

In the same groups, decide what to say and do in each situation. • Compare your decisions with the class.

1. You are in the coat department of a large store. A very aggressive salesperson is trying to sell you a purple coat with a belt. You don't want it. You want . . .
2. You found the sweater you were looking for, but it's black and you want . . .
3. You are looking for pajamas for your three-year-old-nephew, but you don't know what size he wears.
4. It's closing time, and you can't decide which of three sweaters you'd like to buy.

Find Someone Who

Review the vocabulary with your teacher. • Add to this list. • Then interview your classmates and fill in the name of someone who . . .

1. wears bright colors. _____

2. wears trendy shoes. _____

3. prefers casual clothes. _____

4. shops at discount stores. _____

5. _____ _____

6. _____ _____

RETURNS AND EXCHANGES

1. adjust
2. adjustment
3. assemble
4. broken
5. damaged
6. defective
7. dilemma
8. dissatisfaction
9. dissatisfied
10. exchangeable

11. frustrated
12. frustrating
13. frustration
14. hem
15. incomplete
16. manufacturing defect
17. missing part
18. non-refundable
19. poor quality
20. put together

21. refund
22. refundable
23. replace
24. replacement
25. returnable
26. scratched
27. stitching
28. torn
29. under warranty
30. warrantied

See Conversation Springboards on page 212.

Picture Discussion

With your class, answer the questions about the scenes. • *Use the vocabulary list.* • *Add more words.*

1. What is wrong with the tricycle?
2. What will the man do about the tricycle? What will he tell his son?
3. What will the newlyweds do with all their candlesticks?
4. What rights does the man with the lifetime warranty have? What can he do?
5. What is the dissatisfied customer at the customer service counter saying? What happened to her skirt?

Find Someone Who

Review the vocabulary with your teacher. • *Add to this list.* • *Then interview your classmates and fill in the name of someone who . . .*

1. has received a useless gift. _____
2. has exchanged an item of clothing that didn't fit. _____
3. has exchanged something because it was the wrong color. _____
4. has returned an appliance that didn't work properly. _____
5. has used a warranty for repairs. _____
6. _____ _____
7. _____ _____

Partner Role Play

Partner's Name _____

With a partner, answer these questions. • *Then create a role play of this scene.* • *Present your role play to the class.*

1. What is the customer returning?
2. What is the problem?
3. What is your solution?

SCHOOL AND COMMUNITY

1. administration office
2. administrative
3. appointment
4. chaperone
5. detention
6. disciplinary action
7. discipline
8. dress code

9. extracurricular activity
10. intramural sport
11. martial arts
12. meet
13. meeting
14. meeting time
15. office staff

16. parental involvement
17. Parent-Teacher Association (PTA)
18. play chess
19. principal
20. probation
21. suspend
22. suspension

_____
_____
_____
_____
_____
_____
_____

See Conversation Springboards on page 213.

Picture Discussion

With your class, answer the questions about the scene. • Use the vocabulary list. • Add more words.

1. Why are these three students waiting to see the principal?

2. What is each student thinking?

3. What is the boy's father thinking?

4. What do you think the principal will say to each of these students?

5. What is the office staff doing?

6. What intramural sports are there at this school? Where can students sign up?

7. What opportunities are there for parental involvement at this school?

Partner Activity: Ask Aunt Betty

Partner's Name _____

With a partner, read and discuss this letter. • Together, write a response from Aunt Betty giving advice to Bilingual in Biloxi. • Read your letter to another pair.

ASK AUNT BETTY

Dear Aunt Betty:

My son, Bayani, is going to start kindergarten soon. Although he speaks Tagalog fluently, he only speaks a little English. I have to decide whether to place him in a bilingual program. What are the advantages and disadvantages of being in a bilingual program?

Bilingual in Biloxi

Share Your Story

In groups of three, decide what each student's note says. • Write the notes together. • Then read your notes to another group.

Group Discussion

In the same groups, choose a recorder and a conversation monitor. • Discuss these questions. • Report your conclusions to the class.

1. What clubs and other extracurricular activities are available at the schools in your community?

2. What are the physical conditions of the schools in your community?

3. Does this school administration office look like the office in your school? Explain.

4. What are the rules for tardiness and absence?

5. What types of difficulties do students have in school?

6. What can be done about each difficulty?

Cross-Cultural Exchange

In the same groups, choose a conversation monitor and a recorder. • Discuss these questions. • Compare cultures when possible. • Report the results of your discussion to the class.

1. Do students respect teachers in your country? How do they show respect?

2. Do students wear uniforms? Describe them.

3. How much homework do students have every day?

4. How long is the school day? Do students go to school on Saturdays?

5. What extracurricular activities are there?

6. What do parents do to get involved in their children's education?

LIFELONG LEARNING

REGISTRATION   FINANCIAL AID   CASHIER

1. admissions	9. matriculated	17. registration process
2. advise	10. non-credit course	18. required course
3. audit a course	11. non-matriculated	19. scholarship
4. credit course	12. payment	20. school supplies
5. credit hours	13. procedure	21. semester
6. elective	14. register	22. support staff
7. fee	15. registrar's office	23. textbook
8. finance	16. registration form	24. tuition

Picture Discussion

With your class, answer the questions about the scenes. • Use the vocabulary list. • Add more words.

1. What are the students waiting in line for?
2. What are they thinking?
3. What advice are the students giving to each other?
4. What courses are they taking this semester? Which are for credit? Which are non-credit? required? elective?

5. How is this registration process similar to your school? How is it different?
6. What can the students buy in the bookstore?

See Conversation Springboards on page 213.

Share Your Story

In groups of four, tell about your first day at this school. • What do you remember? • How did you feel? • Choose one story to tell the class.

Dialog Journal

Partner's Name _____

*Write a **Journal** entry describing your plans and ambitions. • Use these questions as a guide. • Then read your entry to a partner. • Ask questions about your partner's entry.*

1. What is your ambition?
2. What kind of courses will you need?
3. Where would you like to study?

4. How much money will you need?
5. How long will it take to achieve your goal?

Class Game: Guess Who!

On a slip of paper, write your ambition or educational goal. • Make a pile. • Pick a paper. • Read it to the class. • Guess who wrote it!

Community Activity

Invite a school advisor to your class. • Before the advisor's visit, review these questions. • Add more. • Ask the advisor the questions.

1. What are the opportunities for adult education in your community?

2. What programs are available at your school? What courses?

RECREATION

1. art show
2. baseball diamond
3. baseball league
4. browse
5. cheer
6. community event
7. exhibit
8. exhibition
9. film
10. fine arts
11. marquee
12. matinee
13. motion picture
14. multiplex cinema
15. on-line catalog
16. perform
17. performance
18. playing field
19. popular
20. public library
21. rain or shine
22. root
23. show
24. spectator

_____
_____
_____
_____
_____

 See Conversation Springboards on page 213.

Picture Discussion

With your class, answer the questions about the scenes. • Use the vocabulary list. • Add more words.

1. What are these people doing for recreation?
2. Where is the outdoor concert being held? On what date?
3. Which of these recreational activities are free? Which ones have an admission fee?
4. Where is the art of Asia being exhibited? What are the dates of the exhibit?
5. Where can the public go for recreational reading? What types of recreational reading do public libraries have?
6. How many movies are showing at this multiplex cinema? Which movie do you think you would like best? Why?
7. What is happening in the championship game? Who are the spectators? What are they doing?

Draw with a Partner
Partner's Name _____

With a partner, decide on another recreational activity. • Draw a picture. • Show your picture to another pair. • Tell them about the activity.

Speech

Tell the class about the recreational opportunities in your hometown. • Which was your favorite?

Class Survey

List on the board all the recreational activities available in your community. • Check the things you do. • Compare your answers with classmates. • Total the responses. • What are the trends?

Class Game: *What Would You Like to Do This Weekend?*

On a slip of paper, write an activity you would like to do this weekend. • Make a pile. • Pick a paper. • Read it to the class. • Guess who wrote it! • Ask the person questions about the plans.

Community Activity

Bring in the "Community Calendar" from your local newspaper. • Decide on an interesting activity as a class. • Make plans to do something together!

REVIEW

Advantages/Disadvantages

In groups of three, list the advantages and disadvantages of each topic. • Then compare lists with another group.

	Advantages	Disadvantages
1. Dress Codes		
2. Bilingual School Programs		
3. Shopping in Discount Stores		
4. Recycling		
5. E-mail		

Group Vocabulary Challenge

In groups of four, choose a recorder. • List reasons to return an item to a store. • Work fast! • Read your list to the class. • Which group has the longest list? • Make a class list on the board.

Group Problem Posing/Problem Solving

In the same groups, list five common consumer problems. • State each problem. • Decide how to avoid each problem. • Report your problems and solutions to another group.

Partner Questions and Answers   Partner's Name _____

With a partner, write two questions for each of these topics. • Don't look back in the unit! • Then ask each other the questions. • Report the questions and your partner's responses to another pair.

◆ Shopping in Today's World
◆ Shopping for Clothes
◆ Returns and Exchanges
◆ Utilities

◆ Telephone and Mail Services
◆ Education
◆ Recreation

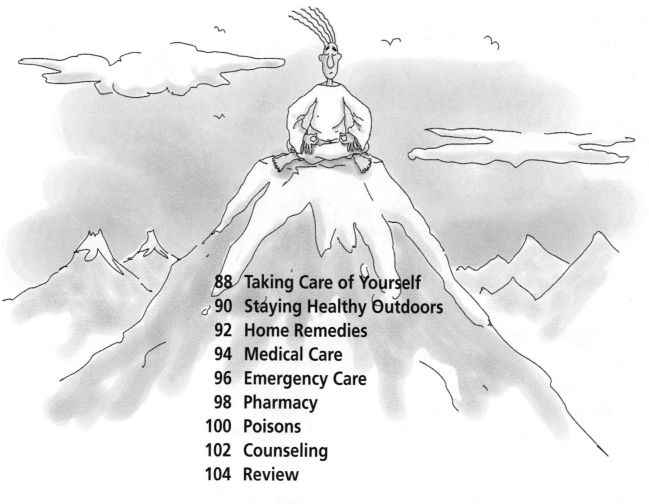

UNIT 5
STAYING HEALTHY

LEARNING STRATEGIES

➤ In the **Journal** section of your notebook, write about a recent illness you had.

➤ Look in newspapers or magazines for advertisements for different brands of medicine. Then go to the pharmacy and list the medicines you recognize from the ads.

➤ What questions do you have about health? What vocabulary do you want to learn in English? List the things you want to learn in this unit. Discuss your list in class.

TAKING CARE OF YOURSELF

1. active	10. empty calories	19. health risk
2. alcohol/liquor	11. energy	20. low-fat diet
3. anorexia	12. excessive	21. nutrition
4. anorexic	13. exercise	22. nutritious
5. appetite	14. fat	23. oily
6. calories from fat	15. fattening	24. overweight
7. carbohydrates	16. fit	25. protein
8. cholesterol	17. fitness	26. saturated fats
9. diet pills	18. greasy	27. sedentary

Picture Discussion

With your class, answer the questions about the scenes. • Use the vocabulary list. • Add more words.

1. What are the two men eating for lunch?
2. Which lunch is more nutritious? Which food has empty calories?
3. What is wrong with the young woman's dinner?
4. What is her mother thinking? What is her father saying?
5. Are the family members watching TV taking good care of themselves? Explain.

6. How is an active lifestyle better for your health than a sedentary lifestyle?
7. What health risks are the people at the party taking? What are the dangers of smoking and drinking?
8. Which of the people in these scenes have a healthy lifestyle? Which do not?

See Conversation Springboards on page 214.

Group Brainstorm

In groups of four, choose a recorder. • List all the things you can do to stay healthy. • Read your list to the class. • Make a class list on the board. • Which advice is most practical?

Partner Activity: *Ask Aunt Betty*

Partner's Name _____

With a partner, read and discuss this letter. • Together, write a reply from Aunt Betty, giving advice to Pudgy in Peoria. • Read your letter to the class.

Community Activity

Bring advertisements for diet products to class. • Discuss the advertisements with your class. • Do you believe what the ads say? • Why or why not?

ASK AUNT BETTY

Dear Aunt Betty:

I am new to this country. In my country, my mother prepared good meals every day. I got plenty of sleep and exercised by walking or running in the country.

Now, I live in the city with my cousins. Everyone works or goes to school. No one is home to shop or prepare meals. I work during the day and go to school at night. I eat out often, and, when I'm home, I have to cook for myself. I don't have time for exercise. I am getting fat, and I don't feel well.

How can I get back to a healthy lifestyle?

Pudgy in Peoria

STAYING HEALTHY OUTDOORS

1. allergic reaction	12. hazard	23. rattlesnake	_____
2. avoid	13. heat exhaustion	24. scorpion	_____
3. bite	14. icy	25. scratch	
4. bug	15. insect	26. skid	_____
5. dehydrate	16. itch	27. slip	_____
6. dehydration	17. itchy	28. slippery	
7. feel faint	18. poison ivy	29. sting	
8. fleas	19. poison oak	30. stinger	_____
9. fly	20. poisonous	31. sunblock/ sunscreen	_____
10. frigid	21. pollen	32. swarm	_____
11. hay fever	22. precaution	33. wasp	_____

Picture Discussion

With your class, answer the questions about the scenes. • *Use the vocabulary list.* • *Add more words.*

1. What is happening in each scene?
2. What animals are in these scenes? Which ones are insects?
3. What health problems do these animals cause?
4. What other health hazards are there at the beach? in the woods? in the desert? in the cold?
5. What other health problems can the weather cause?
6. What precautions can people take to avoid these hazards?

See Conversation Springboards on page 214.

Group Problem Posing/Problem Solving

In groups of five, discuss these situations. • What advice would you give? • Report your solutions to the class.

1. You think you have poison ivy.
2. You were stung by a wasp.
3. You've been picking flowers, and your eyes are starting to itch.
4. You're at the beach and you forgot your sunblock.
5. You've been outside on a hot day, and now you're feeling faint.
6. It's icy outside, and you have to drive to work.

Group Brainstorm

In groups of three, choose a recorder. • Write as many questions as you can about outdoor health hazards. • Ask another group your questions. • Then answer their questions.

Class Game: *Guess What!*

On a slip of paper, write an outdoor health problem. • Make a pile. • Pick a paper. • Read it to the class. • Ask your classmates for the precaution. • Whoever answers correctly picks the next slip of paper.

Cross-Cultural Exchange

In groups of four, choose a conversation monitor and a recorder. • Discuss these questions. • Compare cultures when possible. • Report the results of your discussion to the class.

1. What outdoor health hazards are in your country?
2. What precautions do people take?
3. What remedies are there for outdoor health problems?

HOME REMEDIES

1. acupuncture
2. acupuncture needle
3. alternative medicine
4. back pain
5. bed rest
6. capsule
7. congested
8. copper bracelet
9. drowsiness
10. drowsy

11. heating pad
12. herb
13. herbal tea
14. illness
15. insert
16. liquid
17. massage
18. muscle spasm
19. natural
20. nontraditional medicine
21. recover

22. recovery
23. recuperate
24. respiratory infection
25. rubbing alcohol
26. soothe
27. stuffy nose
28. tablet
29. traditional medicine
30. virus
31. vitamin C

_____
_____
_____
_____
_____
_____
_____
_____
_____

Picture Discussion

With your class, answer the questions about the scenes. • Use the vocabulary list. • Add more words.

1. What illness do the two women have?
2. What different remedies are they using?
3. Which of these remedies do you prefer? Why?
4. What other remedies are there?
5. What health problem do the two men have?

6. What different remedies are they using?
7. Which of these remedies do you prefer? Why?
8. What other remedies are there?
9. Tell the story of each person's illness and recovery.

See Conversation Springboards on page 214.

Partner Interview

Partner's Name _____

Ask a partner these questions. • Then report your partner's responses to another pair of students.

1. What would you do for a dirty cut on your finger?
2. What remedy do you use for a stuffy nose?
3. What remedy do you use for allergies?
4. What do you do for back pain?
5. What do you do if you have a sore throat?
6. What do you do if you have a virus?

Tell the Class

Tell the class about a home remedy that you use or a remedy that is popular in your country. • If possible, bring it to class and explain it to your classmates.

Class Game: *Guess What!*

On a slip of paper, write the name of a home remedy. • Make a pile. • Pick a paper. • Read it to the class. • Ask your classmates what it is used for. • Whoever answers correctly picks the next slip of paper.

Community Activity

List everything in your medicine cabinet. • Bring the list to class. • With your class, make a list on the board. • How many different items did you find?

MEDICAL CARE

SEE RECEPTIONIST BEFORE SITTING.

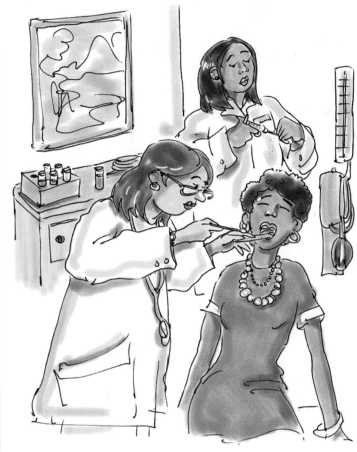

1. blood sample
2. complain
3. complaint
4. contagious
5. cramps
6. examining room
7. flu shot
8. general practitioner
9. immune
10. immunization

11. immunize
12. infection
13. infectious disease
14. inoculate
15. medical history
16. physical examination
17. prescribe
18. primary care physician
19. rash

20. refer
21. referral
22. sign in
23. specialist
24. stethoscope
25. throat culture
26. tongue depressor
27. upset stomach
28. vial

_____
_____
_____
_____
_____
_____
_____
_____

See Conversation Springboards on pages 214 and 215.

Picture Discussion

With your class, answer the questions about the scenes. • Use the vocabulary list. • Add more words.

1. What health problems might the patients in the waiting room have?
2. What complaints might the woman in the examining room have?
3. Which of these health problems are infectious diseases?
4. What might this primary care physician prescribe for each patient?
5. Which patients might she refer to specialists?

Group Vocabulary Challenge

In groups of three, list different health problems. • Work fast! • Read your list to the class. • Which group has the longest list? • Make a class list on the board.

Share Your Story

In the same groups, tell about an experience you had with a serious health problem. • Decide which story to tell the class.

Group Brainstorm

In the same groups, choose a recorder. • List some illnesses people are afraid to talk about. • Read your list to the class. • Make a class list on the board. • Which illness causes the most fear? • Why?

Cross-Cultural Exchange

In groups of four, choose a conversation monitor and a recorder. • Discuss these questions. • Compare cultures when possible. • Report the results of your discussion to the class.

1. What is the most serious health problem in your country?
2. How is it treated?
3. What are the most common health problems in your country?
4. What do people do when they have these problems?
5. What health problem do people fear most?
6. What are the differences in the ways health problems are treated in the U.S. and in your country?

Community Activity

In the same groups, decide on three health problems to research. • Find out what community services are available for each problem. • Report your findings to the class.

EMERGENCY CARE

1. ambulatory	10. fracture	18. injury
2. bandage	11. gurney	19. inpatient
3. blood work	12. health care provider	20. life-threatening
4. compress	13. health insurance card	21. paramedic
5. co-payment	14. health insurance plan	22. sling
6. cover	15. hospitalize	23. swell
7. coverage	16. identification bracelet	24. swollen
8. critical condition	17. injure	25. treat
9. dressing		26. treatment

See Conversation Springboards on page 215.

Picture Discussion

With your class, answer the questions about the scene. • Use the vocabulary list. • Add more words.

1. What is happening in the scene?
2. What is the man doing at the admitting desk?
3. What is wrong with each patient?
4. Who should be treated first? second? third? Why?
5. Could any of these patients go to a doctor's office instead of the emergency room? Which ones?

Group Role Play

In groups of three, choose a medical emergency. • Create a role play. • Present your role play to the class.

Share Your Story

In the same groups, tell about an experience you've had in the emergency room. • Decide which story to tell the class.

Find Someone Who

Review the vocabulary with your teacher. • Add to this list. • Then interview your classmates and fill in the name of someone who . . .

1. has had a broken bone.   _____

2. has had stitches.   _____

3. has been treated in an emergency room.   _____

4. has taken someone to an emergency room.   _____

5. has ridden in an ambulance.   _____

6. has been seriously injured.   _____

7. _____   _____

8. _____   _____

Group Vocabulary Challenge

In groups of five, list as many medical emergencies as you can. • Work fast! • Read your list to the class. • Which group has the longest list? • Make a class list on the board.

PHARMACY

COLDS AND ALLERGIES

VITAMINS AND SUPPLEMENTS

1. addictive	11. expire	21. nonprescription drug (over-the-counter drug) _____
2. antibiotic	12. fill	22. nonrefillable _____
3. anti-inflammatory	13. food supplement	23. no refills _____
4. dosage	14. full stomach	24. painkiller _____
5. dose	15. generic	25. pick up _____
6. drug	16. heart medicine	26. prescription drug _____
7. druggist	17. multiple vitamin	27. refill _____
8. drugstore	18. muscle relaxant	28. relief _____
9. empty stomach	19. narcotic	29. relieve _____
10. expiration date	20. nonnarcotic	30. restriction _____

See Conversation Springboards on page 215.

Picture Discussion

With your class, answer the questions about the scene. • Use the vocabulary list. • Add more words.

1. What is wrong with each of these people?
2. Why are some of the people getting prescription drugs instead of over-the-counter drugs? What's the difference?
3. What are some of the nonprescription drugs used for?
4. Why are some prescription drugs non-refillable?
5. Why is the expiration date important?
6. What are the pharmacist and the woman at the counter saying to each other?

Group Brainstorm

In groups of four, choose a recorder. • List some items you can get in a pharmacy. • Read your list to the class. • Make a class list on the board. • What item do most people get in a pharmacy?

What Do You Say? What Do You Do?

In the same groups, decide what to say and do in each situation. • Compare your decisions with the class.

1. The pharmacist gives you your prescription, but you don't understand the directions.
2. You need to refill your prescription.
3. When you open the new aspirin bottle, you see that the bottle has been opened before.
4. Your health insurance plan won't pay for your prescription.
5. You don't know if the heart medicine you are taking is safe to take with your new prescription.

Cross-Cultural Exchange

In groups of three, choose a conversation monitor and a recorder. • Discuss these questions. • Compare cultures when possible. • Report the results of your discussion to the class.

1. What prescription drugs are most common in your country?
2. How expensive are prescription drugs? nonprescription drugs?
3. How are pharmacies in your country similar to those in the U.S.? How are they different?
4. What else do pharmacies sell in addition to drugs?

Community Activity

In the same groups, visit a local pharmacy. • Research this information and report your findings to the class.

1. What is the name of the pharmacy?
2. Where is the prescription counter?
3. Note three brands of headache remedies, including the size of their containers and their prices.
4. In what aisle can you get cough medicine? Note three brands, including their sizes; their doses; and their prices.
5. What other items can you buy in the pharmacy? List five.

POISONS

1. antidote
2. chemical
3. childproof
4. contaminate
5. contamination
6. contents
7. disinfect
8. disinfectant
9. (do not) induce vomiting
10. eye irritant
11. food poisoning
12. harmful
13. hazardous
14. household chemical
15. household cleaner
16. household poison
17. ingest
18. insecticide
19. irritate
20. irritation
21. kitchen cleaner
22. poison control center
23. prevent
24. prevention
25. spoil
26. swallow
27. warn
28. warning label

Picture Discussion

With your class, answer the questions about the scenes. • Use the vocabulary list. • Add more words.

1. What happened to the little boy?
2. What should his mother do?
3. How could his parents have prevented this danger?
4. Why is the man sick?
5. What advice would you give him?

100

See Conversation Springboards on pages 215 and 216.

What Do You Say? What Do You Do?

In groups of three, decide what to say and do in each situation. • Share your answers with the class.

1. Your child ate a bottle of baby aspirin.
2. The little boy next door drank some disinfectant.
3. You found your neighbor unconscious with an empty bottle of pills in his hand.
4. You accidentally sprayed insecticide in your face.

WARNING:

Contains Sodium Hypochlorite 5.25%. Causes substantial but temporary eye injury. Harmful if swallowed. May irritate skin. Do not get in eyes or on clothing. For prolonged use, wear gloves.

FIRST AID:

*IF IN EYES, remove contact lenses and rinse with plenty of water for 15 minutes.

*IF SWALLOWED, drink large amounts of water. DO NOT induce vomiting.

*IN EITHER CASE, call a physician or poison control center immediately.

*IF IN CONTACT WITH SKIN, immediately remove contaminated clothing and wash skin thoroughly with water.

DO NOT MIX WITH OTHER HOUSEHOLD CHEMICALS, such as toilet bowl cleaners, or products containing ammonia. To do so will release hazardous gases.

Group Activity: *Reading Labels*

In the same groups, answer these questions. • Share your answers with another group.

1. What is the dangerous contents in this bottle of bleach?
2. What should you do if you get bleach in your eye?
3. Who should you call?
4. What should you do if you get bleach on your skin?
5. What will happen if you mix bleach with other household cleaners?

Community Activity

Bring in a product with a caution or warning label. • With your class, make a display of all the products. • Choose one. • Read its label. • Explain the product and any cautions to the class.

1. What is the product?
2. What can it be used for?
3. What cautions or warnings are on the label?
4. Is there a telephone number on the label for questions or comments? Decide what to say. Role-play a phone call to the number.

COUNSELING

ALONE? PREGNANT? GET HELP!
Call a counselor: 555-4231.

Single Parent Support Group
meets every Monday at 7:30 p.m. at the Community Church, 1 Main Street. Child Care available. 555-

ARE YOU HAVING A PROBLEM WITH DRUGS OR ALCOHOL?
Call our counselors at 555-8725.
Alcoholics Anonymous meetings: Tuesdays, 7:30 p.m.
Al-Anon support group for families: Wednesdays, 6:30 p.m.

Are you or your children victims of abuse?
You CAN get help!! Hotline: 555-6758, 24 hours a day.

CANCER SURVIVORS:
You are not alone! Group meetings first Saturday of every month at 10:00 a.m. Families welcome. River Street Center, 2 River Street.
555-3445

1. addict
2. addicted
3. addiction
4. alcohol abuse
5. battered spouse
6. child abuse
7. client
8. coping skills
9. counsel
10. dependency
11. despair
12. desperation
13. drinking problem
14. group therapy
15. improve
16. improvement
17. life change
18. mental health
19. resource
20. self-help
21. social problem
22. spousal abuse
23. stress
24. stress reduction
25. therapist
26. therapy

See Conversation Springboards on page 216.

Picture Discussion

With your class, answer the questions about the signs. • Use the vocabulary list. • Add more words.

1. What social problems do these signs address?
2. Where can someone go to get help for a drinking problem? a drug problem?
3. What group helps single parents? families of alcoholics?
4. What can a pregnant teenager do if she has no help at home?
5. Where can victims of abuse get help?
6. Where can cancer survivors get support?
7. What is the group discussing in this scene?

Partner Vocabulary Challenge   Partner's Name _____

With a partner, list as many mental health problems as you can. • Work fast! • Compare your list with another pair. • Combine lists. • Read your combined list to the class. • Make a class list on the board.

Dialog Journal   Partner's Name _____

*Write a **Journal** entry about a social problem. • State the problem and write about your experiences and feelings about it. • Then read your entry to a partner. • Ask questions about your partner's entry.*

Group Brainstorm

In groups of four, choose a recorder. • Write as many questions as you can about social problems today. • Ask another group your questions. • Then answer their questions.

Cross-Cultural Exchange

In the same groups, choose a conversation monitor and a recorder. • Discuss these questions. • Compare cultures when possible. • Report the results of your discussion to the class.

1. What social problems exist in your country?
2. How do people feel about these problems?
3. What resources are available to help with these problems?

Community Activity

Invite a counselor to visit your class. • Add to this list of questions. • Discuss the questions with the counselor.

1. What is the most serious social problem in your community?
2. What resources are available in your community to help?
3. What are three signs of alcoholism?
4. What are three signs of drug abuse?
5. How can you tell if someone is abusing drugs?
6. What could you do if someone you know had one of these problems?
7. _____
8. _____

REVIEW

Group Vocabulary Challenge

In groups of five, list advice about a healthy lifestyle. • Work fast! • Read your list to the class. • Which group has the longest list? • Make a class list on the board.

Find Someone Who

With your class, add to this list. • Then interview your classmates and fill in the name of someone who . . .

1. has health insurance. _____

2. was stung by a bee. _____

3. has had a serious medical emergency. _____

4. has been bitten by a dog. _____

5. can give first aid. _____

6. knows a home remedy for a cold. _____

7. _____ _____

8. _____ _____

Group Decisions

In groups of five, choose five physical or mental health problems. • Decide what to do in an emergency for each problem. • Share your remedies with the class.

Partner Activity: *The Medicine Cabinet*

Partner's Name _____

With a partner, list the most important items for a medicine cabinet. • Compare your list with another pair. • Combine lists. • Read your combined list to the class. • Make a class list on the board.

UNIT 6
HOUSING

LEARNING STRATEGIES

➤ **Check around your neighborhood for homes to rent or buy. How many homes are for rent? How many are for sale?**

➤ **Find the names of your utility companies on your bills or in your telephone directory. Copy the names and bring them to class. Does everyone in the class have the same utility companies?**

➤ **Look at your lease agreement. List the words you don't understand. Bring the list to class to discuss.**

➤ **Interview a family member or friend (outside of class) and find out what they like and don't like about where they live. Write down your findings in the Activities section of your notebook.**

PLACES TO LIVE

1. congestion
2. countryside
3. farmhouse
4. high-rise
5. housing development
6. land
7. log cabin
8. lot
9. motor home
10. multiple-family dwelling
11. one-story
12. own
13. property
14. ranch house
15. real estate
16. recreational vehicle
17. rental
18. residence
19. semidetached
20. single-family dwelling
21. small town
22. space
23. sprawling
24. suburb
25. tenement
26. town house
27. two-family dwelling
28. two-story
29. village
30. walk-up

See Conversation Springboards on page 216.

Picture Discussion

With your class, answer the questions about the picture story. • Use the vocabulary list. • Add more words.

1. What places to live is this couple looking at? Describe the locations and the types of housing.
2. Which do you think will be most expensive? least expensive? Why?
3. Which property do you think this young couple could buy?

4. What are the advantages and disadvantages of each location? of each type of housing?
5. What other places to live are there? Make lists on the board of locations and types of housing.

What's the Story?

In groups of three, choose a recorder. • Create the young couple's story. • Answer these questions in your story. • Tell your story to another pair of students.

1. Who are they?
2. Where are they from?
3. What do they do for a living?
4. What leisure activities do they enjoy?

5. Where will they decide to live?
6. Why did they come to this area to live?
7. What do they hope to do here?
8. Will they rent or buy their house?

Advantages/Disadvantages

In the same groups, list the advantages and disadvantages of living in a city, a suburb, a small town, and the country. • Read your list to the class. • Make a class list on the board.

Draw with a Partner   Partner's Name _____

With a partner, describe your house or apartment. • From your partner's description, draw a picture of his or her home. • Show the picture to your partner. • Have your partner correct your picture and explain the corrections. • How accurate was your drawing?

INSIDE YOUR HOME

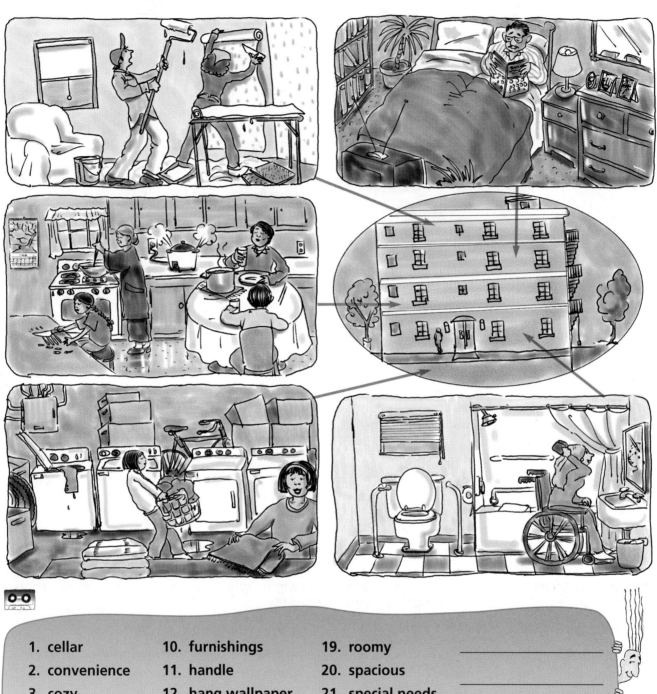

1. cellar
2. convenience
3. cozy
4. cramped
5. customized
6. decorate
7. extra-wide
8. floor covering
9. furnish
10. furnishings
11. handle
12. hang wallpaper
13. mini-blinds
14. modified fixtures
15. occupant
16. privacy
17. redecorate
18. remodel
19. roomy
20. spacious
21. special needs
22. storage space
23. store
24. storeroom
25. wheelchair
26. window treatment

_____

_____

_____

_____

_____

_____

See Conversation Springboards on page 216.

Picture Discussion

With your class, answer the questions about the scenes. • Use the vocabulary list. • Add more words.

1. What are these people doing inside their homes?
2. Where in the building is each apartment located? Where is the laundry room?
3. Describe each room.

4. How will the couple decorate their living room? What furnishings will they have? What floor covering? What window treatment? What will they hang on the walls?
5. Tell the stories of these occupants: Who are they? Where are they from? What are their interests or hobbies?

Group Vocabulary Challenge

In groups of four, list different things people have in their kitchens. • Work fast! • Read your list to the class. • Which group has the longest list? • Make a class list on the board.

Partner Interview

Partner's Name _____

Ask a partner these questions. • Then report your partner's responses to another pair of students.

1. What colors are the walls in your home?
2. What floor coverings are there?
3. What is on the windows?
4. What furniture is in your home? What appliances?

5. What would you like to redecorate? What would you like to change?
6. What would you like to buy for your home?

Class Game: *Pantomime*

In groups of three, choose a redecorating task. • List instructions for the task. • Pantomime your task for the class. • Have your classmates guess what you are doing. • Read your instructions to the class. • Did you forget anything?

Group Decision

In the same groups, discuss this situation and decide what to do. • Report your decision to the class.

◆ Your apartment is bare. You have $1,000 to spend. Your landlord will supply a stove and refrigerator. What will you buy? How much will you pay for each item?

FINDING THE RIGHT HOME

Apartments for Rent

One-bdrm., 1 bath., fncd. yd., utils. not incl. Call ownr.: 555-1582.

Two-bdrm., 1 bath., kitch. w. dishw., utils. incl., excel. loc., $650/mo.

Studio apt. w. bath., bsmt. laundr. avail., no utils., $450/mo.

Three-bdrm., 2 bath., cpt., ht. and elec. not incl., no pets, $600/mo.

Three-rm. bsmt. apt., furnished, utils. incl., nr. public transp.

Houses for Sale

Condo: 3 rms. w. bath, excel. cond., incl. stove, refrig., dishw., w/w cpt., and more. $65,000.

One-acre fncd. lot w. new mobile home; beautiful view, low dn. pmnt. Asking $47,900.

Two-story, 4 bdrm., 2 bath. Excel. loc., fncd. yd. You'll love it! $125,000, as is.

Family size: *2*
Monthly take-home pay: *$850*

Family size: *6*
Monthly take-home pay: *$1,700*

1. apt. (apartment)
2. as is
3. avail. (available)
4. bath. (bathroom)
5. bdrm. (bedroom)
6. bsmt. (basement)
7. cond. (condition)
8. condo (condominium)
9. cpt. (carpet)
10. dishw. (dishwasher)
11. dn. pmnt. (down payment)
12. elec. (electricity)
13. excel. (excellent)
14. fncd. (fenced)
15. ht. (heat)
16. incl. (included)
17. kitch. (kitchen)
18. laundr. (laundry room)
19. loc. (location)
20. mo. (month)
21. nr. (near)
22. open house
23. ownr. (owner)
24. real estate agent _____
25. realtor _____
26. refrig. (refrigerator) _____
27. rms. (rooms) _____
28. studio _____
29. transp. (transportation) _____
30. utils. (utilities) _____
31. w. (with) _____
32. w/w (wall–to–wall) _____
33. yd. (yard) _____

See Conversation Springboards on page 217.

Picture Discussion

With your class, answer the questions about the scenes. • *Use the vocabulary list.* • *Add more words.*

1. Do you understand these newspaper ads? Read them with your class.
2. Which house is the most expensive? the least expensive?
3. Which is the largest apartment? the smallest apartment?
4. What are the advantages and disadvantages of each apartment or house?
5. What are the special needs of each family?
6. Which home will each family choose?

Group Decision

In groups of three, decide which housing in the newspaper ads is best for each family. • *Should they rent or buy?* • *Report your decisions to another group and explain your reasons.* • *Did your groups make the same decisions?*

Partner Interview   Partner's Name _____

With a partner, ask these questions. • *Then report your partner's responses to another pair of students.*

1. Which of these housing ads interests you? What do you like about them?
2. Do you prefer a large or a small home? Why?
3. What is your "dream home"? Describe it.
4. Where would it be?
5. Who would live there with you?
6. Would you rent it or buy it? Why?

Group Role Play

In groups of four, write questions to ask a realtor about an apartment or a house. • *Then create a role play between a realtor and family.* • *Have each family member ask the realtor one of your group's questions.* • *Present your role play to the class.*

UTILITY PROBLEMS

1. air conditioner
2. blow a fuse
3. blow-dryer
4. current
5. cut off
6. dial tone
7. discontinue
8. extension cord
9. furnace
10. fuse box
11. hot water heater
12. ironing board
13. meter
14. nonpayment
15. notification
16. notify
17. oil heat
18. oil tank
19. overload a circuit
20. plug
21. plug in
22. rewire
23. run out
24. thermostat
25. wiring

_____

_____

_____

_____

_____

_____

_____

See Conversation Springboards on page 217.

Picture Discussion

With your class, answer the questions about the scenes. • Use the vocabulary list. • Add more words.

1. What is happening in each scene? What utility problems do these two people have?
2. How can they solve their problems?
3. How could these utility problems be avoided?
4. Tell the story of each of these people.

Group Problem Solving

In groups of four, discuss these utility problems. • State the problem. • What advice would you give? • Compare your solution with another group.

◆ You pick up your telephone receiver, but you can't get a dial tone.
◆ There is a bad thunderstorm, and your power is out.
◆ You want to take a hot shower, but the water is cold.

Partner Interview   Partner's Name _____

Ask a partner these questions. • Then report your partner's responses to another pair of students.

1. In your home, what runs on electricity? on gas? on oil?
2. In your home, where are the circuit breakers or fuse boxes? Have you ever changed a fuse or flipped the switch on a circuit breaker?
3. Where are the meters? How do you read them?
4. Have you ever had any problems with utilities? What happened? What did you do?

Cross-Cultural Exchange

In groups of four, choose a conversation monitor and a recorder. • Discuss these questions. • Compare cultures when possible. • Report the results of your discussion to the class.

1. What month is usually the coldest in your hometown? How cold is it (C°? F°?)?
2. What kinds of heating do people have?
3. In what months do people usually have to heat their homes?
4. What month is usually the hottest? How hot is it (C°? F°?)?
5. How do people stay cool in hot weather? Do many people have air conditioning?

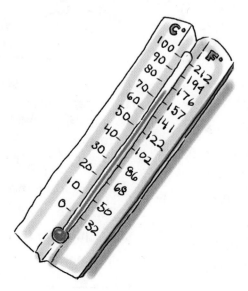

TENANTS AND LANDLORDS

Buy now!
New refrigerators,
$1,000 & $850!

Used refrigerator:
Good condition,
$250. Call
555-1183.

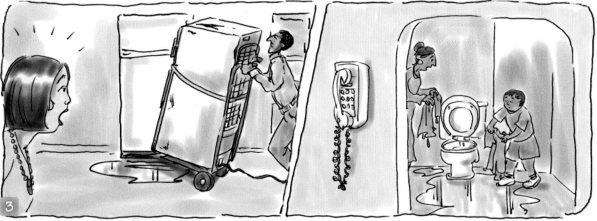

1. afford
2. affordable
3. as good as new
4. brand new
5. decent condition
6. fair
7. functional
8. landlady

9. landlord's responsibility
10. leaky
11. maintain
12. maintenance
13. major appliance
14. makeshift
15. melt

16. obligation _____
17. plumbing _____
18. serviceable _____
19. superintendent (super) _____
20. tenant's rights _____
21. used _____
22. working order _____

See Conversation Springboards on page 217.

Picture Discussion

With your class, answer the questions about the picture story. • Use the vocabulary list. • Add more words.

1. What is happening in each scene? Who are these people? What are they saying to each other?
2. Why doesn't the landlady buy a new refrigerator for the tenant? Why doesn't she buy a new toilet for herself?
3. What responsibilities does the landlady have?
4. What rights does the tenant have?
5. What is the fair thing to do in this situation? Why?
6. How does this story end? Is everyone satisfied with the solution?

Group Problem Solving

In groups of four, discuss these situations. • Find a solution for each problem. • Share your solutions with the class.

Problem 1: The tenants can't pay their rent on time, and the landlord needs the money to fix a broken thermostat.

Problem 2: The tenants want to nail shelves to the apartment walls. The landlord doesn't want nails in the walls.

Problem 3: The tenants are having trouble with their neighbors, so they want to break their lease and move away. The landlord won't let them.

Problem 4: The landlord is raising the rent because property taxes have increased. The tenants cannot afford to pay more rent.

Problem 5: The apartment stairs are broken. The tenants want them fixed. The landlord cannot get a carpenter for six weeks.

Group Role Play

In the same groups, create a role play, illustrating a solution to one of the problems above. • Present your role play to another group.

Cross-Cultural Exchange

In groups of four, choose a conversation monitor and a recorder. • Discuss these questions. • Compare cultures when possible. • Report the results of your discussion to the class.

1. What are tenants' rights in your country? What are landlords' rights?
2. What are tenants' responsibilities? landlords' responsibilities?
3. Who is responsible for cleaning stairways in apartment buildings?
4. Who is responsible for taking the trash outside?
5. Are there limits on the number of people occupying an apartment?
6. Do people hang laundry out of windows to dry?
7. What things do people take outside to clean?
8. Do people wash the sidewalks in front of their homes? How often?
9. Are there restrictions about noise? loud music?

INSURING YOUR PROPERTY

1. assess
2. damage
3. dog bite
4. dwelling
5. fire damage
6. homeowner
7. insurance adjustor
8. insurance coverage
9. liability
10. liable
11. loss of property
12. mandatory insurance
13. optional insurance
14. premium
15. protection
16. repair cost
17. replacement cost
18. smoke damage
19. stolen property
20. storm damage
21. water damage

_____

_____

_____

_____

_____

_____

_____

See Conversation Springboards on page 218.

Picture Discussion

With your class, answer the questions about the scenes. • Use the vocabulary list. • Add more words.

1. What is happening in each scene?
2. What damages or losses do you see in these scenes?
3. What caused the damages or losses?
4. Who are the people? What do you think they are saying?
5. What kind of insurance protection covers each of these situations?

Group Role Play

In groups of three, choose one of the scenes. • Create a role play. • In your role play, explain the situation and discuss the damages or losses and the insurance coverage. • Present your role play to the class.

Group Decision

In the same groups, discuss this scene and decide whether this renter should purchase renter's insurance or not. • If not, think of other ways he can protect his property. • Compare your group's decision with other groups.

Cross-Cultural Exchange

In groups of four, choose a conversation monitor and a recorder. • Discuss these questions. • Compare cultures when possible. • Report the results of your discussion to the class.

1. Do people in your country carry homeowner's or renter's insurance?
2. What kinds of insurance are mandatory? What kinds are optional?
3. How much does insurance usually cost?
4. If people do not have insurance, what do they do when their property is damaged or stolen?

MOVING

1. belongings/possessions
2. breakable
3. bump
4. crate
5. delicate
6. farewell
7. glassware
8. haul
9. household goods
10. leave behind
11. misplace
12. nick
13. organize
14. pack
15. packing box _____
16. put away _____
17. transport _____
18. unload _____
19. unwrap _____
20. utility trailer _____
21. wrap _____
_____

See Conversation Springboards on page 218.

Picture Discussion

With your class, answer the questions about the picture story. • Use the vocabulary list. • Add more words.

1. What is happening in each scene?
2. Did this family have a good experience moving? Why or why not?
3. Was it a good decision for this family to move their own belongings? Why or why not?
4. Why did they move?
5. Do you think they will be happy in their new life?

Group Brainstorm

In groups of four, choose a recorder. • List all the things people do before moving. • Read your list to the class. • Make a class list on the board.

Find Someone Who

Review the vocabulary with your teacher. • Add to this list. • Then interview your classmates and fill in the name of someone who . . .

1. has moved recently. _____

2. has moved many times. _____

3. has helped someone move. _____

4. has lost or broken something in a move. _____

5. hates to move. _____

6. _____ _____

7. _____ _____

Speech

Tell the class about an experience you had while moving. • Was it a good or bad one? • Why?

ANSWERING THE DOOR

1. amazed
2. cautious
3. chain lock
4. charitable
5. charity
6. collection
7. deliver newspapers

8. distrust
9. distrustful
10. door knocker
11. door-to-door
12. fearful
13. Girl Scout
14. lawn mower

15. overgrown
16. pay for
17. special delivery
18. stranger
19. unexpected
20. wary

_____
_____
_____
_____
_____

See Conversation Springboards on page 218.

Picture Discussion

With your class, answer the questions about the scenes. • Use the vocabulary list. • Add more words.

1. What is happening in each scene?
2. How are these people reacting? Why?
3. What are they saying?
4. What will happen next in each scene?

Group Role Play

In groups of three, choose one of the scenes. • Create a role play. • Present your role play to another group.

Group Brainstorm

In groups of four, choose a recorder. • List reasons why people come to your door. • Read your list to the class. • Make a class list on the board.

Group Discussion

In the same groups, choose a recorder. • Discuss these questions. • Compare your answers with another group.

1. Has anyone ever come to your door? Who? What did they want?
2. Do you always open the door? If not, why not? What do you do?
3. What do you say to the people at the door?
4. Do you keep your doors locked? Why or why not?

Partner Activity: Ask Aunt Betty

Partner's Name _____

With a partner, read and discuss this letter. • Together, write a reply from Aunt Betty, *giving advice to* Not His Wife.

ASK AUNT BETTY

Dear Aunt Betty:

We have a problem with our neighbor Matt. My husband and I were friendly with Matt and his wife, Jane. But now Jane has left Matt, and they are getting a divorce.

Ever since Jane left, Matt has come to our door every evening at suppertime. He not only stays for supper but he ends up staying for the whole evening!

I know he is lonely and unhappy, and he likes my home-cooked meals, but I'm getting tired of this. After all, I'm not his wife!

Not His Wife

NEIGHBORHOOD PROBLEMS

1. abandoned	10. hang out	19. run down	_____
2. advocate	11. homeless	20. run over	_____
3. boarded-up	12. inner city	21. stray dog	_____
4. dilapidated	13. junk	22. street light	_____
5. disrepair	14. litter	23. unsafe	_____
6. fire hazard	15. loiter	24. vagrant	_____
7. gang	16. neglect	25. vandal	_____
8. ghetto	17. personal safety	26. vandalism	_____
9. graffiti	18. petition	27. weeds	_____

Picture Discussion

With your class, answer the questions about the scene. • Use vocabulary from the list. • Add more words.

1. Describe this neighborhood.
2. Describe the people in this neighborhood.
3. What are the good things? What are the bad things?
4. What neighborhood improvements is the woman with the petition advocating?
5. Do you think she will be successful? Why or why not?

See Conversation Springboards on pages 218 and 219.

Group Problem Posing/Problem Solving

In groups of four, list all the problems you see in this neighborhood. • Next to each problem, list a solution. • Share your problems and solutions with the class.

Class Brainstorm

With your class, choose a recorder. • List as many neighborhood problems as possible. • Next to each problem, list a solution.

Find Someone Who

Review the vocabulary with your teacher. • Add to this list. • Then interview your classmates and fill in the name of someone who . . .

1. lives in a quiet neighborhood. _____

2. lives in a neighborhood with heavy traffic. _____

3. has parking problems in the neighborhood. _____

4. worries about personal safety in the neighborhood. _____

5. _____ _____

6. _____ _____

Community Activity

With your class, add to this list of housing problems. • Check the problems that apply to your community. • Find out what your community is doing to solve these problems. • Report the results to the class.

☐ not enough housing   ☐ _____

☐ housing too expensive   ☐ _____

☐ housing in poor condition ☐ _____

☐ inadequate water and sewage ☐ _____

NEIGHBORHOOD IMPROVEMENTS

1. alternate-side parking
2. clean-up campaign
3. crime watch
4. friendliness
5. grass-roots organization
6. help out
7. leash law
8. neighborhood association
9. neighborly
10. occupied
11. off-street parking
12. optimism
13. outlook
14. pitch in
15. rainbow
16. refurbish
17. rehabilitate
18. rehabilitation
19. renovate
20. renovation
21. sober
22. urban renewal

_____

_____

_____

_____

_____

_____

Picture Discussion

With your class, answer the questions about the scene. • Use the vocabulary list. • Add more words.

1. What changes have taken place in this neighborhood?

2. What are the people doing? How have they changed?

3. What are the improvements in neighborhood safety? neighbors' attitudes? property maintenance?

4. What does it mean to be neighborly? What neighborly actions are in this scene?

5. Why are grass-roots organizations important?

See Conversation Springboards on page 219.

Group Survey

In groups of four, complete this survey. • Report your results to the class.

1. Who lives in the noisiest neighborhood? the quietest neighborhood?
2. Who lives in the cleanest neighborhood? the dirtiest neighborhood?
3. Whose neighborhood is the safest? the most dangerous?
4. Whose neighborhood has the most parking problems? the fewest?
5. Whose neighborhood has the most children? the fewest?
6. Who likes his or her neighborhood the most? Why?
7. Who likes his or her neighborhood the least? Why?
8. What is the worst neighborhood problem? What do the neighbors do about the problem?

Cross-Cultural Exchange

In the same groups, choose a conversation monitor and a recorder. • Discuss these questions. • Compare cultures when possible. • Report the results of your discussion to the class.

1. What makes a neighborhood "good" in your culture? Describe a "good neighborhood."
2. What makes a neighbor "good" in your culture?
3. Describe a person you know who is a good neighbor. What has this person done that is neighborly?
4. What was your neighborhood like in your hometown?

Group Brainstorm

In groups of three, choose a recorder. • List ways to be neighborly. • Include things to do and things to say. • Read your list to the class. • Make a class list on the board. • How many different ways to be neighborly did your class think of?

Group Role Play

In the same groups, choose one way to be neighborly from your list. • Create a role play. • Present your role play to another group.

Community Activity

Discuss these questions with your class. • Decide how you will find answers to them. • Where can you look? • Whom can you ask? • In groups of four, find the answers and report back to the class.

1. Are there groups that are actively working to make improvements in your community? What are they?
2. What improvements are they making right now?
3. What improvements would you like to see in your community?

REVIEW

Partner Game: *What Do You Remember?*   Partner's Name _____

With a partner, look at the scenes of the neighborhood in Neighborhood Problems and Neighborhood Improvements on pages 122 and 124. • Remember as much as you can. • Close your books. • Describe the differences with your partner. • List everything. • Compare your list with another pair. • Add to your lists. • Open the book and look at the scenes. • What did you forget?

Group Questions

In groups of four, write questions that are important to ask before renting an apartment. • Compare your group's list with another group.

Partner Interview   Partner's Name _____

With a partner, write eight questions to ask about your home and neighborhood. • Ask another pair the questions. • Then report your questions and answers to another group of students.

Draw with a Partner   Partner's Name _____

Draw your dream home. • Describe it to a partner. • Then describe your partner's dream home to another pair of students.

Group Problem Posing

In groups of four, list problems people have with neighbors, neighborhoods, landlords, and tenants. • Compare your group's list with another group.

Group Role Play

In the same groups, choose one of the problems you listed. • Create a problem-solving role play. • Present your role play to the class.

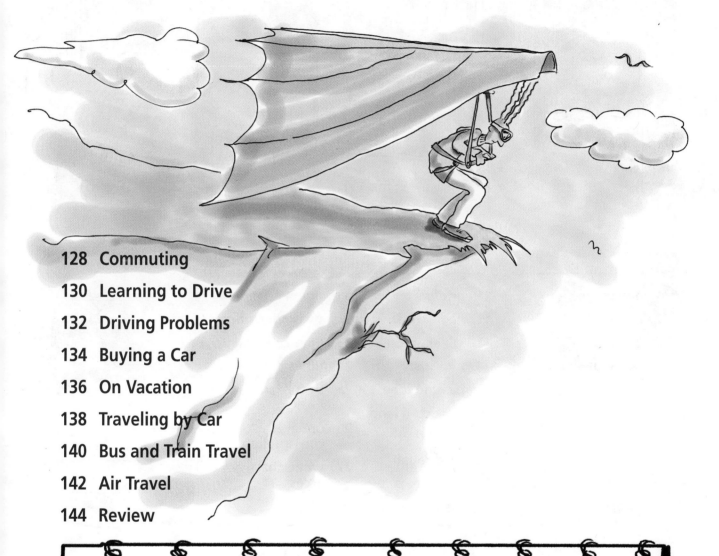

UNIT 7
TRANSPORTATION AND TRAVEL

LEARNING STRATEGIES

➤ Find written information about your local area. Create a class file and bulletin board with brochures, maps, and posters of different local tourist attractions.

➤ Write a letter to a friend coming to visit. Tell your friend about some of your favorite local sights.

➤ Look for good travel deals in advertisements. Bring them to class. Create a bulletin board of travel ads and interesting places to visit.

➤ Tell someone about your ideal vacation trip. Ask them what theirs is and compare your opinions.

COMMUTING

1. accessible
2. bumper-to-bumper
3. bus shelter
4. car pool
5. carpool
6. car pool lane
7. commuter
8. daily commute
9. detour
10. direct

11. gridlock
12. heavy traffic
13. kneeling bus
14. motorist
15. passing lane
16. restricted lane
17. road crew
18. road repair
19. route map
20. rush hour

21. signal
22. stuck in traffic
23. time-consuming
24. timesaving
25. traffic jam/ tie-up
26. under construction
27. wheelchair access

_____
_____
_____
_____
_____
_____
_____
_____

Picture Discussion

With your class, answer the questions about the scenes. • Use the vocabulary list. • Add more words.

1. What are these bus commuters doing?
2. What other things do commuters sometimes do on a bus? What do they do while they're waiting for a bus?
3. How will the man in the wheelchair get on the bus?
4. When can motorists use the carpool lane for carpooling?
5. Why is carpooling a good idea?

6. Why do the cars have to detour?
7. What other reasons are there for detours? for traffic tie-ups?
8. What are the advantages of taking a bus or train to work? What are the disadvantages?
9. What are the advantages and disadvantages of carpooling?

See Conversation Springboards on page 219.

Partner Interview

Partner's Name _____

Ask a partner these questions. • Then report your partner's responses to another pair of students.

1. How do you come to school?
2. How far do you live from school?
3. How long does it take you to get to school?
4. Are there other ways to travel to school? What are they?

5. How do you get to work? Is your commute easy?
6. How long does it take you to get to work?

Community Activity

In groups of four, list every way to commute in your community. • Write the telephone numbers of the transportation companies. • Call and find out the cost of each. • Which is most convenient for you? • Why?

Dialog Journal

Partner's Name _____

*Write a **Journal** entry about an experience you have had commuting to school or work. • Then read your entry to a partner. • Ask questions about your partner's entry.*

LEARNING TO DRIVE

1. back in
2. back up
3. curb
4. driver education
5. driving instructor
6. driving manual
7. experienced
8. fail
9. inexperienced
10. issue
11. knock over
12. motor vehicle bureau (MVB)
13. parallel park
14. pass
15. renew
16. retake
17. reverse
18. road test
19. steer
20. traffic cone/ pylon
21. vision test
22. written test

_____
_____
_____
_____
_____

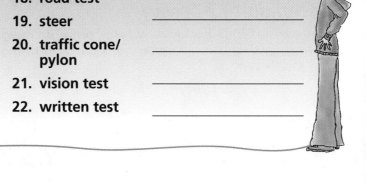

See Conversation Springboards on page 220.

Picture Discussion

With your class, answer the questions about the picture story. • Use the vocabulary list. • Add more words.

1. What class is in the first scene? What is the textbook? What is the instructor saying?
2. What tests are required for a driver license?
3. Which test does the young man fail? Why does he fail?
4. What does he do after he fails? Why is he finally smiling?
5. How will he become an experienced driver?
6. What test will he need to take again to renew his license.
7. Tell the story of this young man's experience learning to drive.

Group Discussion

In groups of four, choose a recorder. • Answer these questions. • Then report your information to another group. • Share the most interesting facts with the class.

1. Do you have a driver license? Where was it issued?
2. What was the fee for your license?
3. Does your license have restrictions? What are they?
4. Where in your community can you apply for or renew a driver license? Can you renew by mail?
5. What other related services are offered at the same office?
6. Do you have an international driver license? Where have you used it?

Conversation Squares

In groups of three, fill in the chart. • First write your own answers. • Then ask your partners the questions and write their answers. • Compare your group's answers with another group.

	You	**Partner 1**	**Partner 2**
Student's Name			
When was the first time you drove?			
Who taught you?			
Did you have any problems learning to drive?			
Did you pass the test the first time?			

Share Your Story

In the same groups, tell about your experience while learning to drive. • Decide which story to tell the class.

DRIVING PROBLEMS

1. accident report
2. blood alcohol level
3. Breathalyzer test
4. change a tire
5. collide
6. collision
7. dent
8. driving under the influence
9. drunk driving

10. emission
11. exhaust
12. fender bender
13. flat tire
14. intoxicated
15. intoxication
16. jack
17. jack up
18. lugnut

19. lug wrench
20. minor accident
21. no-fault/ liability insurance
22. spare tire
23. tail pipe
24. ticket
25. violate
26. violation

_____
_____
_____
_____
_____
_____

See Conversation Springboards on page 220.

Picture Discussion

With your class, answer the questions about the scenes. • Use the vocabulary list. • Add more words.

1. How did the woman get a flat tire? What does she need to do to change her tire?

2. Why did the accident happen? Whose fault was it?

3. What will happen to the intoxicated driver?

4. What will the driver of the other car have to do about the accident?

5. What problems does the man's car have? What will he have to do?

6. What is each police officer doing?

Partner Role Play

Partner's Name _____

With a partner, create thought balloons for each scene. • Compare your balloons with another pair. • Choose one of the scenes and create a role play. • Present your role play to the class.

What Do You Say? What Do You Do?

In groups of four, state the problem. • Decide what to say and do in each situation. • Compare your decisions with the class.

1. Your insurance expired and you forgot to renew it.

2. You are driving down the highway and you hit a dog that runs into the road.

3. You are driving down the street and you notice the car in front of you is losing its tail pipe.

4. A police officer has stopped you for speeding. You are rushing to get home because your mother is very ill.

Cross-Cultural Exchange

In the same groups, choose a conversation monitor and a recorder. • Discuss these questions. • Compare cultures when possible. • Report the results of your discussion to the class.

1. In your country, what kinds of cars are popular?

2. Is insurance required?

3. What happens when there is a minor accident?

4. What happens when a police officer stops someone for driving while intoxicated?

5. What are the most common driving problems in your country?

Community Activity

*In the same groups, bring in an automobile insurance policy. • Discuss the insurance coverage. • Decide what coverage is best. • List the new vocabulary on the board. • Copy the new words in the **Vocabulary** section of your notebook.*

BUYING A CAR

1. add-on
2. bad deal
3. bucket seats
4. car dealer
5. compact car
6. economical
7. economy car
8. 4 × 4
9. four-door
10. good deal

11. make
12. make a deal
13. model
14. negotiable
15. negotiate
16. option
17. optional
18. roof rack
19. sales pitch
20. sedan

21. showroom
22. sports utility vehicle
23. station wagon
24. sticker price
25. sun roof
26. truth in advertising
27. two-door
28. used car lot
29. van

See Conversation Springboards on page 220.

Picture Discussion

With your class, answer the questions about the scenes. • *Use the vocabulary list.* • *Add more words.*

1. What kinds of vehicles are for sale in these scenes?

2. What makes and models do they look like?

3. What are the advantages and disadvantages of each deal?

4. Which car looks like the best deal? Why?

5. What questions should these people ask about each car?

Partner Role Play   Partner's Name _____

With a partner, create a role play about one of the ads. • *Present your role play to the class.*

Group Brainstorm

In groups of three, choose a recorder. • *List options found in a car or other vehicle.* • *Read your list to the class.* • *Make a class list on the board.*

Community Activity

In groups of four, bring in car ads from the newspaper. • *Read them together.* • *List the abbreviations on the board and discuss them.* • *Choose a car you would like to buy.* • *Tell the class about the car and why you chose it.*

ON VACATION

1. beach house
2. bungalow
3. castle
4. exotic
5. faraway places
6. hammock
7. hike
8. hiker
9. mountain bike
10. mountain climbing
11. package tour
12. rental car
13. scenery
14. scenic
15. sea
16. snowcapped
17. travel agent
18. traveler
19. vacationer
20. view
21. vista
22. youth hostel

_____
_____
_____
_____
_____
_____
_____

Picture Discussion

With your class, answer the questions about the scenes. • Use the vocabulary list. • Add more words.

1. Where are the students dreaming of going on vacation?
2. Where will they stay? What will they do?
3. How long will each vacation last?
4. What kind of preparations does each student have to make for the vacation?
5. How much will each vacation cost?
6. Which vacation would you enjoy most? least? Why?

See Conversation Springboards on pages 220 and 221.

Partner Role Play

Partner's Name _____

With a partner, decide on a place to go for a vacation. • *Create a role play between a traveler and a travel agent.* • *Present your role play to the class.*

Partner Activity: Ask Aunt Betty

Partner's Name _____

With the same partner, read and discuss this letter. • *Together, write a response from Aunt Betty, giving advice to Illegal in Illinois.* • *Read your letter to the class.*

Share Your Story

In groups of four, tell about the best or worst vacation you have ever had. • *Decide which story to tell the class.*

Community Activity

Choose a place you would like to visit. • *Go to a travel agent and get brochures and information.* • *Tell the class what you learned.*

ASK AUNT BETTY

Dear Aunt Betty:

I am planning to visit my family in my home country. I'm not sure how to do this because I am living in this country illegally. I meant to renew my student visa, but since I was busy working and going to school, I forgot.

Now it's my grandmother's birthday, and my family wants me to come home. What should I do?

Illegal in Illinois

TRAVELING BY CAR

1. access road	10. highway	19. road trip
2. back seat	11. highway patrol	20. roadside motel
3. barrier	12. interstate	21. shoulder
4. billboard	13. main road	22. speeding ticket
5. exact change lane	14. night clerk	23. station attendant
6. expressway/ freeway	15. pump gas	24. toll
7. family reunion	16. registration desk/front desk	25. toll booth
8. fill up	17. rest stop	26. toll road
9. full-service station	18. roadkill	27. turnpike

See Conversation Springboards on page 221.

Picture Discussion

With your class, answer the questions about the picture story. • Use the vocabulary list. • Add more words.

1. What is the family doing in this story?
2. Where are they going?
3. How many miles do you think they have to travel?
4. What time do they leave? How many days does the trip take? What time do they arrive?
5. How fast do they drive?
6. What might they do at rest stops along the way?
7. What is the highway patrol officer doing?
8. What do the adults do in the car? What do the children do? What does the dog do?

Advantages/Disadvantages

In groups of three, discuss the advantages and disadvantages of traveling by car. • Share your information with another group. • Report the most interesting ideas to the class.

What Do You Say? What Do You Do?

In the same groups, state the problem. • Decide what to say and do in each situation. • Compare your decisions with the class.

1. You need directions to get to the main highway.
2. You don't know how much the toll is.
3. You don't know where the nearest gas station is.
4. You are driving on a highway and are completely lost.

Cross-Cultural Exchange

In groups of five, choose a conversation monitor and a recorder. • Discuss these questions. • Compare cultures when possible. • Report the results of your discussion to the class.

1. In your country, do people take long road trips? Where to?
2. What are the speed limits on highways in your country?
3. Are there toll roads? How much are the tolls?
4. Are there rest stops? What are they like?

BUS AND TRAIN TRAVEL

1. arrive	9. distressed	17. ticket agent
2. board	10. inform	18. ticket counter
3. bus station	11. information board	19. time change
4. coach	12. information booth	20. time zone
5. conductor	13. locomotive	21. train platform
6. depart	14. porter	22. train station
7. destination	15. sleeper car	23. waiting area
8. dining car	16. terminal	

Picture Discussion

With your class, answer the questions about the scenes. • *Use the vocabulary list.* • *Add more words.*

1. What are all the people doing in each scene? What are their destinations?

2. What is the ticketing agent at the bus station ticket counter saying to the young man?

3. Why does the train station have three clocks showing different times?

4. Why is the man at the train station information booth so distressed? What is he shouting? What will the agent at the booth do to help him?

5. What is similar about bus travel and train travel? What is different? What are the advantages and disadvantages of each?

See Conversation Springboards on pages 221 and 222.

What's the Story?

In groups of four, choose a recorder. • Tell a story about one of these travelers. • Where is the traveler going? • Why? • Everyone in the group should contribute at least two sentences. • Read your story to the class.

What Do You Say? What Do You Do?

In the same groups, decide what to say and do in each situation. • Compare your decisions with the class.

1. Your friend is arriving on the 8:12 train from Boston. It's 8:30 and the train hasn't arrived.

2. You need information about taking a bus from Dallas to Los Angeles. Find out the departure times and the prices.

3. You are waiting in line at the bus station. The person in front of you is trying to buy a one-way ticket to New York, but he doesn't speak English very well—he speaks your first language. Try to assist him.

Group Brainstorm

In the same groups, choose a recorder. • List questions travelers ask at an information booth in a bus or train station. • Read your list to the class. • Make a class list on the board.

Partner Interview

Partner's Name _____

Ask a partner these questions. • Then report your partner's responses to another pair of students.

1. When was the last time you traveled by bus or train?

2. Where did you go?

3. What was the fare?

4. How long did the trip take?

5. Describe the trip: Was the bus or train crowded? Were you able to get a seat? Where did you sit? What did you do? Who else was traveling with you?

AIR TRAVEL

1. aisle seat
2. baggage carousel
3. baggage cart
4. baggage claim
5. boarding pass
6. carry-on bag
7. check baggage
8. check-in counter
9. claim check
10. customs

11. customs declaration form
12. disembarkation card
13. embarkation card
14. flight attendant
15. gate
16. immigration
17. in-flight meal
18. metal detector

19. overhead compartment
20. security check
21. special meal
22. ticket stub
23. tilt
24. tray
25. tray table
26. upright position
27. window seat

See Conversation Springboards on page 222.

Picture Discussion

With your class, answer the questions about the picture story. • Use the vocabulary list. • Add more words.

1. What is happening in each scene?
2. What are the airport procedures for departure? for arrival?
3. What procedures are different for international travel?
4. Tell the story of this young man's trip.

Partner Role Play

Partner's Name _____

You are at the airport, checking in for an international flight. • With a partner, create a role play between the passenger and the ticket agent. • Present your role play to the class.

What Do You Say? What Do You Do?

In groups of four, state the problem. • Decide what to say and do in each situation. • Compare your decisions with the class.

1. You go through the security check, and the buckle on your belt sets off the alarm.
2. You are on an airplane, and a little girl behind you is kicking the seat.
3. You are on an airplane and you don't feel very well.
4. After you leave the terminal with one suitcase, you remember you left a bag on the carousel.

Community Activity

In the same groups, research these questions. • Report your findings to the class.

1. Where can you apply for a passport in your community?
2. Where can you get travel information in your community?
3. What is the closest airport? How long does it take to get there from your home? from the school? Is there public transportation to the airport?

REVIEW

Group Vocabulary Challenge

In groups of four, list as many types of transportation as you can. • Work fast! • Read your list to the class. • Which group has the longest list? • Make a class list on the board.

Draw with a Partner
Partner's Name _____

What kind of car would you like to have? • Draw a picture. • Then list all the features you would like. • Explain your dream car to a partner. • How much does it cost? • Find an ad in the newspaper that comes the closest to your dream car.

Partner Questions
Partner's Name _____

With a partner, write five questions about traveling. • Then ask your questions to another pair of students. • Present your questions and answers to the class.

Partner Activity: Ask Aunt Betty
Partner's Name _____

With a partner, write to Aunt Betty, asking for advice about a transportation problem. • Then exchange with another pair. • Respond to their letter. • Read their letter and your reply to the class.

Partner Game: What Do You Remember?

Partner's Name _____

With a partner, look at one of the stories or scenes in this unit. • Remember as much as you can. • Close your books. • Describe the scene with your partner. • List everything. • Which pair of students has the longest list in the class?

Partner Lists
Partner's Name _____

With a partner, list as many driving and commuting problems as you can. • Compare lists with your classmates. • Who has the longest list? • Choose three problems from your list. • Find solutions with your partner. • Read your solutions to another pair.

UNIT 8
FINDING A JOB

LEARNING STRATEGIES

➤ In the **Vocabulary** section of your notebook, list the jobs you see people doing every day and the skills required for each job.

➤ Watch the news and commercials on TV every day. Add to your list the different jobs you see.

➤ Do you have questions about your list? Ask your family, friends, teacher, and classmates about the jobs on your list.

➤ Write about your list in the **Journal** section of your notebook. Divide your list into jobs you think you would like and jobs you think you would not like. Explain your reasons.

JOBS IN YOUR COMMUNITY

1. agriculture
2. arts
3. banking
4. beauty care
5. commerce
6. communications
7. design
8. entertainment
9. food service
10. government

11. health care industry
12. industry
13. law enforcement
14. manufacturing
15. money management
16. news media
17. occupation
18. office work
19. photography

20. private sector
21. public service
22. retail sales
23. security
24. service industry
25. shipping
26. tourism
27. vendor

See Conversation Springboards on page 222.

Picture Discussion

With your class, answer the questions about the scenes. • Use the vocabulary list. • Add more words.

1. What kinds of workers do the students see in these scenes? Make a list on the board.

2. Describe the job each person does.

3. What general occupation does each worker fit into?

4. What other kinds of jobs fit into these occupations?

Group Brainstorm

In groups of four, choose a recorder. • Fill in the five charts with answers to the questions. • Report your information to the class.

1. What fruits, vegetables, trees, and flowers are grown in your community? What jobs in agriculture are available there?

Agriculture	Jobs

2. What industries are in your community? What large companies? What kinds of jobs are available there?

Industries/Large Companies	Jobs

3. What small businesses are in your community? What kinds of jobs are available there?

Small Businesses	Jobs

4. What places in your community provide food services? What food service jobs are available there?

Places with Food Services	Jobs

5. What other kinds of services are provided in your community? What service-related jobs are there?

Other Services	Jobs

Cross-Cultural Exchange

In the same groups, choose a conversation monitor and a recorder. • Discuss these questions. • Compare cultures when possible. • Report the results of your discussion to the class.

1. What businesses and industries are in your hometown?
2. What jobs are most common there?
3. What are the wages?
4. What is the training necessary for each job?

Class Interview

Who has a job in your community? • With your class, write a list of questions on the board about the different jobs people have. • Conduct class interviews with them. • Interview your teacher first!

Community Activity

In groups of three, choose a place in your community to research. • Go there, and list all the workplaces, workers, kinds of work, and occupation categories you see. • Report your findings to the class.

YOUR OCCUPATION

1. administrative assistant
2. auto worker
3. blue collar
4. certification
5. clerical
6. executive
7. first shift

8. hospital worker
9. inspector
10. management
11. night shift
12. office worker
13. overtime
14. second shift

15. secretarial
16. self-employed
17. shift
18. third shift
19. underemployed
20. unqualified
21. white collar

See Conversation Springboards on pages 222 and 223.

Picture Discussion

With your class, answer the questions about the scenes. • Use the vocabulary list. • Add more words.

1. What is happening in each scene?
2. What occupations do these students have?
3. What shift does each person work?
4. What kind of preparation did each student need for his or her occupation?
5. The hospital aide was a doctor in her country. Why is she underemployed?
6. Do any of these jobs require certification? What other jobs require certification?
7. Which of these occupations are hazardous? Why?
8. Are these people happy with their occupations? Why or why not?

Group Vocabulary Challenge

*In groups of four, list as many occupations as you can. • Work fast! • Read your list to the class. • Which group has the longest list? • Make a class list on the board. • Copy the new words in the **Vocabulary** section of your notebook.*

Group Brainstorm

In the same groups, choose a recorder. • List questions to ask about someone's job. • Read your list to the class. • Make a class list on the board.

Class Survey

With your class, add to this list of questions. • Interview your classmates. • Report your results to the class. • How many members of your class . . .

1. have worked full time? _____
2. have worked part time? _____
3. have been unemployed? _____
4. have worked overtime? _____
5. have worked the first shift? _____
6. have worked the night shift? _____
7. have been self-employed? _____
8. have been underemployed? _____
9. _____ _____
10. _____ _____

Speech

Present a two-minute speech to your class about your job or occupation. • Use notecards, but do not read your speech. • Practice your speech with a partner first.

THE RIGHT JOB FOR YOU

1. analytical	10. heavy equipment operator	18. presentation _____
2. analyze	11. independent	19. professional _____
3. build	12. interesting	20. skilled _____
4. builder	13. job training	21. solve problems _____
5. challenge	14. manual labor	22. technical _____
6. challenging	15. medical technician	23. unskilled _____
7. construction site	16. men's apparel/ fashion	24. work environment _____
8. coordinate		_____
9. elementary school teacher	17. paraprofessional	_____

Picture Discussion

With your class, answer the questions about the scenes. • Use the vocabulary list. • Add more words.

1. What jobs is this student imagining?
2. What work would he do in each job?
3. What would he wear for each job?

4. What would be the advantages of each job?
5. What would be the disadvantages of each job?

See Conversation Springboards on page 223.

Draw with a Partner

With a partner, fill in the empty bubble with one more job possibility. • Decide which job the student should choose. • Explain your decision to another pair.

Partner Interview

Partner's Name _____

With a partner, ask the questions on this Job Interest Inventory Survey about job preferences. • Then report your partner's responses to another pair.

JOB INTEREST INVENTORY SURVEY

1. Which are more important to you in a job?

   ☐ friendly co-workers ☐ convenient location ☐ other: _____

   ☐ a good supervisor ☐ interesting work

   ☐ good pay ☐ chance for advancement

   ☐ convenient hours ☐ challenging work

   Explain your answer: _____

2. Do you prefer to work quickly or slowly? Explain your answer:

   _____

3. Which are important in your work environment?

   ☐ noise level ☐ temperature ☐ lighting ☐ other: _____

   ☐ odors ☐ space ☐ indoors/outdoors

   Explain your answer: _____

4. Are you willing to travel? to live in another country? Explain your answer:

   _____

5. Which of these do you like to do?

   ☐ make things ☐ perform or make presentations

   ☐ help people ☐ solve problems

   ☐ buy or sell things ☐ other: _____

   Explain your answer: _____

6. How much preparation or training time are you willing to spend?

   ☐ a few weeks ☐ six months

   ☐ two years ☐ four years

   ☐ six years ☐ other: _____

   Explain your answer: _____

7. What is your ideal job?

   Explain your answer: _____

LOOKING FOR A JOB

1. bulletin board
2. classified advertisement (ad)
3. employment agency
4. employment counselor
5. entry level
6. experience necessary
7. help wanted sign
8. inquire
9. job lead
10. job qualification
11. job search
12. make an inquiry
13. no experience required
14. position
15. post
16. recommend
17. recommendation
18. seek employment
19. telephone interview
20. word of mouth

_____
_____
_____
_____
_____
_____
_____

Picture Discussion

With your class, answer the questions about the picture story. • Use the vocabulary list. • Add more words.

1. What is happening in the story?
2. What are the people saying in each scene?
3. What different methods is this man using to look for a job?
4. What other methods could he use to find a job?

See Conversation Springboards on page 223.

Partner Role Play

With a partner, choose one of the scenes. • Create a role play. • Present your role play to another pair of students.

Find Someone Who

Review the vocabulary with your teacher. • Add to this list. • Then ask your classmates and fill in the name of someone who . . .

1. has found a job from a newspaper ad. _____

2. has found a job through an employment agency. _____

3. has found a job through a HELP WANTED sign in a window. _____

4. has found a job through a friend. _____

5. is looking for a job now. _____

6. _____ _____

7. _____ _____

Group Decision

In groups of four, read the employment opportunities listed in this sample newspaper classified section.

◆ Discuss the abilities, experience, and job needs of each member of your group.

◆ Discuss the advantages and disadvantages of each job.

◆ Do any of these jobs appeal to anyone in your group?

◆ Choose the best job for each member of your group.

◆ If there is no appropriate job listed, write one.

◆ Report your decisions to the class.

CLASSIFIED/HELP WANTED

DOUG'S DELIVERY IS LOOKING FOR friendly, courteous, and effective customer service representatives and meal couriers. Call 555-2173 for details.

HAIRDRESSER
Immediate opening for colorist/stylist for upscale French salon/treatment center. No following necessary. To apply, fax resume to Béatrice at 555-6252.

MANAGEMENT TRAINEE
Entry-level position available with Arizona branch of nation's leading motor carrier. Applicant must be willing to work all shifts in fast-paced environment. College degree preferred. Send resume to: T6400 Tribune 85890

OFFICE MANAGER
Bright, energetic & take-charge person needed by a downtown giftware co. Resume to: T5411 Daily Star 10024

PEST CONTROL TECHNICIAN
needed. Apply at Pacific Pest Control, 34 S. 8th St., M-F 9am-1pm.

PHOTOGRAPHER'S ASSISTANT
Will train; must be energetic, friendly, outgoing. Apply in person: Jake's Old Time Photo, 24th and Adams, Millville.

SALES
PERSONALITY PLUS
Co. in growth stage seeking 2 key people; above-average attitude; neat appearance a must. Call 555-2316. Training available.

SECRETARY/RECEPTIONIST
Prefer. exp. in construction industry, Woodbury location. Computer skills required. Busy office. Fax resume: 555-7655.

STEP AEROBICS INSTRUCTOR
Certification required. Sierra Athletic Club, Sierra, 555-1398.

SUPERINTENDENT
Wanted with exp. & tools. Interviews to be held this week betw. 10am & 1pm at 22 92nd St., Newtown, 555-8342. Call for directions only.

APPLYING FOR A JOB

1   **2**

1. applicant
2. availability
3. career objective
4. contact
5. director
6. first impression
7. hire
8. human resources
9. interview

10. interviewer
11. job application
12. job offer
13. job reference
14. minimum wage
15. personnel department
16. position desired
17. proper appearance

18. punctual
19. recruit
20. recruiter
21. recruitment
22. requirement
23. resume
24. starting salary
25. well qualified
26. work history

_____
_____
_____
_____
_____
_____
_____

Picture Discussion

With your class, answer the questions about the picture story. • Use the vocabulary list. • Add more words.

1. What is happening in each scene? What are the people saying?

2. What is each applicant wearing? Are the clothes appropriate? Why or why not?

3. What information does the job application ask for?

4. What information would be on each applicant's resume?

5. How does each applicant feel about this interview?

6. How does the personnel director feel about each applicant?

See Conversation Springboards on page 224.

What's the Story?

In groups of three, tell the story of one of these job applicants. • Report your story to the class. • Answer these questions.

1. What job is the person applying for?
2. What is the starting salary?

3. What is the person's work history? What special skills does he or she have?
4. Does he or she get the job? Why?

Group Discussion

In groups of four, discuss these questions. • Use the words from the vocabulary list. • Then report your information to the class.

1. Should you include all of your work history on a job application? Explain your answer.
2. What should you do if you cannot arrive on time for your interview?
3. What should you wear to an interview?
4. What would you do if the interviewer said the company could not meet your salary requirements?

5. What would you say if the interviewer tells you that the company cannot give you the job you want?
6. What could you list as special skills, awards, training certifications, or other abilities?
7. Who would you use as a job reference? Why?

Group Questions

In groups of four, list two sets of job interview questions: (1) questions the interviewer will ask and (2) questions the applicant should ask. • Read your questions to the class. • Make a class list of the two sets of questions.

Partner Role Play   Partner's Name _____

With a partner, create a role play of a job interview. • Use your group interview questions from above. • Present your role play to another pair.

WAGES AND BENEFITS

1. accidental death and dismemberment insurance (AD&D)
2. annual
3. benefits package
4. bimonthly
5. biweekly
6. bonus
7. child care
8. commission
9. compensation
10. contract
11. dental coverage
12. dependent coverage
13. early retirement
14. group insurance
15. income
16. insurance policy
17. insurance premium
18. leave of absence
19. life insurance
20. medical coverage
21. monthly
22. paid vacation
23. profit sharing
24. reimburse
25. reimbursement
26. remuneration
27. salary
28. savings plan
29. unpaid leave

See Conversation Springboards on page 224.

Picture Discussion

With your class, answer the questions about the scenes. • Use the vocabulary list. • Add more words.

1. What benefit does each scene illustrate? Describe each one.
2. What other benefits are there? Fill in the empty bubble with one example.
3. What forms is the new employee signing?
4. Who is he talking to?
5. What are some reasons to take a leave of absence?
6. Why is life insurance important?
7. What are some advantages of early retirement?

Group Decision

In groups of three, decide which one of these jobs you would choose. • In each job, the work is exactly the same. • The only differences are the wages, hours, benefits, and commute. • Report your decision and reasons to the class.

Job 1: Pays $14 per hour. Part-time job. At least 15 hours per week guaranteed, with possibly up to 40 hours some weeks. No benefits. Fifteen-minute walk.

Job 2: Pays $8 per hour, plus time-and-a-half for overtime. Full-time job, 40 hours per week. Benefits package includes health, one-week paid vacation plus four paid holidays, and child care available on site. Half-hour commute by car; no public transportation.

Job 3: Pays $10 per hour. Full-time job, 40 hours per week. Complete benefits package includes health and life insurance, two-week paid vacation plus five paid holidays, and company retirement plan. No child care. One-hour commute by train.

Group Brainstorm

In the same groups, choose a recorder. • List reasons to ask for a raise. • Read your list to the class. • Make a class list on the board. • Which are the best reasons?

Community Activity

Bring a local newspaper to class. • With a partner, list the best jobs, wages, and benefits from the Help Wanted section. • Report your list to the class. • Make a class list on the board. • What jobs are available? • How much do they pay? • What benefits are offered?

Cross-Cultural Exchange

In groups of four, choose a conversation monitor and a recorder. • Discuss these questions. • Compare cultures when possible. • Report the results of your discussion to the class.

1. What job benefits are common in your country? Describe them.
2. What benefits do people have when they lose their job?
3. What are the best paying jobs?
4. Which jobs are the most secure?

REVIEW

Partner Game: *What Do You Remember?* Partner's Name _____

With a partner, make four lists about jobs in your community. • Include as many items as you can remember. • Compare your lists with another pair.

Places Where People Work	Jobs People Have	Ways to Find a Job	Job Benefits
_____	_____	_____	_____
_____	_____	_____	_____
_____	_____	_____	_____
_____	_____	_____	_____
_____	_____	_____	_____
_____	_____	_____	_____
_____	_____	_____	_____
_____	_____	_____	_____

Partner Interview   Partner's Name _____

With a partner, ask these questions. • Then report your partner's responses to another pair of students.

1. What different kinds of jobs have you had? Describe them.
2. Which job did you like best? What did you like about it?
3. How did you find that job?
4. What kind of job would you like to have? What appeals to you about that job?
5. What preparation will you need for that job?
6. How long will the preparation take?
7. What is most important to you in a job?

Partner Role Play   Partner's Name _____

With a partner, write five good questions for an interviewer to ask in a job interview. • Write five good questions for the job applicant to ask. • Create a role play for a job interview with these questions. • Present your role play to the class.

Group Brainstorm

In groups of four, choose a recorder. • List some good advice for someone who is looking for a job. • Report your advice to the class.

LEARNING STRATEGIES

➤ In the **Journal** section of your notebook, write an entry about all the skills you have. Write a second entry about all the skills you would like to have and why you would like to have them.

➤ Listen carefully to what people say as they do their work in everyday life. Also, watch and listen carefully to TV programs that involve people at work. Take notes in the **Vocabulary** section of your notebook. Report your findings to the class.

➤ Visit a place where people are working. Notice if people are doing a good job or bad job. Notice their attitude, too. Report your findings to the class.

STARTING A NEW JOB

1. anxiety
2. anxious
3. awkward
4. colleague
5. complicated
6. eager
7. embarrassed
8. enthusiasm
9. enthusiastic
10. haste
11. hasty
12. impatience
13. intimidate
14. intimidating
15. knowledgeable
16. lunch break
17. mistake
18. paper jam
19. probationary period _____
20. rushed _____
21. show how _____
22. task
23. uncertain
24. unclear _____
25. unfamiliar _____

_____

See Conversation Springboards on pages 224 and 225.

Picture Discussion

With your class, answer the questions about the picture story. • *Use the vocabulary list.* • *Add more words.*

1. What is happening in each scene?
2. What is good about this woman's first day on the job? What is bad?
3. How do her co-workers treat her? Why?

4. Why does she have each problem?
5. How does she feel at the end of the day? Why?

What's the Story?

Partner's Name _____

With a partner, create a story for this new employee. • *Tell the story to another pair of students.* • *Be sure to answer these questions.*

1. What is her name?
2. What is her job?

3. What work experience has she had?
4. Will she succeed at this job? Why or why not?

Group Problem Solving

In groups of four, discuss possible solutions to the young woman's problems at work. • *Decide what advice to give her for the next day at work.* • *Report your advice to the class.*

Share Your Story

Tell the class about a good or bad experience at a new job.

INSTRUCTIONS AT WORK

1. assume
2. check
3. clarification
4. clarify
5. confused
6. confusion
7. demonstrate
8. demonstration
9. double-check
10. expect

11. expectation
12. figure out
13. follow
14. illustrate
15. illustration
16. instruction manual
17. misunderstand
18. mix up
19. mix-up

20. overlook
21. perplexed
22. puzzled
23. repeat
24. request
25. sequence
26. skip a step
27. specific
28. specifically
29. take for granted

_____
_____
_____
_____
_____
_____
_____
_____

Picture Discussion

With your class, answer the questions about the scenes. • Use the vocabulary list. • Add more words.

1. What is happening in each scene?
2. What went wrong in these situations? Why?

3. What will happen next in each scene?
4. How is it possible to avoid these problems?

See Conversation Springboards on page 225.

What Do You Say? What Do You Do?

In groups of three, decide what to say and do in each of these situations. • Share your solutions with another group. • Role-play one solution for the class.

◆ You don't know how to switch a phone call to another employee's extension. You have no instructions.

◆ You are typing a report which is due at the end of the day. Your computer just "crashed." You don't have the instruction manual.

◆ You work at the counter in a cafeteria and can't understand a customer.

◆ You deliver packages to a house where a very large dog chases you every time you approach.

Community Activity

Find a set of instructions at home, at work, or in an office or agency in your community (how to operate a washing machine, how to use a copy machine, how to use an ATM card). • Bring the instructions to class. • Read them with your classmates and figure them out together. • Are the instructions clear?

Write with a Partner   Partner's Name _____

With a partner, choose one of the following tasks. • Write a set of instructions for the task. • Read your instructions to another pair, and have them pantomime the task. (Make sure you include every step of the task!)

◆ wash clothes in a washing machine

◆ connect a VCR to a TV

◆ operate a standard shift car

◆ hang a picture on a wall

◆ plant a tree

◆ other: _____

Speech

Demonstrate a procedure for your class. • Choose a procedure that you know well (preparing a special dish, explaining a math problem, performing a special dance step, using a special piece of equipment). • Bring to class everything you need to make your demonstration clear. • Use the board for written instructions.

DOING A GOOD JOB

1. alert
2. bad attitude
3. bag groceries
4. careful
5. careless
6. clock in
7. conscientious
8. courteous
9. crush
10. diligent
11. discourteous
12. good attitude
13. hardworking
14. industrious
15. initiative
16. interested
17. pride
18. reach
19. stack
20. teamwork
21. work habits
_____
_____
_____
_____
_____

Picture Discussion

With your class, answer the questions about the scenes. • Use the vocabulary list. • Add more words.

1. What is happening in each scene?
2. In what ways are these workers doing a good job?
3. Which workers need to improve their work habits? Why?
4. What other ways are there to doing a good job in a supermarket? in a factory? in a fast food restaurant? in a bank? in an office? Make a list on the board.

See Conversation Springboards on page 225.

Group Problem Solving

In groups of three, discuss this problem and agree on a solution. • Report your solution to the class.

◆ You are one of the workers in these scenes who is doing a good job. Your co-worker is *not* doing a good job. What can you do to improve the situation?

Group Role Play

In the same groups, create these two role plays. • Present your role plays to the class.

◆ The manager is talking to a worker who is doing a good job.
◆ The manager is talking to a worker who is doing a bad job.

Partner Activity: Ask Aunt Betty

Partner's Name _____

With a partner, read and discuss this letter. • Together, write a response from Aunt Betty, giving advice to Frustrated in Fresno. • Read your letter to the class.

ASK AUNT BETTY

Dear Aunt Betty:
  I work in an office with four co-workers. Three of us arrive on time every day, work hard, and often stay late to finish our work. One person, however, is often late, takes long breaks, and doesn't work very hard. The three of us usually have to finish <u>his</u> work! What should we do?

Frustrated in Fresno

167

INJURIES AT WORK

1. beaker
2. blow up
3. burst
4. chemical experiment
5. combustible
6. combustion
7. conveyor belt
8. explode
9. explosion
10. flammable
11. flask
12. fumes
13. ignite
14. inflammable
15. laboratory
16. protective gear
17. recoil
18. shatter
19. shoot/fire
20. throw one's back out
21. warning sign

_____
_____
_____
_____
_____
_____

Picture Discussion

With your class, answer the questions about the scenes. • Use the vocabulary list. • Add more words.

1. What is happening in each scene?
2. What injuries will each worker have?
3. What kinds of protective clothing or gear should some of these workers be wearing? What other kinds of protective clothing do people wear at work? Make a list on the board.
4. What kinds of warning signs are in the scenes? What other warning signs do you see at work? Make a list on the board.
5. Will workers' compensation pay for the medical care of these workers? Why or why not?
6. Which jobs are more dangerous than others?

🔊 *See Conversation Springboards on pages 225 and 226.*

Group Problem Solving

In groups of three, discuss ways to prevent the problem in each scene. • Decide on the best prevention. • Report your preventive solutions to the class.

Group Brainstorm

In the same groups, choose a recorder. • List hazards at your jobs and in your homes. • Read your list to the class. • Make a class list on the board.

Share Your Story

In the same groups, answer these questions and share your stories. • Tell your best stories to the class.

1. Did you ever get hurt at work? What happened?
2. Did you ever get hurt doing work at home? What happened?

Community Activities

In groups of four, visit a work site in your community.

◆ Look for safety signs.
◆ Ask about safety regulations.
◆ Report your observations to the class.

Find safety regulations at your job. • Bring a copy of the regulations to class, and tell the class about them.

Draw with a Partner   Partner's Name _____

With a partner, discuss any safety signs you have seen around your community. • Draw the signs. • Explain them to another pair of students.

DEDUCTIONS FROM PAY

1. city withholding tax
2. credit union
3. direct deposit
4. earn
5. employee contribution
6. Federal Insurance Contributions Act (FICA)
7. federal withholding tax
8. gross earnings
9. gross pay
10. insurance deduction
11. labor union
12. Medicare tax
13. net earnings
14. payday
15. pay period
16. paystub
17. retirement contribution
18. salary after taxes
19. Social Security (FICA)
20. statement of earnings and deductions
21. state withholding tax
22. take-home pay
23. union dues

Picture Discussion

With your class, answer the questions about the scene. • Use the vocabulary list. • Add more words.

1. What is happening in this scene?
2. Why is the one employee unhappy?
3. What deductions show on her paycheck?
4. What is her co-worker telling her?

5. Do you understand each of these payroll deductions?
6. Why does her co-worker's paycheck look different?

See Conversation Springboards on page 226.

Partner Role Play

With a partner, create a role play between an employee and a payroll office clerk. • Present your role play to another pair of students.

The employee wants to do three things:

1. change his or her paycheck to direct deposit.
2. open an account in the employee credit union and have $5 deducted every week.
3. report an error—he or she worked 3 hours overtime last week, but didn't get paid for the overtime.

Cross-Cultural Exchange

In groups of four, choose a conversation monitor and a recorder. • Discuss these questions. • Compare cultures when possible. • Report the results of your discussion to the class.

1. Are taxes withheld from paychecks in your country?
2. What other deductions from paychecks are there?
3. Are paychecks deposited directly into banks?
4. What workers belong to unions? Are unions powerful?

Class Survey

With your class, ask these questions. • Compare your responses with your classmates.

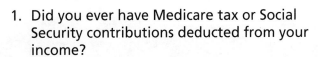

1. Did you ever have Medicare tax or Social Security contributions deducted from your income?
2. Do you know anyone who receives Social Security checks?
3. Do you think Social Security is a good government program?
4. Do you think income tax withholding is a good government program?
5. Did you ever belong to a labor union?
6. Did you ever have paychecks direct-deposited?

Group Brainstorm

In groups of three, choose a recorder. • List things that can be deducted from paychecks. • Compare and combine your list with another group. • Read your combined list to the class. • Make a class list on the board.

SPENDING MONEY

1. bad credit	11. expenses	20. moderation
2. budget	12. extravagance	21. overspend
3. common sense	13. extravagant	22. owe
4. credit rating	14. financial responsibility	23. prudent
5. credit risk		24. repossess
6. debt	15. good credit	25. sensible
7. disposable income	16. good sense	26. simple pleasures
8. economize	17. impress	27. spendthrift
9. entertainment expenses	18. live above one's means	28. splurge
10. expenditure	19. live within one's means	29. waste
		30. wasteful

Picture Discussion

With your class, answer the questions about the picture story. • Use the vocabulary list. • Add more words.

1. How do these co-workers spend their paychecks?

2. What other differences do you think there are in their lives?

3. What do you think their beliefs are about spending money?

4. Tell each story.

See Conversation Springboards on page 226.

Group Brainstorm

In groups of three, choose a recorder. • List ways to save money in everyday expenses. • Read your list to the class. • Make a class list on the board. • Which advice is the most useful?

Conversation Squares

In the same groups, fill in the chart. • First write your own answers. • Then ask your partners the questions and write their answers. • Compare answers with another group.

	You	**Partner 1**	**Partner 2**
Student's Name			
What do you waste money on?			
Are you saving for anything? What?			
When you have extra money, what do you do with it?			

Group Problem Posing/Problem Solving

In the same groups, discuss ways people get into trouble spending money. • State each problem. • What advice would you give? • Report your problems and solutions to the class.

Class Game: Guess Who!

On a slip of paper, write one item you would like to splurge on. • Make a pile. • Pick a paper. • Read it to the class. • Guess who wrote it!

PAYING TAXES

1. accountant	11. exemption	20. overpay
2. annual income	12. file a tax return	21. pay interest
3. auditor	13. Form 1040	22. resident
4. back taxes	14. Form 1040EZ	23. taxable income
5. computation	15. Form W-2	
6. compute	16. income tax	24. tax credit
7. deadline	17. Internal Revenue Service (IRS)	25. tax evasion
8. deductible		26. tax form(s)
9. dependent	18. late penalty	27. taxpayer
10. exempt	19. nonresident	28. tax withheld

Picture Discussion

With your class, answer the questions about the scenes. • Use the vocabulary list. • Add more words.

1. What is happening in each scene?
2. What is the happy woman looking at?
3. Why is one woman employee worried?
4. What is her co-worker explaining to her?
5. How many dependents does the co-worker have?

6. Who is L. Ross? What is she discussing with the man?
7. What did the unhappy man receive? Why is he so upset? What advice is he getting?

See Conversation Springboards on pages 226 and 227.

Partner Activity: Ask Aunt Betty

Partner's Name _____

With a partner, read and discuss this letter. • Together, write a reply from Aunt Betty, giving advice to Worried in Washington. • Read your letter to the class.

Ask Aunt Betty

Dear Aunt Betty:

My husband has a small business repairing lawn mowers and doing odd jobs, and I baby-sit for my neighbor's children. We make just enough money to pay for the rent and food. We can't even afford to take our kids to the dentist. But that's not the problem. I'm writing to you because we haven't filed an income tax return for three years. My husband says, "Forget it!" But I'm worried. What should I do?

Worried in Washington

Group Brainstorm

In groups of four, choose a recorder. • List things that the government spends tax money on. • Compare and combine your list with another group. • Read your combined list to the class. • Make a class list on the board.

Cross-Cultural Exchange

In the same groups, choose a conversation monitor and a recorder. • Discuss these questions. • Compare cultures when possible. • Report the results of your discussion to the class.

1. Compare taxes in different countries.
2. Is there a national income tax in your home country?
3. Who has to pay income tax?
4. What percentage of annual income do people have to pay?

5. When is the income tax due?
6. Is income tax withheld from people's wages?
7. What other kinds of taxes are there?

175

LEAVING A JOB

1. advance
2. advancement
3. career change
4. career decision
5. career opportunity
6. career path
7. career training
8. give notice
9. leer
10. low pay
11. maternity leave
12. move away
13. overworked
14. regret
15. resign
16. resignation
17. seasonal layoff
18. self-improvement
19. sexual advance
20. stare
21. stressful
22. technical training
23. underpaid
24. working conditions

_____
_____
_____
_____
_____
_____
_____

Picture Discussion

With your class, answer the questions about the picture story. • Use the vocabulary list. • Add more words.

1. What is happening in each scene?
2. What was this woman's reason for leaving each job?
3. What career opportunities did she have?
4. When did she retire? How old was she?
5. Tell the story of this woman's working life.

176

See Conversation Springboards on page 227.

Partner Role Play

Partner's Name _____

With a partner, choose one of the scenes. • Create a role play between the woman and her employer. • Include the reason for leaving, the employer's response, and the final goodbye. • Present your role play to the class.

Partner Interview

Partner's Name _____

Ask a partner these questions. • Then report your partner's responses to another pair of students.

1. Have you ever left a job? Why or why not?
2. Would you keep a bad job if you really needed the money? Why or why not?
3. What makes a job good?
4. What makes a job bad?

Group Brainstorm

In groups of four, choose a recorder. • List reasons for leaving a job. • Read your list to the class. • Make a class list on the board.

Group Decision

In the same groups, decide whether to keep each of these jobs or leave it. • Explain your decisions to the class.

◆ You have worked at this job for three years, but you have never had a raise. You are a good worker, but your employer cannot afford to pay you more.

◆ Your boss always tells the workers that they are lazy, slow, and incompetent. In fact, you and your co-workers are responsible, efficient, and careful.

◆ One of your co-workers has been making sexual advances towards you. You have tried to discourage this, but the situation continues to get worse.

REVIEW

Group Brainstorm

In groups of three, choose a recorder. • List the differences between doing a good job and doing a bad job. • Read your list to the class. • Make a class list on the board.

DIFFERENCES

Doing a Good Job	Doing a Bad Job
_____	_____
_____	_____
_____	_____
_____	_____

Partner Questions   Partner's Name _____

With a partner, make a list of questions to ask when starting a new job. • Include questions about job benefit details, payroll deductions, and income taxes. • Ask another pair your questions, and answer theirs. • Report your questions and answers to the class.

Partner Activity: *Ask Aunt Betty*

Partner's Name _____

With a partner, write a letter from Aunt Betty, *giving advice to someone starting a new job. • Read your letter to the class.*

Partner Game: *What Do You Remember?*

Partner's Name _____

With a partner, list as many employment problems from this unit as you can remember. • Check your list with another pair. • Look back through the unit. • Did you forget any of the problems?

Group Discussion

In groups of three, choose a recorder. • List reasons for leaving a job and reasons for staying at a job. • Compare your reasons with another group. • Discuss these questions.

1. When is it good to leave a job?
2. When is it better to stay?

UNIT 10
IN THE NEWS

LEARNING STRATEGIES

➤ Every day that you are studying this unit, bring in a related article from a newspaper or magazine and tell the class about it.

➤ Watch a newscast every day in English. Note the channel, time, and newscasters. Note the news of the day. Make a list of the different topics covered. Then write down questions about the newscast. What was confusing? What didn't you understand?

➤ Watch sports news on TV or read the sports section of a local newspaper. Then answer these questions:

- What sports are in the national news now? Why?

- What athletes are in the news now? Why?

- What is the biggest current sports story?

- What local sports are in the news now?

CLASS NEWS

1. catch up
2. champion
3. championship
4. ecstatic
5. elated
6. embrace
7. homecoming
8. hug
9. MVP (Most Valuable Player)
10. overjoyed
11. overwhelmed
12. personal news
13. reunion
14. reunite
15. separation
16. shock
17. slip and fall
18. special occasion
19. teammate
20. tears of joy
21. thrill
22. thrilled
23. thrilling
24. triumph
25. trophy
26. unforgettable moment
27. victorious
28. victory

See Conversation Springboards on page 227.

Picture Discussion

With your class, answer the questions about the scenes. • Use the vocabulary list. • Add more words.

1. Why is the woman's arm in a sling? Tell the story of her accident.
2. Why are the young man's teammates carrying him? Tell the story of their victory.
3. Why does the young woman look so surprised? Tell the story of her happiness.
4. Why is the man hugging his twin brother? Tell the story of their reunion.

Draw with a Partner
Partner's Name _____

Decide what news you have to share. • Draw a picture of your news. • Explain your picture to a partner. • Show your pictures to another pair. • Explain your partner's picture.

Group Superlatives

In groups of four, answer these questions. • Report your answers to the class.

1. Who has had the best week?
2. Who has had the worst week?
3. Who has had the best news this year?
4. Who has the most exciting plans for this weekend?
5. Who has the most unusual news story to tell?

Write with the Class

With your class, write a newsletter or make a bulletin board for class news. • Bring pictures and make a headline for each news story.

Community Activity

Call a friend or relative to catch up on the latest news. • Take notes on your friend's or relative's news. • In groups of four, report on your telephone conversation.

NEWS MEDIA

1. anchorperson
2. article
3. at the scene
4. bulletin
5. cable network news
6. current event
7. front page
8. headline
9. live broadcast
10. newscast
11. newscaster
12. newsmagazine
13. newsperson
14. on location
15. on-line news
16. reporter _____
17. report the news _____
18. satellite news _____
19. station
20. telecast _____
21. top story _____
22. weekly

Picture Discussion

With your class, answer the questions about the scenes. • Use the vocabulary list. • Add more words.

1. In what different ways does this family get the news?
2. What time do you think it is? Why?
3. What TV program are they watching? Why?
4. What is the top story on the TV news?
5. What is the headline on the front page of the newspaper?
6. What kind of magazine is the mother reading?
7. What news is the student looking at on his computer?

See Conversation Springboards on page 228.

Find Someone Who

Review the vocabulary with your teacher. • Add to this list. • Then interview your classmates and fill in the name of someone who . . .

1. reads a daily newspaper. _____

2. reads a weekly newsmagazine. _____

3. listens to the news on the radio. _____

4. watches cable network news. _____

5. watched the news on TV yesterday. _____

6. _____ _____

7. _____ _____

Class Discussion

With your class, make a list on the board of people in the news. • How many names does everyone recognize? • Why are these people in the news?

Group Role Play

In groups of four, create a role play between a person in the news and news reporters. • Plan questions for the reporters to ask, and prepare answers to the questions. • Present your role play to the class.

Community Activity

Watch the news on TV in English and take notes. • Report back to the class. • Include answers to these questions.

1. What stories were in the news?
2. Where did they occur?
3. What happened?
4. How much did you understand?

WEATHER AND NATURAL DISASTERS

1. avalanche
2. blizzard
3. burn down
4. catastrophe
5. collapse
6. deadly
7. destroy
8. destruction
9. devastating
10. drought
11. dry up

12. earthquake
13. erupt
14. eruption
15. escape
16. evacuate
17. evacuation
18. forecast
19. forest fire
20. hurricane
21. lava
22. level

23. powerful
24. rescuer
25. rubble
26. shake
27. survival
28. terrify
29. thunderous
30. tidal wave
31. tornado
32. towering
33. volcano

_____
_____
_____
_____
_____
_____
_____

Picture Discussion

With your class, answer the questions about the scenes. • Use the vocabulary list. • Add more words.

1. What natural disaster is shown on each TV screen?

2. What is happening in each catastrophe?

3. What other natural disasters are there? Describe them, and add them to the list.

4. Where can these catastrophes occur?

5. Which natural disasters can be forecast? Which cannot?

See Conversation Springboards on page 228.

Cross-Cultural Exchange

In groups of four, choose a conversation monitor and a recorder. • Discuss these questions. • Compare cultures when possible. • Report the results of your discussion to the class.

1. What kind of natural disasters occur in your country?

2. How often do they occur? Are they seasonal? When was the last one? How many people were affected?

3. How do people prepare for the disaster? What precautions are taken in extreme conditions? What do they do afterward?

4. Who has experienced a natural disaster? Ask questions about the experience.

Group Vocabulary Challenge

*In the same groups, list different kinds of weather. • Work fast! • Read your list to the class. • Which group has the longest list? • Make a class list on the board. • Copy the new words in the **Vocabulary** section of your notebook.*

Community Activity

Watch a weather report on TV, and read a weather forecast in a newspaper. • Answer these questions.

1. What is today's high temperature?

2. What was last night's low temperature?

3. What is the forecast for tomorrow?

4. What is the extended forecast for the week?

5. Are there any extreme weather conditions being forecast? Where? What are they?

Cross-Cultural Role Play

Pretend you are a TV weather reporter in your hometown. • Create a role play, reporting the weather for a typical day there. • Present your role play to the class.

◆ Include the high and low temperatures and an extended forecast.

◆ Refer to a map.

◆ Use visual aids.

SPORTS NEWS

1. amateur athlete
2. athlete
3. athletic
4. balance beam
5. bronze medal
6. commentator
7. compete
8. competition
9. competitive
10. figure skating
11. finalist
12. gold medal
13. indoor sport
14. international competition
15. medalist
16. mixed pairs
17. Olympics
18. outdoor sport
19. pole vault
20. professional athlete
21. semi-finalist
22. silver medal
23. skating rink
24. sports event
25. stadium
26. track and field

_____
_____
_____
_____
_____
_____
_____

See Conversation Springboards on pages 228 and 229.

Picture Discussion

With your class, answer the questions about the scenes. • Use the vocabulary list. • Add more words.

1. What sports event is on each TV screen?
2. What international competition could this be?
3. Are these athletes amateurs or professionals? Explain your answer.
4. Which sports are indoor sports? Which are outdoor sports? Where do people play each sport?
5. What other track and field events are there? Make a list on the board.
6. In what other sports events do athletes compete internationally? Make a list on the board.

Group Vocabulary Challenge

*In groups of three, choose one sport that you know well. • List vocabulary for that sport. • Work fast! • Read your list to the class. • Which group has the longest list? • Make a class list on the board. • Copy the new words in the **Vocabulary** section of your notebook.*

Speech

Tell the class about a sport you have played, or a sport that you like very much. • Bring related equipment to class, if possible. • Explain the sport. • Show the class how to play it.

Group Discussion

In groups of three, choose a recorder. • Discuss these questions. • Share your information with another group.

1. What sports injuries are common?
2. How do they happen?
3. How can they be prevented?
4. Are any sports too dangerous or too violent?

Cross-Cultural Exchange

In the same groups, choose a conversation monitor and a recorder. • Discuss these questions. • Compare cultures when possible. • Report the results of your discussion to the class.

1. What sports are most popular in your country?
2. Which sports season is it in your country now?
3. Who are the most famous athletes in your country?

ENTERTAINMENT NEWS

1. acrobat
2. celebrity
3. classical music
4. clown
5. conduct
6. conductor
7. entertain
8. entertainer
9. entertaining
10. family entertainment
11. limited engagement
12. magic
13. magical
14. magician
15. performer
16. stage
17. star
18. symphony orchestra
19. theme park
20. tightrope walker
21. trapeze artist

See Conversation Springboards on page 229.

Picture Discussion

With your class, answer the questions about the scenes. • Use the vocabulary list. • Add more words.

1. What kind of entertainment does each scene show?
2. What is happening in each scene?
3. What kind of entertainment will this family choose? Why?
4. What other kinds of entertainment would the daughter enjoy? Draw one example in the empty bubble.
5. What other kinds of entertainment are there?
6. What kinds of entertainment are most popular? Why?
7. What kinds of entertainment are in the news now? Why?
8. What entertainment celebrities are in the news? Why?

Who Else?

List three of your favorite forms of entertainment. • Then find classmates who have the same favorites. • Write their names in the chart and report your findings to the class.

	Favorite Form of Entertainment	Student's Name
1.		1. _____ 2. _____ 3. _____
2.		1. _____ 2. _____ 3. _____
3.		1. _____ 2. _____ 3. _____

Group Role Play

In groups of three, create a role play of a TV or radio talk show host interviewing two celebrities. • Present your role play to the class. • Have the class participate by asking questions.

Community Activity

*Bring a newspaper to class. • In groups of four, look for any local entertainment. • Is there an event that everyone would like to attend? • Make arrangements with the class, and attend the event together. • Then write a **Journal** entry and discuss the event in class afterwards. • Answer these questions.*

◆ Did you enjoy the event?
◆ What did you like about it?
◆ What didn't you like?

CRIME IN THE NEWS

1. acquit	14. defend	27. murder
2. acquittal	15. defendant	28. prosecute
3. assault	16. defense	29. prosecution
4. attorney	17. guilty	30. punish
5. bailiff	18. handgun	31. punishment
6. capital punishment	19. innocent	32. rob
7. cell	20. jail	33. robbery
8. commit	21. juror	34. sentence
9. convict	22. jury	35. testify
10. conviction	23. justice	36. testimony
11. courtroom	24. lawyer	37. trial
12. criminal	25. mug	38. verdict
13. deadly weapon	26. mugging	39. witness stand

See Conversation Springboards on page 229.

Picture Discussion

With your class, answer the questions about the picture story. • Use the vocabulary list. • Add more words.

1. What crime, or crimes, did the man commit?
2. Who is the witness at the trial? What is her testimony?
3. What will the jury's verdict be?
4. What sentence will the judge give?
5. Tell the whole story of this crime in the news.
6. What would you do if you were the victim in this crime? the witness? the attorneys? the jury?
7. What other kinds of crime are there?

Cross-Cultural Exchange

In groups of four, choose a conversation monitor and a recorder. • Discuss these questions. • Compare cultures when possible. • Report the results of your discussion to the class.

1. What kinds of crime are most common in your country?
2. What kinds of punishment are there?
3. Are there different punishments for children and for adults?
4. Is capital punishment used in your country?

School Survey

Ask three people in your school this question. • Fill in their answers. • Report your findings to the class. • What are the total class results?

Do You Approve of Capital Punishment?

1. Yes ☐   No ☐   Not Sure ☐
2. Yes ☐   No ☐   Not Sure ☐
3. Yes ☐   No ☐   Not Sure ☐

Community Activity

Bring in local newspapers. • Discuss articles about crimes in the newspapers with your class. • Watch local TV news. • List crimes reported on TV. • Bring your list to class. • Compare the list with the newspaper articles and discuss with your class.

HEROES IN THE NEWS

1. admiration
2. admire
3. brave
4. bravery
5. cause
6. courage
7. courageous
8. dedicated
9. die for

10. heroic
11. heroism
12. honor
13. leader
14. martyr
15. medal
16. memorial
17. monument
18. patriot

19. patriotic
20. patriotism
21. protect
22. risk
23. sacrifice
24. saint
25. statue
26. strength
27. veteran

_____
_____
_____
_____
_____
_____
_____

See Conversation Springboards on page 230.

Picture Discussion

With your class, answer the questions about the scenes. • Use the vocabulary list. • Add more words.

1. Where are the boy and his mother visiting? What statue is the boy looking at? What do you think his mother will tell him?
2. What heroes are pictured on coins and bills in the currency of your country?
3. What heroic actions did these people perform?
4. In what ways do we honor heroes? List them on the board.

Draw with a Partner

Partner's Name _____

With a partner, choose a hero you admire. • Draw a picture of the hero and write a caption for your picture. • Explain your picture and caption to another pair. • Report your choices to the class.

Conversation Squares

In groups of three, fill in the chart. • First write your own answers. • Then ask your partners the questions and write their answers. • Compare answers with another group.

	You	**Partner 1**	**Partner 2**
Student's Name			
Who is your personal hero?			
Why?			

Group Decision

In the same groups, decide who should win the "Local Hero Award" this year. • Report your decision to the class and explain your choice.

◆ A fireman who rescued a family from a fire. The fireman was badly burned during the rescue.

◆ A twelve-year-old girl who has AIDS. She is very brave and has made many speeches to help raise money for AIDS research.

◆ A fifteen-year-old boy who rescued an elderly woman from an attacker. The boy was shot in the arm during the rescue.

◆ A woman astronaut who was chosen to be the captain of a space shuttle mission.

Cross-Cultural Exchange

In the same groups, choose a conversation monitor and a recorder. • Discuss these questions. • Compare cultures when possible. • Report the results of your discussion to the class. • Make a class list on the board.

1. What international heroes, martyrs, and saints does everyone in the class know about?
2. How are heroes honored in your country? Give some examples.
3. What martyrs are admired in your culture? What did they do?

LOCAL NEWS

1. car crash
2. cleanup
3. dumpsite
4. fall apart
5. head-on collision
6. health hazard
7. human interest story
8. illegal dumping
9. kidnap
10. local issue
11. missing
12. multi-vehicle accident
13. overcrowded
14. pileup
15. pollutant
16. pollute
17. polluter
18. toxic waste
19. unsafe conditions

_____
_____
_____
_____
_____
_____
_____

See Conversation Springboards on page 230.

Picture Discussion

With your class, answer the questions about the scenes. • Use the vocabulary list. • Add more words.

1. What is happening in each TV news scene?
2. What do you think caused the car accident?
3. What is the condition of the school? What improvements are needed?
4. What do you think was dumped illegally?
5. What do you think happened to the child?
6. What local issues are in this TV newscast?

Group Role Play

In groups of three, choose one of the stories in this TV newscast. • Create a role play of a news reporter interviewing people at the scene of the story. • Ask questions about the story. • Explain what happened. • Present your role play to the class.

Community Activity

Bring a local newspaper to class. • In the same groups, find headlines and page numbers of the items below. • Report your findings to the class. • Discuss the most interesting local news together.

◆ local events coming soon
◆ local problems and issues in the news
◆ local good news

Class Brainstorm

With your class, choose a recorder. • List on the board the local problems and issues. • How many items are on the list? • Now list the local good news. • How many items are on this list?

Group Problem Posing/Problem Solving

In groups of four, choose one local problem or issue in the news. • Define the problem or issue. • Decide on a solution. • Report your solution to the class.

Cross-Cultural Exchange

In the same groups, choose a conversation monitor and a recorder. • Discuss these questions. • Compare cultures when possible. • Report the results of your discussion to the class.

1. What local problems and issues are most common in your hometown?
2. What is the current local news in your hometown? Tell it to your group.

WORLD NEWS

1. aid
2. armed
3. battle
4. breakthrough
5. famine
6. fighting
7. hijack
8. hostage
9. humanitarian
10. international incident
11. military
12. oil spill
13. Red Cross
14. refugee
15. research scientist
16. scientific discovery
17. starvation
18. starve
19. supplies
20. tank
21. terrorism
22. terrorist
23. Third World
24. underdeveloped
25. war
26. wipe out

See Conversation Springboards on pages 230 and 231.

Picture Discussion

With your class, answer the questions about the scenes. • Use the vocabulary list. • Add more words.

1. What is happening in each TV news scene?

2. Where in the world is there a war or fighting right now?

3. Where in the world has there been a famine recently? terrorism?

4. What scientific discoveries have been reported in the news recently?

5. What effect will the oil spill have on the environment? Explain.

6. What good news has been in the world news recently?

Group Decision

In groups of four, decide what the story is for each TV news scene and where each story is happening. • Write one headline for each story, and report your headlines to another group.

Group Problem Posing

In the same groups, list some current world problems. • Report your list to the class. • Make a class list on the board. • With your group, decide on the three most serious problems in the world today. • Report your problems to the class. • Which problems does the whole class think are the most serious?

Class Brainstorm

With your class, choose a recorder. • List on the board ideas for solving the three most serious world problems. • Which are the best ideas?

Community Activity

Watch the world news on TV, and take notes on these questions. • Report your notes to the class.

◆ What countries are in the world news?

◆ What problems are in the world news?

◆ What good news did you see?

Cross-Cultural Exchange

In groups of four, choose a conversation monitor and a recorder. • Discuss these questions. • Compare cultures when possible. • Report the results of your discussion to the class.

1. What is the most serious problem or issue in your country right now?

2. What people are in the news in your country right now? Why are they in the news?

3. What good things are happening in your country right now?

POLITICS AND GOVERNMENT IN THE NEWS

1. assassinate
2. assassination
3. ballot
4. ballot box
5. bodyguard
6. campaign
7. candidate
8. debate
9. democracy
10. democratic
11. dictator
12. dictatorship
13. elect
14. election
15. legislature
16. march
17. military coup
18. official
19. overthrow
20. picket
21. political party
22. politician
23. protest
24. protestor
25. rally
26. representative
27. riot
28. speaker
29. supporter
30. vote

_____
_____
_____
_____
_____
_____

Picture Discussion

With your class, answer the questions about the scenes. • Use the vocabulary list. • Add more words.

1. What political events do these news scenes show? What is happening in each scene?

2. In what countries could each of these events be happening?

3. How many kinds of government can you think of? List them on the board.

198 *See Conversation Springboards on page 231.*

Cross-Cultural Exchange

In groups of four, choose a conversation monitor and a recorder. • Discuss these questions. • Compare cultures when possible. • Report the results of your discussion to the class.

1. What kind of government exists in your country? Describe it.

2. Who is the head of the government? What is the leader's title?

3. Do people trust election results in your country? Why or why not?

4. What political parties are in your country? Who supports each party?

Find Someone Who

Review the vocabulary with your teacher. • Add to this list. • Then interview your classmates and fill in the name of someone who . . .

1. doesn't like politics. _____

2. is a member of a political party. _____

3. has voted in an election. _____

4. has participated in a protest. _____

5. has voted by absentee ballot. _____

6. _____ _____

7. _____ _____

Dialog Journal

*Write a **Journal** entry about one of your political views. • Then read your entry to a partner. • Ask questions about your partner's entry.*

Guest Speaker

Write a class letter inviting a local politician or elected official to speak to your class. • Prepare questions for the speaker. • Take notes during the speech. • Write a class thank-you letter after the speech.

REVIEW

Group Vocabulary Challenge

In groups of four, make two lists: Good News and Bad News. • Add the appropriate news stories to the lists. • Which list is longer? • Why? • Compare your lists with another group.

Partner Role Play

Partner's Name _____

With a partner, choose a celebrity to interview on a TV newscast. • Write ten questions for the interview. • Create a role play of the interview. • Present the role play to the class.

Conversation Squares

In groups of three, fill in the chart. • First write your own answers. • Then ask your partners the questions and write their answers. • Compare answers with another group.

	You	**Partner 1**	**Partner 2**
Student's Name			
Who are your personal heroes?			
What do you think is the worst crime?			
What do you think is the best world news recently?			
What do you think is the worst world news recently?			
Who are your favorite entertainers? What do they do?			

Class Role Play

With your class, plan a complete TV newscast. • Divide into groups to cover each aspect of the news. • Include these news segments. • Present them to your teacher!

- ◆ headline news
- ◆ world trouble spot satellite report
- ◆ on-the-scene crime report
- ◆ sports
- ◆ weather
- ◆ entertainment report

APPENDIX

CONVERSATION SPRINGBOARDS

INTRODUCTIONS AND GREETINGS (pp. 2-5)

Conversation Springboard: *What's happening?*

F1: Oh, hello, Dr. Nichols! I'm so glad you could come. Your assistant said you were probably going to be busy.

M1: You know I never miss these International Student parties, Helen. The food is always wonderful! And it gives me a chance to get acquainted with some of the students.

F1: Well, the food this time is as good as ever. And here's someone I'd like you to meet.

M2: Oh, hi, Mrs. Berry. It's a great party! Did you try the Vietnamese spring rolls? They're delicious!

F1: Yes, I did, Harry. They are! Dr. Nichols, I'd like you to meet one of our new international students, Harry Chen. Harry, this is Dr. Nichols, the president of the university.

M2: Oh! Excuse me! It's a pleasure to meet you, Dr. Nichols. I'm sorry, I can't shake hands.

M1: Glad to meet you, Harry. Don't worry about it. I can see you've got your hands full. Are those the spring rolls?

M2: Yes, they are.

M1: They do look good. Maybe you could show me where to get some, too?

M2: Oh, yes! I'd be glad to, Dr. Nichols. Right this way.

M1: I'll see you later, Helen. It looks as though I'm in good hands here!

Picture Springboard: *Finish the conversation.*

F1: Hi, Phyllis. Hi, Donald. How's everything going?

M1: Hi, Marilyn. Just fine.

F2: Me, too. How are you, Marilyn?

F1: Great! Is it OK if I sit here?

M1: _____

F2: _____

F1: _____

MORE ABOUT YOU (pp. 6-9)

Conversation Springboard: *What's happening?*

M1: What's your main reason for studying English, Mi Sook?

F1: I want to get a better job, Alexander, and for the kind of employment I want, English is an important qualification.

M1: What kind of job do you want to qualify for?

F1: Well, I love to travel, and I already have a degree in business management. I'd like to work in international business. But for that, I need to speak English more fluently.

M1: I see. Good luck, Mi Sook. I think your English sounds really good already.

F1: Thanks, Alexander. *Your* English is wonderful. Why are you studying it?

M1: Oh, I have a lot of reasons. Probably the most important one is my girlfriend. She's Australian, and we're planning to live in Australia after we get married.

F1: Then you'll need English for everything, won't you?

M1: I guess so.

F1: That's exciting, Alexander. You'll have a whole new life!

M1: You will, too, Mi Sook.

Picture Springboard: *Finish the conversation.*

M1: Why are you studying English, Anita?

F1: Me? Well, I guess it's really for social reasons, Yannis. You know I love to talk. I'm a pretty sociable person.

M1: That's true. You get along really well with everybody.

F1: Thanks, Yannis. I like my neighbors, too, and I want to get to know them better. That's why I'm studying English—all my neighbors speak English. What about you? What are your reasons for studying English?

M1: _____

_____

F1: _____

_____

CONGRATULATIONS (pp. 10-11)

Conversation Springboard: *What's happening?*

M1: Hey, Simone, congratulations! I just heard about your promotion!

F1: Thanks, Ted. I just heard about it, too.

M1: Well, it's not surprising to me. You really deserve it. You've worked hard for this.

F1: I appreciate your saying that, Ted.

M1: It's the truth! You've done a wonderful job here, Simone.

F2: He's right! Hi, Simone. Congratulations! I think it's terrific! We need to celebrate the occasion. How about it, Ted? We can go over to the Jolly Onion.

M1: Good idea, Lila! That's a great place. Let's take Simone out to lunch. What do you say, Simone? Can you come out for lunch with us?

F1: I wish I could, Ted. But, I'm not going to get any time for lunch today. I have meetings all afternoon, and, in fact, I'm late for one now.

M1: *(teasing)* Uh-oh. Now that you're a big shot, you're too busy to go out with us little guys, huh?

F1: I'm a big shot now? Wow, that happened fast! I'm impressed!

F2: Oh, don't tease her, Ted. We'll do it when you have time, Simone.

F1: Thanks, Lila. Actually, tomorrow would be great.

Picture Springboard: *Finish the conversation.*

F1: Oh, what beautiful babies! They're adorable!
M1: Thank you.
F1: They're twins, aren't they?

M1: _____
_____

F1: _____
_____

APOLOGIES (pp. 12-13)

Conversation Springboard: *What's next?*

F1: Hi, guys! Sorry I'm late!
M1: What kept you, Sue? No, wait, don't tell me—I bet I know. Your alarm didn't go off.
F2: Or maybe your hair dryer didn't work, like last time.
F1: No, no, that's not what happened.
M1: Let's see. . . The bus broke down, and you had to walk.
F1: Hey, guys, what's the matter? I said I was sorry.
F2: I know, Sue, but this happens all the time. We always have to wait for you.
F1: But I don't mean to be late! There's always a reason!
M1: I know, I know. So, what was the reason this time?
F1: I know you're not going to believe me. . .

Picture Springboard: *Finish the conversation.*

F1: Oh! Oh, dear! My groceries!
M1: Oh, I'm sorry, Miss! I didn't see you. Are you OK?
F1: Yes, I'm. . . Oh, my bag's torn. Oh, no—the eggs!
M1: Oh, gee, what a mess! I'm very sorry! Here, let me help you.

F1: _____
_____

M1: _____
_____

GOOD AND BAD MANNERS (pp. 14-15)

Conversation Springboard: *What's your opinion?*

F1: It's OK, honey. Mama's finished. We'll be home soon and we'll have some nice lunch. . . Hey! What's that truck doing? He's stopping right behind us! *(Woman beeps horn.)* Unbelievable! He's not moving! He's blocking us in!
M1: I want lunch, Mama!
F1: I know, honey, I'm sorry. Oh, I don't believe it! They're unloading the truck! What an inconsiderate, thoughtless, rude thing to do!
(She beeps horn again.)
M1: Mama, I want lunch. . .
F1: Hey, Mister! You're blocking me in!
M2: What?
F1: Look, I've got a baby crying here. I've got to get out. You can park somewhere else!
M2: No problem, lady. We'll just be a minute.
F1: It *is* a problem! Why can't you park somewhere else?

M2: We're just unloading, lady. Won't be long.
F1: That's it! You can't get away with this! I'm going to report you!
M2: Go ahead. Report me, lady. I'm just doing my job.

Picture Springboard: *Finish the conversation.*

F1: *(teacher)* . . . And that's the biggest difference between the past tense and the present perfect. Is that clear?
M1: *(whispering)* Psst! Hey, Gordy! Gordy!
M2: *(whispering)* Yeah? What do you want, Duc?
M1: My pencil just broke. Do you have an extra?
F2: Sh! I can't hear the teacher!
M2: Just a second. I'll check. . .

M2: _____
_____

F1: _____
_____

HELPING EACH OTHER (pp. 16-19)

Conversation Springboard: *What's next?*

M1: Excuse me. Would you mind answering a few questions for a survey?
F1: What kind of a survey?
M1: It's for my English class. It's about people helping each other. We have to ask three people in the school these questions.
F1: People helping each other, huh? OK, sure.
M1: Here's the first question: Would you pick up a hitchhiker?
F1: A hitchhiker? No, I wouldn't. It's too dangerous. He might want to rob me—or worse!
M1: OK. Here's the second question: Would you help a stranger in distress?
F1: Mmm, that's a hard one. I guess it depends.
M1: On what?

Picture Springboard: *Finish the conversation.*

F1: Come in. Hi, Monica. Here, have a seat. It's nice to see you.
F2: Thanks, Professor.
F1: You look a little worried. Is there something I can help you with?
F2: I don't want to bother you, Professor Jones, but if you have a minute. . .
F1: Of course. My next class isn't for another hour. Just tell me how I can help.

F2: _____
F1: _____
F2: _____
F1: _____

Conversation Springboard: *What happened?*

F1: Hi, Gregory. You don't look very happy. Is everything OK?

M1: Well, this week has been pretty terrible for me.

F1: Really? I'm sorry to hear that. What happened?

M1: Well, on Monday my grandfather died.

F1: Oh, I'm very sorry, Gregory. Were you very close to your grandfather?

M1: Yes, I was. But he was very old, and he was sick for a long time, so his death wasn't really a shock. Still, it was very sad. I can't believe he's gone.

F1: Of course. It's always hard to lose someone you love.

M1: Yeah, I guess so. Then, after the funeral, when I got home, I discovered that my apartment had been burglarized! Everything was a mess, and my TV and stereo were stolen.

F1: Oh, Gregory, how awful! Is there anything I can do to help?

M1: No, but thanks, anyway, Jenny. This hasn't been my best week, that's for sure.

F1: I'm sure next week will be better for you.

M1: Thanks. I hope so.

Picture Springboard: *Finish the conversation.*

F1: Oh, Dolores, I'm so sorry.

F2: Thank you, Emi.

F1: Can I do anything to help?

F2: Just having you here with me is a comfort, Emi. I think I'm still in a state of shock.

F1: Of course. It's hard to believe that it's true. How did it happen?

F2: _____

_____

F1: _____

_____

UNIT 2: PERSONAL LIFE

Conversation Springboard: *What's happening?*

F1: How do you get along with your roommate, Teresa?

F2: Maggie? She's great—we get along very well, except. . .

F1: Except what?

F2: Well, we're really very different, you know.

F1: How so?

F2: I guess Maggie is a little disorganized and messy; I'm organized and neat.

F1: That must be difficult!

F2: Yes, it is sometimes. Life is frantic in the mornings because we have such different lifestyles. And at night, I like to study and go to bed, but Maggie watches TV all night, and doesn't do her homework till the last minute.

F1: I like to live alone for that reason. I'm asleep by 10:00 every night, but I get up at 5:00 and cram in all my homework between 5:00 and 7:00!

F2: I could never do that! But Maggie does!

Picture Springboard: *Finish the conversation.*

F1: How do you get along with your roommate, Sam?

M1: Tad? He's great. We get along very well, except. . .

F1: Except what?

M1: Well, we're really very different, you know.

F1: _____

M1: _____

F1: _____

Conversation Springboard: *What's next?*

M1: Let's try to get a list together for our party! We should try to include everyone's favorite foods. What's your favorite food, Sylvia?

F1: Party food. Well, let's see. . . crunchy things— carrots, cauliflower, broccoli. . . and dips, of course!

F2: How about dipping sauces—lots of different ones. . . salsa, hot sauce, sweet sauce, and something creamy.

M1: What about you, Doug? What's your favorite food?

M2: Let's see. . . I have to think for a minute what my *favorite* food is—I love all food! Hmm. . . pizza, I guess—for our party, mini pizzas would be great!

F2: Let's get some fried stuff, too. My favorite is fried bananas.

M2: Fried bananas?! What's that?

F1: Fried plantains—they're great. Yes, let's make those, too! Great idea!

F2: Yes, and crackers and chips and different types of fruit!

M1: That's so boring. Every party I go to has crackers and chips. You know, before we go any further, we should collect money and figure out how much we want to spend.

Picture Springboard: *Finish the conversation.*

M1: What's your favorite dessert, Gloria?

F1: Ice cream. I love all flavors, too! What about you?

M1: I don't care much for ice cream. It's too sweet for me.

F1: Really? Oh, I love sweet things. What do you like, Johnny?

M1: _____

F1: _____

M1: _____

Conversation Springboard: *What's your opinion?*

F1: What a great day to be in the park!

M1: Yes, it's not often we get to enjoy this park—we should come more often!

F1: I know, but I get so involved with my work, I hardly ever take time to get outdoors.

M1: I know—I always mean to, but I don't seem to ever find the time to relax.

F1: Being here makes me cheerful, and I feel much more lively around music and energetic people.

M1: It's funny, though—with all this noise and activity, look at that woman taking time to smell the flowers. That's really great. She looks so meditative.

F1: She does. . . Oh, but that poor man over there looks so melancholy. I wonder what's wrong. His dog looks bewildered—like he wants to help his master, but can't.

M1: Maybe the guy is just shy—he'd like to have friends, but is too introverted to take a risk.

F1: I don't think so. . . Should we go sit down next to him and say hello?

Picture Springboard: *Finish the conversation.*

M1: From my hiding place behind this tree, I can see so many different types of people. . . Let's see. . . Oh, here's an active type, this woman, power walking with her barbells. She sure is working off the pounds! And there's a baby, getting used to exercise early—the mom and dad are having a good run. . . Talk about starting early—do you see that father and son with the bat and ball? Looks like he's getting his son ready for the major leagues! This couple on the bench doesn't want anyone to sit next to them, that's for sure. . . Oh, I see my friend, Paco. He's all alone, with his dog. He looks so sad. . . I'd better go cheer him up. I wonder what's wrong. . . Paco, what's wrong?

M2: _____

M1: _____

M2: _____

FRIENDS (pp. 30-31)

Conversation Springboard: *What's happening?*

F1: Who is your best friend, Jose?

M1: Well, that's a difficult question to answer, Tanya. I have a lot of friends, both male and female. I don't know who I would call "best." What about you?

F1: I have a lot of friends, too, but my best friend is Susie—she's been my friend since we were kids.

M1: That's really nice. It takes a long time to find out if someone is trustworthy and sincere. People you think are your friends for years sure can disappoint you.

F1: I know. Susie is kind and loyal—and she's so supportive. I try to be that way for her, too.

M1: I've met some really nice people, but when the chips are down, they often turn out to be insensitive and self-centered, and worst of all, two-faced.

F1: What does two-faced mean, Jose?

M1: It means exactly what it says: It's the kind of person who has a face for me, and a different face for you, depending on what they want. That person smiles to your face and says bad things about you behind your back.

F1: Wow! I know some people like that—that's so insincere and selfish. That's the kind of person I want to avoid if I can!

M1: Me, too! Those are phony types—I can't stand them!

Picture Springboard: *Finish the conversation.*

M1: Thanks so much, Ken, for letting me borrow your new car! I have a new girlfriend and I really want to make an impression!

M2: That's OK, Jeff. But please be careful.

M1: No sweat. . . Well, I'll see you later. I'll be sure to bring it back by midnight.
(Jeff is careless and gets into an accident.)

M2: _____

M1: _____

M2: _____

CHILDHOOD MEMORIES (pp. 32-33)

Conversation Springboard: *What happened?*

F1: I get so nostalgic sometimes when I see little girls playing together. I always used to play with my sister.

F2: I never had sisters or brothers, but I lived in a neighborhood with lots of kids my age. What kinds of things did you do?

F1: Our favorite thing was playing with dolls. We had so many dolls—big ones, small ones—all sorts. And we *loved* to dress up in our mother's clothes and shoes. We'd pretend the dolls were our children, and we were the mothers. It seems so silly now, but we would spend hours playing house and having tea parties.

F2: When I was little, I played with the boys a lot. They loved to pretend to fight with swords and have imaginary wars. But to tell the truth, it was rough for me. The boys sometimes played with matches and lit fires. It scared me—I guess they were a little more adventurous than I was.

F1: What did you do when you got scared?

F2: I just went home and asked my grandma to read me a fairy tale. I loved to sit on her lap and listen to her read aloud to me. It felt safe to be away from those boys!

F1: That brings back good memories. My grandpa read to me all the time, too. My sister and I used to fight to sit on his lap, but it was always big enough for both of us—till we got too old!

F2: It's so nice to reminisce. Not everyone has such good childhood memories.

Picture Conversation: *Finish the conversation.*

M1: I sure hope my kids don't do the things I did as a kid!

M2: Me, too! I really was a handful—my poor parents!

M1: I was fascinated with fire. I used to play with matches and start fires in the backyard.

M2: I did that, too! I got in big trouble for it.

M1: _____

M2: _____

M1: _____

Conversation Springboard: *What's the process?*

M1: *(to himself)* Time for the Find Someone Who activity. OK, here goes. Excuse me, do you enjoy meeting people from different cultures, Diana?

F1: Oh, yes, Fred. Who doesn't?

M1: OK, I do, too. How do you spell your name? I want to write it here.

F1: D-i-a-n-a. I'll put your name down, Fred.

M1: Thanks. *(to himself)* Hmm. . . Number Two. Oh, Jose, can you answer Number Two for me?

M2: What is it? Let's see. . . "likes to travel to foreign countries." Sure, I do.

M1: Great! How do you spell your name?

M2: J-o-s-e.

M1: Thanks. Great. This is a breeze! *(to himself)* Who can I get next? Aha! Chris, do you love to speak foreign languages?

F2: Are you kidding? I'm having such a hard time learning English! No way!

M1: *(to himself)* Oops! What do I do now? I know, I'll ask the teacher! What's his name again?

Picture Springboard: *Finish the conversation.*

M1: We finally all remembered to bring in our photos! They're so interesting—look at all the differences.

M2: Yes. Funny, here at school, our lives are so similar, but when we go back home, they are *so* different.

F1: I guess traditions, cultures, and climate really affect the way people live.

M2: _____

M1: _____

F1: _____

Conversation Springboard: *What's the process?*

Teacher: Let's get together now and compare our stories, class. What group wants to go first?

F1: We do! Who wants to read this?

M1: I'll do it. OK, we wrote about Picture One, where the crazy guy with the glasses was telling an amusing story. We think he was telling about the time that he left his glasses in the bus. . .

F1: No, we decided not to use that story, remember?

M1: Oh, yes. . . We decided to make up a story about a bizarre adventure he had in Alaska. He was on vacation in Alaska. . .

F2: I think he was on vacation in the Rockies, not Alaska. Remember?

M1: Oh, yeah. . . He was on vacation in the Rockies with his family when this really embarrassing thing happened.

M2: Didn't we say he was on vacation with his friends? And something frightening happened?

F1: I don't think so. I really don't think we're ready to present our story yet. We should have taken notes. We all remember it differently!

Teacher: Do you need more time? How many of you need more time?

Students: We do! Yes! We do, too!

Picture Springboard: *Finish the conversation.*

F1: Oh, Sara, that's such a sad beginning to the story!

F2: Well, it was so dreadful—and the worst part is, it's a true story.

M1: How does it turn out, Sara?

F2: _____

M1: _____

F2: _____

Conversation Springboards: *What's your opinion?*

M1: I'm so bored; life is so much the same every day. Sometimes I wish I had enough money to just quit my job and do nothing!

M2: That would be nice for a few weeks, or even a few months, but then what? Is that *really* your objective in life—to do nothing?

M1: I guess not. . . But, I often fantasize about living on a tropical island and not having to work so hard.

M2: You don't have to live on an island to avoid overworking, Mo. I think part of life should be accomplishing your goals, but another part should always be having enough leisure time to enjoy both work and play.

M1: I guess you're right. I have a lot of ambitions, but it seems that the way to reach these goals is to study, study, study, and then work, work, work.

M2: Well, you have to persevere to accomplish your goals. We all do, but we also have to plan to have time to "stop and smell the roses," as they say.

M1: I must be working too hard and not smelling any roses—I've really lost sight of my objectives. This studying routine is so overwhelming!

M2: Sounds like you need a vacation!

Picture Springboard: *Finish the conversation.*

F1: I've been thinking a lot about what to do after I graduate. I really want to be a teacher.

F2: A teacher! Why do you want to be a teacher? I thought you wanted to make a lot of money.

F1: Well, I've been fantasizing about what my life would be like as a teacher.

F2: _____

F1: _____

F2: _____

Conversation Springboard: *What's happening?*

M1: I'm never going to get through this assignment. I have so much trouble doing these papers.

F1: Well, the professor didn't give us much time to complete this one, and it's all individual research.

M1: I enjoy doing projects much more in a group. I learn so much from collaborating. And the projects turn out better, too.

F2: It's funny, I'm much better at independent study. I love to do research on the Internet. Besides, I hate those oral presentations. I'm always worried about messing up the group's work.

M1: Everyone worries about that. But if you discuss the presentation beforehand and practice, it can actually be fun!

F2: You're kidding! Fun? I get so nervous, I can't sleep the night before I have to give a presentation. I take pages of notes and then memorize them.

M1: You memorize your notes? How can you do that? I just write up everything the group decides on my word processor, print out the notes, and refer to them during the presentation.

F1: Listen, Cindi—next time we have a project due, would you like to work with me? I've taken a study skills course; maybe I can help you.

F2: Thanks, Linda. That would be great!

Picture Springboard: *Finish the conversation.*

M1: This peer tutoring is so helpful to me, Paul. Thanks for being so patient.

M2: No problem, Luis. I'm glad to help. I've got some good study tips for you.

M1: That would be great. I have so many problems trying to remember everything.

M2: _____

M1: _____

M2: _____

UNIT 3: FAMILY LIFE

FAMILIES (pp. 44-45)

Conversation Springboard: *What's happening?*

F1: You come from a large family, Sammi, don't you?

F2: Pretty big. I have a sister and twin brothers. My mother died when I was seven, and my father remarried, so I ended up with three half brothers.

M1: That's seven children! Must have been expensive to take care of everyone!

F2: I guess so. It was pretty noisy, too. But we got along really well—still do. What about you guys? What kind of families do you have?

F1: I have an adopted sister. She's six years younger than I am.

M2: I bet that was nice growing up with a baby sister, eh? What about you, Sid?

M1: Well, I have a twin brother. We're identical; our parents *still* can't tell us apart.

M2: That must have been fun growing up, having a twin! I'm an only child. I got a lot of attention from my parents, but I always wanted a brother or sister. I used to *invent* an imaginary twin brother for myself.

M1: Did you have any cousins?

M2: Oh, yes, and our extended family lived upstairs, so there were always relatives around. There were four generations in our house!

F1: Four generations! Maybe you didn't have any brothers or sisters, but at least you had someone around to help you with your homework!

Picture Springboard: *Finish the conversation.*

M1: What's your family like?

M2: Funny you should ask. I have two sisters—and two moms!

M1: Two moms?!

M2: _____

M1: _____

M2: _____

FALLING IN LOVE (pp. 46-47)

Conversation Springboard: *What happened?*

F1: I saw the announcement for your parents' 25th anniversary in yesterday's paper. It was really neat. Do you know how your parents met?

F2: Yes, it was really incredible, actually, very romantic. They met in college, found they were compatible, and began to date. Their courtship lasted all through school.

F1: No kidding! When did they get engaged?

F2: When they were still in college. They got married after they graduated. Then my mother worked to put my father through graduate school.

F1: That's a lot of years they've been together—really true love. Did you have an anniversary party?

F2: Yes, we had a big party. The best part was the photos from their courtship, their engagement, their wedding, and their honeymoon!

F1: You know, they met so young. Did they ever have another boyfriend or girlfriend?

F2: No, not really. They were attracted to each other from the start. . . and they're still really in love. They were acting like newlyweds at the party!

F1: That's really beautiful. I haven't noticed anyone in class that I could fall in love with!

F2: Me, neither. Oh, well, maybe next semester!

Picture Conversation: *Finish the conversation.*

F1: It's so nice of you to help me with this activity. I didn't understand it at all. The instructions were confusing.

M1: Well, I was glad to help. By the way, if you're not too busy, do you think you might want to. . . maybe. . . go to the movies with me sometime?

F1: _____

M1: _____

F1: _____

Conversation Springboard: *What's the process?*

M1: Will you be my partner for this Ask Aunt Betty activity?

F1: Sure, Larry. What do we have to do?

M1: We have to write to Aunt Betty, asking for advice about a marriage problem. Gee, what should we write about?

F1: Let's look at the pictures and try to get some ideas.

M1: I have an idea. . . How about a letter about a husband spending all of his and his wife's savings on new clothes?

F1: Wouldn't it be more likely that the *wife* spend money on clothes?

M1: Not necessarily. Besides, this is just pretend. We can do whatever we want.

F1: OK. It sure will be different. OK, how do we start?

M1: Let's start with "Dear Aunt Betty. . . My husband keeps spending our hard-earned money on clothes."

F1: Shouldn't we start by stating the situation: How long they've been married, how many kids there are, and stuff like that?

M1: I guess so. . .

Teacher: Time's up! Time to exchange your letter with another pair.

M1, F1: Now we're in trouble! We don't have a letter.

Picture Conversation: *Finish the conversation.*

F1: Grandpa, please, no more photos! You've taken so many already.

M1: Can't ever take too many photos of my girls. Grandma and I are so proud of you!

F2: The graduation was so lovely. It made me cry.

M1: _____

F1: _____

F2: _____

Conversation Springboard: *What's happening?*

F1: When is your baby due, Cecilia?

F2: In a month. I'm getting very nervous. We don't have everything we'll need.

F1: What do you need? I don't think the baby needs much for the first few months.

F2: Well, for right now, we have a crib and a car seat.

F1: That seems like enough for now. Infants just eat, sleep, and cry for a few months.

F2: Oh, don't say "cry." I'm so worried my baby will cry a lot, and I won't know what to do.

F1: All babies cry, Cecilia—that's how they tell you they need something. It's pretty simple: It's either hungry, tired, or you have to change its diaper.

F2: That's all there is to it? How do you know which one to do?

F1: Well, you try one thing. If it doesn't work, try something else.

F2: Oh, I'll never be a good mother!

Picture Springboard: *Finish the conversation.*

F1: The baby has such a high fever. I'm so worried.

M1: If he would only stop crying. . .

F1: Do you think you should call the pediatrician?

M1: _____

F1: _____

F2: _____

Conversation Springboard: *What's your opinion?*

M1: Mr. and Mrs. Gomez, come in.

M2: Thanks for seeing us, Mr. Jones. We're so grateful that the teachers at Mary's school are so concerned about her.

F1: We're still concerned about Mary, Mr. Jones, but we're also worried about her sister, Elizabeth.

M1: Elizabeth? She's doing so well.

F1: Elizabeth is doing well in school, but she does have a problem. You see, Mary confides in her, and we are at least glad about that. But Elizabeth doesn't want to violate Mary's confidence by telling anyone else. She really doesn't know what to do.

M2: We know Mary is skipping school and is doing all the rebellious teenage things we always hear about but didn't think our daughter would do. But she's hanging out with a bad crowd, and we think it's more than adolescent rebellion.

F1: We all established some rules for Mary the last time we met together, but Mary has decided they're unacceptable.

M1: Perhaps we should have another meeting with all of us together. Do you think Mary will be honest with us?

M2: Frankly, I think we're beyond meetings. I just don't have any answers at this point.

Picture Springboard: *Finish the conversation.*

F2: Hi, Mom! Hi, Dad! Why are you awake?

M2: Mary! It's 2 a.m., and it's a school night!

F1: We were so worried. Why didn't you call?

F2: _____

M2: _____

F1: _____

Conversation Springboard: *What's next?*

M1: Our baby is due any day. Let's ask our friends about their experiences with their kids.

F1: Yeah, maybe we can get some tips about how to bring up ours.

M1: Carla, can you give us some advice about parenting? We're really nervous about it!

F2: Well, they are really great—babies, I mean. When they start to grow up, you have to keep your eye on them all the time!

M1: What do *you* think? Can you give us any advice, Ali?

F3: Me? I'm in the middle of the terrible two's—with twins! They were so sweet when they were babies, but now I'm at my wits' end!

F1: When do children start to misbehave? Do they *all* misbehave? Are they all disobedient?

M1: Maybe we should rethink this parent thing.

F1: Ahem. It's a little late for that. We need to call the doctor—I think I'm in labor.

Picture Springboard: *Finish the conversation.*

F1: I'm so glad you two will be having a baby soon! There's nothing like it!

M1: I remember those baby years—they were the best. Now, I have a defiant eleven-year-old daughter who causes us all kinds of problems.

F2: My kids are always fighting with each other now. But when they were babies, they were so sweet. I guess it's all a part of growing up.

M2 *(father of boy & girl)*: _____

F3 *(mother-to-be)*: _____

M3 *(father-to-be)*: _____

AFTER SCHOOL (pp. 56-57)

Conversation Springboard: *What's the process?*

M1: OK, everyone. We have to do this Community Activity. How should we start?

F1: Well, let's look over the questions first. Then let's try to figure out how to get the information.

F2: I wouldn't even know how to start!

M1: Well, that's why we're doing this together, Rosie. Oh, boy. . . Where do we find the answers?

F1: Don't panic! Let's see: For the information on after-school programs, let's call a school. Or should we call the board of education?

M1: No, let's call an elementary school. We have a better chance of getting an answer there.

F2: OK, I'll do that.

F1: What about the stuff about the library?

F2: I live near the library. I'll stop by and ask.

M1: No, Rosie, you're doing the other stuff. It wouldn't be fair for you to do all the work. I'll do it. Hey, Rosie, since you live near the library, how about if I give you a ride home that day?

F2: That would be great!

F1: I'll try to get the answer to Number Four about special learning problems. Isn't that called "special education"?

M1: Sorry, Gloria. What did you say?

Picture Springboard: *Finish the conversation.*

F1: Hi, Zia! What's new?

F2: What's all the noise in the background? I can hardly hear you!

F1: Oh, those are my brothers playing baseball in the house and my sister singing along to a music video.

F2: _____

F1: _____

F2: _____

Conversation Springboard: *What's next?*

F1: Did you hear that Phil and Sharon are getting divorced?

F2: No. How can that be? They seem so compatible.

F1: Well, I think he's suing her for abandonment. She has a boyfriend, you know.

F2: She does?! How could she do that?! They have two little kids—one is just a baby!

F1: Who knows the real story? I guess they are both agreeing that there are irreconcilable differences; they're going to court next week.

F2: Already? What about counseling? Have they seen a marriage counselor?

F1: I guess so. They are both just frustrated and disagree on everything, and the bottom line is Sharon has a boyfriend now.

F2: That's really too bad. What about the children?

F1: Well, of course, Phil is suing her for child custody, but Sharon wants to keep the children.

F2: Oh, that's a terrible situation. I guess the judge will decide.

Picture Springboard: *Finish the conversation.*

M1: My client is insisting on full custody—and that Sharon pay alimony and child support.

F3: That's thoroughly ridiculous. Phil is a doctor. How will he ever have time for the children? And *alimony?* He makes ten times what Sharon makes!

M1: Phil says he'll give up his practice; then he won't have any money. The children mean everything to him.

F4: _____

M2: _____

F3: _____

M1: _____

Conversation Springboard: *What's happening?*

(telephone conversation)

M1: Hi, Grandma. How are you?

F1: Hi, Dan! It's so nice to hear your voice.

M1: Well, I've been so busy at college; sorry I haven't called you this week.

F1: Don't apologize. I'm happy you called. How are things?

M1: Everything is fine. How are you? I was sorry your friend Dorothy passed away.

F1: Oh, Danny, it makes me so sad. I have such fond memories. . . and so many of my friends are dying, or having all sorts of problems.

M1: So how are things with you? Are you feeling OK, Grandma?

F1: I'm feeling fine. I've been very busy since I retired. I enrolled in the community college, and I'm taking an advanced computer course. I take yoga in the evening, and sometimes when I can't sleep, I stay up late and surf the net!

M1: Grandma, you need to get your rest.

F1: I know, but sometimes I can't get on line during the day.

M1: Gee, Grandma, I hope having a long, healthy life is a gene I inherited from you!

Picture Springboard: *Finish the conversation.*

M1: Hi, Harold. Long time, no see.

M2: Yes, since I retired, I've been keeping busy. Getting older isn't so bad if you have the right attitude.

M3: So, what's keeping you busy these days?

M2: _____

M1: _____

M3: _____

UNIT 4: COMMUNITY AND CONSUMER LIFE

AROUND TOWN (pp. 64-65)

Conversation Springboard: *What's the process?*

M1: Oh, another Vocabulary Challenge. These things give me a headache!

F1: I think they're fun, Frank. Anyway, I love shopping, so this should be easy!

M1: Oh, really? Where do you shop, Daisy?

F1: It depends. I buy my food at a health food store, The Wild Mushroom. And I love to buy bread at the Golden Bakery on Lake Boulevard.

M1: Wait a second, let's get this down—The Wild Mushroom: food; Golden Bakery: bread. But what can we fill in for "What can you do?"

F1: That's easy—"buy food/buy bread." Let's try another.

M1: OK, what about the jewelry store? Oops, I mean the cleaner's.

F1: The cleaner's or the jewelery store? Which do you want to do first?

M1: The cleaners. What can you buy there?

F1: *Buy* at the cleaners? You don't buy anything. You get your clothes cleaned there. Well, I guess some of these columns can be blank.

Picture Springboard: *Finish the conversation.*

M1: Excuse me, we seem to be lost. Could you tell us how to get to a coffee shop called Coffee and More?

F1: We're meeting my brother there, and we've been driving around in circles.

F2: Let's see, I'm not exactly sure. Katy, do you know?

F3: _____

F2: _____

F1: _____

Conversation Springboard: *What's your opinion?*

M1: One thing I've noticed about the U.S. is that there are a lot more community services here than in my country.

F1: Yes, in my country there are hardly any. Here there are all sorts of things available.

M1: Yup. My kids' school has a really good after-school program, and my church runs a soup kitchen. I think it's great.

M2: Well, I don't agree. I don't think all these public services are such a good idea.

F1: Why not, Jimmy?

M2: In my country, families take care of each other. We don't need day-care centers and senior citizen centers and soup kitchens.

F1: What about people who don't have any family?

M2: Everybody has a family! You don't see homeless people on the street in my country. And old people are at home with their families, where they belong!

M1: Well, I think it's nice for senior citizens to have something to do instead of being bored at home. It gives them new friends and fun in their lives.

M2: What's so boring about being at home? At my family's house, it's never boring!

F1: Well, I'm glad we have community services here, Jimmy. If this college didn't have a day-care center, I wouldn't be able to come to this class!

Picture Springboard: *Finish the conversation.*

M1: Don't worry, friend. You're going to be OK.

M2: What happened? I guess I blacked out.

M1: Yeah, it looks like the heat got to you. How do you feel now?

M2: _____

M1: _____

M2: _____

Conversation Springboard: *What happened?*

F1: The storm knocked out our power last night. Our power lines actually came down. What a pain!

M1: Good thing it wasn't too cold.

F1: Well, it wasn't the cold we were worried about. The gas company thought we had a gas leak because of the storm.

F2: Really? That can be dangerous. Sometimes, you can't smell the gas.

F1: We sure smelled it. Our dog got sick from the gas.

M1: Did other apartments have the same problem?

M2: Hi, guys. Are you talking about that gas leak in my building?

F1: Steve, don't tell me you live at 47 Essex Street, too?

M2: Sure. You live there, Mari? What a coincidence. Were you OK last night?

F1: Not really. My dog got sick from the gas leak.

M2: Oh, that's too bad. Are *you* OK?

Picture Springboard: *Finish the conversation.*

M1: I don't know what's wrong with this TV, sir. The cable wire seems fine.

M2: I really want to see the basketball game tonight. I've been waiting all week.

M1: _____

M2: _____

M1: _____

MAILING SERVICES (pp. 70-71)

Conversation Springboard: *What happened?*

(telephone conversation)

F1: Hi, Mom! We got the package! Michael just loves it!

F2: Oh, hi, Christie! Good, I'm glad it arrived. I was worried it wouldn't get there in time for his birthday.

F1: Michael had a wonderful birthday, Mom. Besides his party, he got lots of cards. Some even came priority mail, and, of course, your package was so exciting for him.

F2: Can I speak with him?

F1: Sure. Mike. Grandma's on the phone!

M1: Grandma?

F2: Hi, Michael. Happy birthday!

M1: I got an e-mail, Grandma. Someone sent me a birthday card e-mail!

F1: *(whispers)* Tell Grandma "thank you" for the piñata.

M1: What's a pitanya?

F1: Piñata. It's the donkey with the flowers that Grandma sent.

M1: Grandma, thanks for the pitanya!

Picture Springboard: *Finish the conversation.*

F2: I'd like to send this package by overnight delivery.

M2: Where's it going?

F2: New Bedford, Massachusetts. Is there overnight service to New Bedford?

M2: _____

F2: _____

M2: _____

TELEPHONE SERVICES (pp. 72-73)

Conversation Springboard: *What's your opinion?*

(telephone conversation)

F1: Hello.

M1: Hello. Are you the head of the household?

F1: Who is this, please?

M1: This is Mr. Moore from MTA Telephone Service. This evening only, I have a special deal for you. I just have a few questions for you first.

F1: Sorry, I'm not interested. Thank you, anyway.

M1: Oh, but this new service will save you a lot of money. And there's no obligation to you. Try the service for three months and if you are not satisfied, you can. . .

F1: Excuse me. I like the telephone service I have. I'm not interested.

M1: Well, I think you'll find MTA Telephone Service has many special advantages that other phone companies do not provide.

F1: I'm really sorry, Mr. Moore. It's dinnertime, I've just gotten home, and my children are hungry. Besides, I've got a very good deal with my current company.

M1: Oh, can you tell me what it is?

F1: I'd like to, but I'm really too busy. But thanks, anyway.

Picture Springboard: *Finish the conversation.*

(telephone conversation)

M1: Hi, Jeanie! How are you?

F1: Oh, hi, Dad. Fine. Listen, I'm on another call. Can you call back?

M1: Jeanie, I'm calling from an airplane. Is Mom home?

F1: _____

M1: _____

F1: _____

Conversation Springboard: *What happened?*

M1: Good evening, ladies and gentlemen. I'm talking with Sara Mendez—the world's oldest shopper. Sara is 100 years old today and is celebrating her birthday here at the Midtown Mall. Happy birthday, Sara!

F1: Hello, thank you.

M1: Sara, we're curious. Why the mall? You're having a party here at the mall. Why?

F1: Well, I've always loved to shop. I still do—I love the mall. I get a chance to get out in all sorts of weather and see people. I don't buy too much any more, but I like the action here!

M1: Can you tell us about the changes you've seen in terms of shopping?

F1: Well, when I was a girl, we used to hang around the general store. We got everything there—food, fabric to make clothes, shoes, ribbons, you name it.

M1: And now, what do you see?

F1: Goodness, people shop by phone, and lately, through computers. This modern world amazes me!

M1: Did you ever shop by phone?

F1: Well, by mail. When I first got married, we lived on a farm, and we did all our shopping through catalogs. We were very excited when the mailman brought our packages!

M1: What about shopping via the Internet?

F1: My great, great grandchildren do that all the time. It's really incredible!

M1: Well, here's your family, Sara. Happy shopping with your free gift certificate, compliments of the Midtown Mall in honor of your 100th birthday!

Picture Springboard: *Finish the conversation.*

(telephone conversation)

M1: Home Shopping TV. How can I help you?

F1: Well, I just saw that great handbag on TV. I'd like to order it.

M1: Sure. Let me get some information from you. . .

F1: _____

M1: _____

F1: _____

Conversation Springboard: *What's your opinion?*

F1: I don't know when I'll get a chance to go Christmas shopping. I'm so busy between work and school.

M1: Why don't you just order everything through a catalog? I do—no muss, no fuss.

F2: Yes, but where's the fun of going to the stores with your friends? Checking out the bargains?

F1: And going to the outlet stores?

M1: Doesn't sound like fun to me! I just get what I need in one shot.

F2: By the way, have you gone to that new outlet mall? I hear the prices are outrageous—totally unreasonable! They say the clothes are pretty trendy, but so impractical. Who would buy them?

F1: Well, I shop there whenever I can. I think the clothes are really tasteful. And I'm a pretty thrifty shopper, too. There are good prices there, if you look.

F2: Really? Do you *really* like it? I love the clothes you wear, Elke! They're always so stylish. Do you think we could go to that outlet mall sometime together?

F1: Sure. I just need to find the time. I'm so busy these days, it's crazy.

F2: How about this afternoon? Class is cancelled. The teacher is at a meeting or something. And the outlet is only about ten minutes away. I'll drive.

F1: All right. Maybe I can get all my Christmas shopping done. Hey, Young Soo, want to come along?

M1: No, thanks. That's not my kind of fun.

Picture Springboard: *Finish the conversation.*

M1: Hey, check these out. Aren't these high-tops cool?

M2: Yeah, they're like mine. See? What did they cost?

M1: I don't know. My dad bought them for me.

M2: He did?

M1: _____

_____

M2: _____

_____

Conversation Springboard: *What's next?*

M1: Look, Louisa! Another candlestick set!

F1: I guess it's the trendy gift this year, Tom. What will we do with so many, though?

M1: I suppose we have to return them. Do we know where they are from—all four sets?

F1: Well, the names of the stores are on the boxes, but we don't have the sales receipts.

M1: But what if some of these people come to our house for dinner and don't see their candlesticks? Or worse, see another set instead of theirs?

F1: Do we have to keep track of who gave us what and put it out when they come over?

M1: Gee, I never thought about that. That would be a little frustrating—and difficult.

F1: Let's not worry about that. How about if we try to return some of them now and worry about the rest another time. . .

M1: Oh, no!

F1: What's wrong?

M1: You're not going to believe this, but guess what Barb and Jim got us!

Picture Springboard: *Finish the conversation.*

M1: I'm sorry, Billy—this bike is missing the front wheel. It's not in the box.

M2: But, Daddy, you promised I could ride it when we got home.

M1: I know I did, Billy, but there's no wheel. You can't ride a bike without a wheel.

M2: _____

M1: _____

M2: _____

Conversation Springboard: *What's your opinion?*

M1: Mrs. Esposo, your son really does need to go into a bilingual program in kindergarten.

F1: Excuse me, Mr. Keene, but Bayani doesn't read in English or in Spanish. I have to insist that he be put in an English-speaking kindergarten.

M1: I can't agree with you. In the bilingual program, he'll learn to read and write in Spanish first, then when he's ready, he'll go into an English classroom.

F1: My nephew who is 16 was in a bilingual program, and he never really learned to read or write in either language. He had a lot of trouble in school and finally dropped out. I want Bayani in a regular English class. He's smart; he'll learn quickly.

M1: He'll be lost in the class; he won't be able to talk to the other boys and girls.

F1: Not for long. He's a friendly boy and he'll make friends in any language. Besides, he'll learn from his classmates.

M1: I'm sorry, but I have to disagree.

F1: Mr. Keene, what kind of support services will be available to Bayani in his class? Will he get some extra help in English? He's entitled to that.

M1: Yes, I know. But you are insisting on making life hard for him.

F1: I know my child best. And I have to insist that he be placed in a regular program.

Picture Springboard: *Finish the conversation.*

M1: Dad, I told you it wasn't my fault.

M2: Well, if it wasn't your fault, what happened? Why did you get suspended?

M1: _____

M2: _____

M1: _____

M2: _____

Conversation Springboard: *What's next?*

M1: Joe! Nice to see you. How was your summer?

M2: Great! My kids were all away at camp. It was quiet, but restful. Now everyone is back in full swing!

F1: Hi, Harry! Hi, Joe! What courses are you taking this semester?

M1: I'm not sure yet. I'm on my way to see my advisor. I'd like to finish my required courses this semester, but I also have a lot of electives to take. What about you?

F1: I've finished my electives, so now I have to take my required courses. I'm off to the registrar to pay my tuition.

M2: I'm taking only a few credit hours this semester. I'm taking a non-credit course in the adult education program.

F2: Hi, Joe. I see you signed up for the same non-credit course I did. It'll be fun.

M2: Yeah, I'm really looking forward to it.

M1: What's the course?

Picture Springboard: *Finish the conversation.*

F1: Excuse me. Do you know where the English section is?

M1: I'm not sure. This is the school supply section. I'll help you look.

F1: I'm looking for three different textbooks.

M1: _____

F1: _____

M1: _____

Conversation Springboard: *What's next?*

(telephone message)

M1: Hello, this is the Metropolitan Museum. We are proud to present our special exhibit this month, Treasures of Asia. It will run from September 2nd through October 4th. Tickets are $8.00 for adults, $2.00 for children under 12, $6.00 for senior citizens with identification, and $4.00 for students. Our hours are nine to five, Tuesday through Thursday, Friday and Saturday, nine to nine, and Sunday ten to six. We are closed on Monday. If you need further assistance, press "star" for upcoming events, "one" for special group rates, "nine" for the administrative offices, "eight" for the gift shop, or "zero" to repeat this message.

F1: Gee, I hardly understood anything. . . What should I press to repeat the message? I don't remember. I guess I'll press "star." No, that's for upcoming events. "One." Oops, that's for special group rates. Darn, I can't remember!
(hangs up and calls again)

M1: Hello, this is the Metropolitan Museum. We are proud. . .

Picture Springboard: *Finish the conversation.*

F1: I'm so glad we came to this concert, Grandpa. Athena is enjoying it, too!

M1: I still think it's silly to bring a dog to a concert!

F1: But, Grandpa, Athena loves music. Look how nicely she's behaving.

M1: Melissa, where's the picnic basket?

F1: _____

M1: _____

UNIT 5: STAYING HEALTHY

TAKING CARE OF YOURSELF (pp. 88-89)

Conversation Springboard: *What's next?*

M1: Gee, Don, don't you think you should cut out some of those high-calorie foods?

M2: What do you mean, Pete? Everyone eats burgers and hot dogs.

M1: I think it's OK once in a while, but you're always eating this stuff. It's really not good for you. That pie, for example, is just empty calories. And the calories are all from fat!

M2: I don't think I'll have a heart attack from this lunch. Besides, eating low-fat foods is no fun!

M1: Don, look, I'm your brother. I'm worried about you. The sedentary life you lead and the saturated fats you consume are really bad.

M2: Well, if I get too fat, I can always take diet pills. At least I'm not anorexic!

M1: Don't be foolish. You can eat nutritious meals that are enjoyable. We're getting older and have to watch out for our health more now.

M2: I do. I eat enough to satisfy my appetite. Nutritious foods just don't do it for me.

M1: How about trying to change just a little at a time? Look, I'll help you—I'll cook for you. Just try to start taking care of yourself.

M2: You'll cook for me?! What did you have in mind?

Picture Springboard: *Finish the conversation.*

F1: I'm really worried about my husband. His health habits are just awful.

F2: How so? You're so health conscious—you exercise, eat a low-fat diet, and you're very active.

F1: Yeah, but not my husband. Well, he used to exercise, but now all he does is watch TV and eat greasy, fattening foods. It's a bad example for the kids. I don't know what to do.

F2: _____

F1: _____

F2: _____

STAYING HEALTHY OUTDOORS (pp. 90-91)

Conversation Springboard: *What's next?*

M1: I didn't think the desert would get so hot this early in the morning!

M2: Look at that sun! It's like a furnace! I'm really starting to feel weird!

M1: I wish we had brought that sunblock. I'm burning up.

M2: Me, too. I'm kind of dizzy and I feel a little dehydrated.

M1: Oh, boy; I hope you aren't getting heat exhaustion. Let's sit here for a while. There's no shade, though!

M2: Well, let's at least have some water. Uh-oh, empty. . . I think my stomach is upset.

M1: *(to himself)* Gee, what'll I do if he faints? Wait, Mike. Let's get out of here—there's a scorpion heading for your leg!

M2: A scorpion! Where?

M1: Over there—behind you!

M2: That's nothing! There's a rattlesnake on that big rock next to you!

M1: Oh, no! What do I do?

Picture Springboard: *Finish the conversation.*

F1: Dad, let's go home! I'm getting attacked by a swarm of bees or wasps or something!

M1: OK, but try not to move too fast—you'll get stung. . . Oh boy, my hay fever is acting up again.

M2: Dad! I think I stepped in poison ivy. I'm itchy all over!

M1: _____

M2: _____

F1: _____

HOME REMEDIES (pp. 92-93)

Conversation Springboard: *What's happening?*

(telephone conversation)

F1: Hi, Simon. I won't be in class today. I'm sick as a dog.

M1: Who is this?

F1: It's Mona. No wonder you don't recognize my voice because I'm *so* sick.

M1: Right. I didn't even know it was you. What's going on?

F1: I don't know. I must have caught a cold. I have such a bad stuffy nose, I can hardly breathe. And I ache all over.

M1: Well, sounds like a respiratory infection, or maybe the flu. What are you doing for it?

F1: Well, I'm staying in bed with a heating pad and lots of vitamin C.

M1: That's a good idea. Whatever you have, it's probably contagious. Do you think you need to see a doctor?

F1: Well, I would rather get some acupuncture for the pain in my neck—or a massage would help. I prefer nontraditional medicine.

M1: Don't forget to drink lots of herbal tea.

F1: Yeah, thanks for the advice. Could you call me later with the assignment? I don't want to fall behind in class.

M1: Sure. Take care. Talk to you later.

Picture Springboard: *Finish the conversation.*

M1: My back is killing me!

F1: Lie still and I'll put some rubbing alcohol on and give you a massage.

M1: Oh—that hurts! Paul, walk on my back gently, please.

M2: Like this, Daddy?

M1: _____

F1: _____

M1: _____

MEDICAL CARE (pp. 94-95)

Conversation Springboard: *What's next?*

F1: Hi again, Mrs. Weston.

F2: Hello, Dr. Wolff.

F1: Hi, Abby. You don't look very happy today. Does your ear hurt?

214

F3: Yes, it does.

F1: May I take a look at it? Don't worry, I won't hurt you.

F3: OK.

F1: Hmm. . . Yes, that one's infected. Let's see your other ear now.

F3: That one doesn't hurt. . .

F1: OK. It looks fine. Thanks, Abby. When did the earache start this time, Mrs. Weston?

F2: Two days ago, and it's been getting worse.

F1: It looks like she'll need an antibiotic again. I'll give you another prescription. This is Abby's third ear infection this winter, isn't it?

F2: Yes, it is.

F1: I think it's time to look into this more. I'd like to refer you to a specialist.

F2: That's a good idea, Doctor.

Picture Springboard: *Finish the conversation.*

F1: Janice, looks like you have a throat infection.

F2: No wonder I feel so awful. What should I do?

F1: _____

F2: _____

F1: _____

EMERGENCY CARE (pp. 96-97)

Conversation Springboard: *What's happening?*

M1: Grandma, when are we going to get out of here?

F1: Dan, just be patient. There are so many sick people here.

M1: But Grandma, I want to go home. *(starts to cry)* I want Mommy.

F1: Honey, don't cry. How do you feel? Does your arm hurt?

M1: Not much, Grandma. I'm hungry. This sling hurts, though.

F1: Dan, your arm is fractured. Please try not to move it. It's getting pretty swollen. Stay here. I'll talk to the nurse.

M2: Can I help you?

F1: Yes, I've been here with my grandson for four hours. He's just a little boy and he's scared. When will the doctor be back with his X-rays?

M2: I don't really know, ma'am. We've got people with life-threatening illnesses coming in.

F1: I understand that, but I've got a frightened little boy who is also in pain.

M2: I'll see what I can do.

F1: Thanks. I appreciate it.

Picture Springboard: *Finish the conversation.*

F1: Have you been a patient at this hospital before?

M1: No, I haven't.

F1: What kind of insurance coverage do you have?

M1: I have an HMO, the Partner's Health Plan.

F1: I'll need to make a copy of your insurance card.

M1: _____

F1: _____

M1: _____

PHARMACY (pp. 98-99)

Conversation Springboard: *What's next?*

M1: What a day—I haven't stopped filling prescriptions since we opened this morning!

F1: Winter's here—lots of illnesses. Boy, being a pharmacist in flu season is no picnic!

M2: Excuse me. Where can I find an over-the-counter anti-inflammatory drug?

M1: Over on the shelf to the right. That one used to be a prescription drug, but you can get a low dosage over-the-counter generic for half the cost of the prescription.

M2: Where did you say?

F1: Right there, next to the painkillers.

M1: Be sure to take it on a full stomach.

M2: Oh, here it is. Thanks.

F2: I'm here to pick up my prescription. The doctor called it in about an hour ago.

M1: What's your name?

Picture Springboard: *Finish the conversation.*

M1: I'd like to pick up my prescription for a painkiller. I broke my ankle this afternoon. Last name is Riggs.

M2: Just a second. OK, this is pretty strong medicine. Be sure to follow the instructions: maximum four a day—one tablet every four hours. And there are no refills on this prescription.

M1: _____

M2: _____

M1: _____

POISONS (pp. 100-101)

Conversation Springboard: *What's happening?*

F1: Hi, Cloe. I'm home. How was your day?

F2: Oh. . . not so good.

F1: What's the matter? You look awful!

F2: I've been so sick all afternoon, with a very bad stomachache and a fever.

F1: Did you take any medicine?

F2: Yes, but it didn't do any good. I feel worse.

F1: What did you eat?

F2: Not much. Just a hamburger for lunch.

F1: How was it cooked?

F2: Rare.

F1: Rare?!

F2: I always eat my hamburgers rare.

F1: Cloe, sounds like it might be food poisoning!

F2: Oh! What do I do now?

F1: I'll take you over to the clinic. Do you think you can make it?

F2: Well, I'm pretty weak. I've been vomiting all afternoon.

F1: Well, let's try. You really do need to see a doctor.

Picture Springboard: *Finish the conversation.*

F1: Oh, no! Sean! What did you do?! Look at you! Oh, what do I do now? Oh, my goodness, he swallowed drain cleaner! Where did I leave that number for the poison control center. . . Here it is!

M1 *(poison control center)*: _____

           F1: _____

           M1: _____

COUNSELING (pp. 102–103)

Conversation Springboard: *What's the process?*

M1: OK, the four of us can probably knock off this Cross Cultural Exchange pretty quickly. Who'll be the monitor?

F1: I will.

M2: I'll record, OK? We'll have to report back after we finish.

M1, F1, F2: Sure. Fine. Great! Let's get started.

F1: First question: What social problems exist in your country?

M1: Aren't they all the same? Drugs, alcohol, poverty. . .

F1: What about child abuse?

F2: And don't forget spousal abuse and mental problems.

M2: Wait, it has to be country by country. It says in *your* country.

M1: But we're all from the same country. What do we do?

F2: How about by province? We can look at our country by province and see if there are any differences.

M2: I don't think there are. Although, maybe things are different in the rural areas. Let's try that. . .

Picture Springboard: *Finish the conversation.*

F1: I'm so glad the three of you came to our group tonight. So, how was your week?

F2: Well, the group therapy is really helping me, but this was a really bad week.

F1: Oh, I'm sorry, Elaine. Would you like to share it with us?

F2 *(patient 1)*: _____

F3 *(patient 2)*: _____

M1 *(patient 3)*: _____

UNIT 6: HOUSING

PLACES TO LIVE (pp. 106–107)

Conversation Springboard: *What's happening?*

M1: We just sold our house!

F1: Wow, that was fast!

M1: Yeah, the people who bought from us live in a high-rise in the city. They think our little ranch house is big!

F2: Yeah, the house sold quite easily. The real estate market is strong because the area is really growing.

M1: Yes, there are housing developments being built everywhere—it's no longer the village it once was. That's why Anne and I are moving out—this town is getting too congested. There's just no space anymore.

F1: Where do you think you'll live?

M1: Oh, I don't know. Maybe a log cabin, somewhere in the countryside.

F2: Excuse me, Tom? A log cabin in the countryside? I think I'd rather move back to the city—to a town house.

M1: A town house, Anne? I didn't think you wanted to move *back* to the city—and to live in a *town house!*

Picture Conversation: *Finish the conversation.*

M1: It's been so discouraging looking for a place to live!

F1: We've seen some pretty nice places, but they're all so different!

M1: Well, which do you prefer, Maria? We have to make a decision soon!

F1: _____

M1: _____

F1: _____

INSIDE YOUR HOME (pp. 108–109)

Conversation Springboard: *What's next?*

M1: Sylvia, I sure am glad we found this town house! It's perfect for us! Let's try to finish putting up the wallpaper and mini-blinds tonight before we go to bed.

F1: I never hung wallpaper before. It's a good thing we didn't put the carpets down yet—we're making such a mess!

M1: You said it! And it's a good thing the furniture doesn't arrive until next week.

F1: That's for sure. You know, this room is going to look really nice after all the furnishings are in place.

M1: It sure will. The last occupant's taste was pretty awful—I mean, I couldn't live with black walls and ceilings—it would feel like a cave!

F1: I know. Lighter colors make a room look so much more spacious.

M1: By the way, how do you want to redecorate the bedroom?

Picture Springboard: *Finish the conversation.*

F1: I really like our new neighbors.

M1: Yeah? I haven't met them yet.

F1: They're very nice. You should see their apartment. It's decorated beautifully.

M1: Really? What's it like?

F1: _____

M1: _____

F1: _____

Conversation Springboard: *What's your opinion?*

(TV commercial)

M1: Today's Homes Realtor offers a special group of homes in your area. We have a lovely one-family home on a large lot—a handyman's dream. Three bedrooms, two baths, and an above-ground pool—asking price is $55,000. A great bargain!

Or, if you prefer a mobile home, we have several available within your price range. Great condition, some with dishwashers and wall-to-wall carpeting. All in Shady Oaks Trailer Park.

Condos your style? How about a two-bedroom town house for $100,000. Low down payment and low interest loans available! Near transportation, shopping, and schools.

We have great rental properties, too! How about a studio for $400 a month. This apartment is in excellent condition. Believe it or not, a new refrigerator, dishwasher, heat, and utilities are included in this great bargain! Fenced-in yard and laundry room, too—what a deal!

Picture Springboard: *Finish the conversation.*

M1: We've been looking for weeks, Sheldon. I'm not sure that we'll ever find something that will fit our budget.

M2: Dad, don't worry—we will. Be patient. We know exactly what we need and the real estate agent is working hard to help us.

F1: Oh, look at this house! What do you think? Do you like it?

M2: _____

M1: _____

F1: _____

Conversation Springboard: *What happened?*

M1: What a storm last night!

M2: Don't remind me!

M1: Why? What happened?

M2: The power went out, and. . .

M1: You, too? The power was out in our neighborhood for over an hour.

M2: The funny thing is the power *did* go out—but the storm wasn't the cause.

M1: Oh?

M2: That's right. We were sitting in the dark for hours waiting for the power to come back on, when the entire time a fuse had just blown.

M1: You're kidding!

M2: No. I found out later that my kids had their computer, blow-dryer, TV, and CD player plugged into the same extension cord! It's no wonder the house didn't burn down!

M1: That *is* pretty dangerous.

M2: Yeah. You know, I never even thought to check the fuse box. I mean, I just figured it was the storm outside that knocked out the power. . . Hmm, I really should get an electrician to come in and rewire the place. . .

Picture Conversation: *Finish the conversation.*

M1: Good morning. Star Oil.

M2: Yes, this is Juan Ramirez. My oil tank just ran out of oil.

M1: Please hold. . .

M2: Wait! I'm calling from a pay phone—you see, my phone was. . .

M1: Could you please repeat that, sir?

M2: _____

M1: _____

M2: _____

Conversation Springboard: *What's next?*

M1: We really want to get out of our lease. We've got such terrible conditions in our apartment, we can't stand living there any more!

M2: Since when? I thought you loved that apartment, David.

M1: Well, since the new owner took over, the place has really deteriorated. Most of the major appliances don't work, and they refuse to fix them or replace them. They're not even functional! The fixtures in the bathroom are leaking. And they don't maintain the building.

M2: It's really the landlord's responsibility to keep everything serviceable.

F1: Rick's right—you don't need brand-new appliances, but it's fair to ask for decent, second-hand models if the ones you have can't be fixed.

M1: Oh, I've asked the landlord so many times. It doesn't do any good!

F2: You have rights to have the appliances be in working order. Why don't you call the tenant's rights organization? They can give you good advice.

M1: Great idea, Eliza. I'll do that today.

Picture Springboard: *Finish the conversation.*

F1: Mrs. Patel? This is Jean Samuels in Apartment 3C. The refrigerator really *does* need to be replaced. It's completely stopped working. All my food is spoiled, and the ice cream is melting all over the freezer.

F2: Are you sure? Check the temperature controls. Maybe the temperature needs to be adjusted.

F1: Mrs. Patel, it's not the temperature controls. We've been talking about replacing this refrigerator for a year now. I'm sorry, but I'm really annoyed about this.

F2: _____

F1: _____

F2: _____

217

Conversation Springboard: *What's happening?*

(telephone conversation)

M1: Hello, Mrs. Jones? Good evening. This is Sam Slick, Alpha Insurance representative in your neighborhood. How are you tonight?

F1: Excuse me. Alpha Insurance? I don't think you're my representative.

M1: Well, not right now. But I'm going to offer you a homeowner insurance protection plan against loss, burglary, storm, water, smoke and fire damage with the lowest premium on the market today.

F1: Excuse me. I don't understand. Could you speak more slowly, please?

M1: Sure. I'm about to offer you, tonight only, the best insurance plan you can get.

F1: Well, I don't really need an insurance plan.

M1: Mrs. Jones, everyone needs insurance. What if you are burglarized? What coverage would you have? What if a fire ruins everything you own?

F1: Mr. Slick, first of all I don't need any insurance. I live in a rented apartment, and all the furniture is rented, too. Secondly, my dinner's getting cold. So thanks, anyway. Bye.

Picture Springboard: *Finish the conversation.*

F1: Do you think our insurance will cover the fire and smoke damage?

M1: Let me get my clipboard and write up a report. As the insurance adjustor, all I can do is send in the report. I don't know about the extent of your coverage.

F1: I know my deductible is $250, but I sure hope the insurance covers the replacement cost.

M1: _____

F1: _____

M1: _____

Conversation Springboard: *What's happening?*

F1: They're gone just for a day, and I miss them already!

M1: Oh, Mom, Jeff got such a good job—it was too good to pass up. It was nice to help them pack, wasn't it?

F1: Well, I guess. With the children around, Lucy was having a hard time wrapping and packing all the glassware. She has so many fragile things.

M1: Well, you were great to help organize their belongings. There was so much confusion that so many of their things could have been broken or scratched. Hard to believe we did it ourselves without professional movers.

F1: Still, transporting everything in that utility trailer worries me. I hope we packed everything OK.

M1: Mom, don't worry. I'm sure everything's fine.

F1: Well, how will Lucy help Jeff with all those heavy boxes?

M1: Don't worry. They'll be fine. . . Oh, no!

F1: What? What's wrong?

M1: Look—Christopher forgot his teddy bear!

Picture Springboard: *Finish the conversation.*

M2: Christopher, don't cry. Tell Daddy what's wrong.

F2: Do you think he's sick?

M2: I can't imagine why he's so miserable.

F2: _____

_____

M2: _____

_____

Conversation Springboard: *What's the process?*

M1: We don't have much time for the Partner Activity.

F1: Let's try to finish before class is over.

M1: There's not much to do here.

F1: What do we have to do?

M1: Let's see, we need to read the letter and discuss it, and then write a reply.

F1: Hmm, I wonder if Aunt Betty is a real person. She looks real.

M1: And I wonder if her dog is real. The dog looks real, too. What do you think its name is?

F1: I don't know. A good name would be Sugar, though. . .

M1: Oops! We forgot to do the activity. Let's see. "With a partner, read and discuss this letter. . .

Teacher: OK, class, that's it for today.

Picture Springboard: *Finish the conversation.*

(knocking at door)

F1: Who is it?

F2: It's Mary, Mrs. Smith. Mary Martinez.

F1: What do you want?

F2: _____

F1: _____

F2: _____

Conversation Springboard: *What's next?*

(TV reporter)

F1: This is Mary Wu reporting live from Williams Street. This neighborhood will be our first experiment in urban renewal. Let's see who we can talk to. Raf, you've lived here for 30 years. What can you tell our viewers?

M1: I've seen a lot of changes over the years. The neighborhood has really gotten run down. Lots of abandoned cars, boarded-up houses, gangs, and garbage on the streets.

F1: Thanks, Raf. . . Lilian Mendez, you have been an advocate for this neighborhood, trying to organize your neighbors now for a year. Have there been any improvements?

F2: Well, I'm sorry to say, very few. There's graffiti all over the place, vagrants hanging out on the street corners, and homeless people who have nothing to do. People are worried about their personal safety.

do. People are worried about their personal safety. It's sad, but I'm not ready to give up. We've got a petition going around to give to the mayor.

F1: Thanks, Lilian. Looks like you're doing a great job, but there's more work to be done! Back to you, Tom.

Picture Springboard: *Finish the conversation.*

M1: Lilian, you talked to the reporter. What did she say to you?

F2: Not much, Raf. But maybe with the publicity, we'll have a chance with our petition.

M1: I'm really tired of this dangerous neighborhood. I used to love it here. I felt safe and good about the community. Now, I'm almost ready to give up!

F2: _____

M1: _____

F2: _____

NEIGHBORHOOD IMPROVEMENTS (pp. 124-125)

Conversation Springboard: *What's happening?*

F2: Well, Raf, we did it! We really did it! Can you believe our neighborhood is going to be on the evening news as a good example of urban renewal?!

M1: *You* did it, Lilian. You never gave up. And look at it now.

F2: We *all* did it, Raf! One person can't change a neighborhood alone.

F1: Raf, Lilian, hi! The neighborhood looks wonderful! Your grass roots organization really succeeded. Mind if I interview a few people for the newscast?

F2: Go right ahead.

F1: Sir, what do you think of the changes in this neighborhood?

M2: I'm proud to be part of refurbishing the neighborhood. I used to be homeless, but the neighborhood association gave me a job. I'm leading the clean-up campaign, and everyone is helping. In all the years I've lived here, I haven't seen such warm, neighborly attitudes. It's wonderful!

F1: Thank you. Well, folks, you've seen it—this is amazing! Your tax dollars at their working best. And what it took were two really dedicated residents to start the ball rolling. This is Mary Wu, reporting live from Williams Street.

Picture Springboard: *Finish the conversation.*

M3: Look at this neighborhood. I moved away two years ago.

F1: And you don't recognize it, right?

M3: Yeah, so much has changed. I don't know where to begin!

F1: What do you think is the biggest change?

M3: _____

F1: _____

M3: _____

Conversation Springboard: *What happened?*

M1: Hi, honey, you're home early.

F1: Boy, was I ever glad to be carpooling today!

M1: Really? I thought you said commuting with Andy and Joan was a waste of time and a bother, and you didn't like to have to listen to them talking all the way to work every day.

F1: Well, that's true sometimes, but today it was a real timesaver.

M1: Why? What happened?

F1: Well, you know how bad Friday afternoon rush-hour traffic can be, even without any problems. Well, today was a nightmare! There was a road crew doing construction work on the highway. . .

M1: Really?

F1: Yeah, the cars were backed up for miles. It was one of the worst traffic jams I've ever seen.

M1: So, how did you manage to get home early?

F1: If we hadn't been in the car pool lane, I'd still be stuck in traffic right now. All the traffic in the other lanes had to detour off the highway onto a little, two-lane road. But we just zipped along with no delays, and here I am—home early!

Picture Springboard: *Finish the conversation.*

F1: *(daughter)* Mama? Mama?

F2: What is it, honey?

F1: Are we going to get on the bus here?

F2: Yes, that's right, honey. This is a bus shelter, and it's where we get our bus.

F1: Are all the people here going to get on the bus?

F2: Uh-huh. Well, maybe not on our bus, but everybody's going to get on some bus.

F1: But what about that man in the wheelchair? How's he going to get on the bus?

F2: _____

F1: _____

M1 *(man in wheelchair)*: _____

Conversation Springboard: *What happened?*

M1: What's the matter, Bandar? You look like you just lost your best friend!

M2: Oh, hi, Kenji. No, I just failed the stupid road test for my driver license, that's all.

M1: That's too bad. What happened?

M2: I knocked over one of the cones parallel parking.

M1: You took a driver ed class, didn't you?

M2: Yeah, but I failed, anyway.

M1: Aw, don't worry about it. A lot of people fail the road test the first time, you know.

M2: Really? I don't know anybody else who did.

M1: My cousin had to retake the road test three times! The first time his steering wasn't so good, and he drove over the curb.

M2: Gee!

M1: The second time he forgot to look in the mirror before he backed up.

M2: Uh-oh. Did he hit anything?

M1: Yep. He backed right into a police car!

M2: Oh, no, you're kidding! So what happened the third time?

M1: By then the examiner was so nervous that she passed him just to get rid of him!

M2: Wow, I don't feel so bad now. I guess I'll go practice some more and take the test again.

Picture Springboard: *Finish the conversation.*

M3: All right, let's try the parallel parking again. Are you ready?

M2: I think so.

M3: See those two cones? They're the markers.

M2: OK, I see them.

M3: You have to park between them without touching either one. Think you can do that?

M2: _____

M3: _____

M2: _____

Conversation Springboard: *What's happening?*

M1: Hey, Mom! Look at that! That guy in front of us is going to lose his tailpipe!

F1: Do you think so? It does look a little wobbly.

M1: More than a little! It's hanging way down. If he goes over a bump, it'll hit the road for sure!

F1: I hope you're wrong, but I'm afraid you may be right, honey. The whole muffler looks really low.

M1: Well, do something, Mom. Beep the horn at him. I'll wave at him to pull over.
(beeps horn)

F1: I don't think he understood. He's speeding up! Oh, my gosh! It's scraping the road!

M1: You'd better slow down, Mom! It's going to fall off! Look out! *(Muffler falls off car.)*

F1: Oh, no! I don't believe it, I don't believe it! Right in the middle of the road!

M1: Good driving, Mom! I thought we were going to hit it for sure!

F1: I don't believe it! And he isn't even slowing down!

M1: I guess he doesn't even know what happened?

Picture Springboard: *Finish the conversation.*

F1: Just my luck! What a place for a flat tire, right in the middle of the desert! It's a good thing I'm prepared for it. . . Whew, it's hot! Boy, that's flat, all right. Now, let's see, where's the stuff to fix it . . . I think everything's in the trunk. *(opens trunk)* Yup. Here's the spare, and the jack. The lug wrench has to be here somewhere. Oh, there it is. That's everything. . . OK, now what do I do first? Hmm. . .

F1: _____

_____

_____

_____

Conversation Springboard: *What's the process?*

M1: List car options, huh? Who wants to be the recorder. . . Nobody? Oh, come on, somebody has to do it. How about you, Miyako?

F1: I always have to do it! I think you guys expect me to do it just because I'm a woman. It's not fair!

M2: OK, OK, I'll do it. Just don't go too fast.

M1: All right, car options. Are there any in the vocabulary list?

M2: Yes, sun roof and bucket seats.

F1: And four-by-four, I think. I'm not exactly sure what that is.

M1: It's four-wheel drive. And, yes, it's optional. Can you think of any others?

M2: How about power options—power locks, power windows. . .

F1: And power brakes, power steering. . .

M1: I don't think power brakes and power steering are optional anymore. Don't all cars have them nowadays?

M2: Yes, I think so.

Teacher: OK, class, time's up. Let's see what you've got.

Picture Springboard: *Finish the conversation.*

M1: OK, here we are. Now remember, just let me do the talking.

F1: Oh, I don't trust these used car places at all! They always sell you a car with problems.

M2: Hi, there. Can I help you folks?

M1: _____

M2: _____

F1: _____

Conversation Springboard: *What's your opinion?*

F1: Hey, Oscar!

M1: Huh?

F1: Are you daydreaming? You look like you're a million miles away.

M1: Oh, this lesson on vacations got me started thinking about the kind of vacation I'd like to take, Mi Sook. . .

F1: I thought so. What is your dream vacation, Oscar?

M1: Well, you know I'm from The Dominican Republic. That's a beautiful tropical island in the Caribbean—like a paradise. I'd like to take my wife and kids back there for a vacation—stay in a beach house, lie in a hammock under the palm trees, with a big beach umbrella . . . That would be heavenly for me.

F1: Oh, Oscar, it sounds wonderful. You should do it!

M1: That's easier said than done. My wife and I have to work, and the children have school. It's hard to find the time and the money to do it. What about you, Mi Sook? What's your dream vacation?

F1: Mine's with my family, too. I haven't been back to Korea for more than a year, and I really miss my family. Sometimes I get so homesick that it's hard for me to study! I would love to just climb on a plane tomorrow, call my family from the airport in Seoul, and say, "Surprise, I'm home!"

M1: That sounds like an important vacation. I know you can't fly off tomorrow, but when *will* you be able to get back home to visit?

F1: I don't know. . .

Picture Springboard: *Finish the conversation.*

M1: Mmm, that's a beautiful travel brochure, Anita. Are you planning a trip to Germany?

F1: Yes, but not only Germany, Luigi. I love castles. I want to visit castles and cathedrals all over Europe! You're planning to go to Europe next summer, aren't you?

M1: Yes, with Mohammed. He's never been to Italy. We're going hiking in the Alps.

F1: Oh, that sounds like an adventure! Tell me more.

M1: _____

F1: _____

M1: _____

TRAVELING BY CAR (pp. 138–139)

Conversation Springboard: *What's happening?*

M1: Fill her up?

M2: Yes, and would you check the oil and radiator, too, please.

M1: Sure thing.

M2: We're not making very good time. The highway patrol's out in full force today. I've counted ten patrol cars in the past hour.

F1: Well, we don't want a speeding ticket, that's for sure.

F2: (daughter) Hey! Gimme that!

M3: (son) No! Let go of me! Mommy!

F2: You gimme that back! It's mine! Mom! (Dog barks.)

F1: Settle down, kids. Adriana, leave your brother alone.

F2: But he's got my earphones!

M3: No, they're mine!

F2: He broke his, and now he took mine!

F1: Tony, give your sister back the earphones. (Dog barks again.) How about it, kids. Let's take Cody for a walk on the grass over there. I think we all need a little rest!

F2: Not Grandpa. He's getting plenty of rest. He's been sleeping all day!

Picture Springboard: *Finish the conversation.*

M1: Honey?

F1: (waking up) Mmm. . . Oh. Where are we?

M1: At a motel just off the exit from the highway. I got too sleepy—had to stop for the night. The vacancy sign is on. I'll go in and register us for a room. (grandfather snoring)

F1: Just one room? I don't think we'll get much sleep with your father snoring all night!

M1: _____

F1: _____

M1: _____

BUS AND TRAIN TRAVEL (pp. 140–141)

Conversation Springboard: *What's next?*

M1: (son) Who was that man—the one that put our suitcases up there on the rack?

F1: That was the porter, honey.

M1: Can we eat on the train, Mommy?

F1: Yes, dear. They have a dining car, but we have some food with us, too. Are you hungry?

M1: No. When will we get to Washington, Mom?

F1: Tomorrow afternoon, dear.

M1: Where will we sleep tonight?

F1: Right here, dear. The seats fold down, and we can stretch out. They'll give us pillows and blankets.

M1: How come we can't sleep in a bed?

M2: Tickets, please.

F1: Oh, yes. Let's see now, where did I put those. . .

M1: We're going all the way to Washington to visit my grandma.

M2: Are you, now. That's a long trip.

M1: But Mommy says we're not sleeping in beds tonight. I saw a bed in a little room in that other car over there.

M2: Yes, that's a sleeper car. This is a coach.

F1: Honey, don't bother the conductor.

M2: Oh, that's all right, ma'am.

F1: I don't know what I did with those tickets. . . I had them right here. . .

221

Picture Springboard: *Finish the conversation.*

M1: May I help you, ma'am?

F1: Yes, please. Could you tell me what time it is here? The clocks say all different times, and I'm not sure what time zone I'm in anymore!

M1: It's 3:00 Mountain Standard Time.

F1: Oh, thank goodness! I was afraid I'd miss my train. Which track is the train to Chicago on, and how soon does it leave?

M1: _____

F1: _____

M1: _____

AIR TRAVEL (pp. 142–143)

Conversation Springboard: *What's happening?*

M1: Hi, can I help you with that?

F1: Thanks, I think I've got it now. This overhead compartment is kind of unusual.

M1: I think this is my seat. My ticket stub says 12A. Is that the window or the aisle seat?

F1: It's the aisle seat, but if you'd prefer the window, that's OK with me.

M1: Thanks, the aisle's fine with me.

M2: *(pilot's voice over PA system)* This is your captain. We are cleared for takeoff. Please make sure your seatbelts are securely fastened and all carry-on bags are stowed in the overhead compartments or under the seat in front of you. Flight attendants will be in the aisles to demonstrate safety equipment, and a safety manual is in the seat-back in front of you.

M1: Hmm. . . I can't find the other end of my seatbelt. . .

F1: Oh, sorry! I think I'm using it here! No wonder it didn't attach properly! Here you are. Now I wonder where the other part of mine is. . .

M1: I think you're sitting on it.

F1: Oh, for goodness sake, you're right! Thanks!

Picture Springboard: *Finish the conversation.*

M1: Can I take that for you, sir?

M2: Yes, thanks. I'm finished.

M1: Would you care for something more to drink?

M2: _____

M1: _____

M2: _____

UNIT 8: FINDING A JOB

JOBS IN YOUR COMMUNITY (pp. 146–149)

Conversation Springboard: *What's the process?*

F1: Do you think it'll be OK that we didn't all do this Community Activity together?

F2: It has to be OK, Mari! We couldn't go together!

M1: And we each did the activity. We probably got more information this way. What about you, Ilse? What did you find?

F2: Well, yesterday was such a beautiful day. I didn't want to waste the day doing homework. . .

M1: You mean you didn't do it?

F2: Oh, no, I did it, Tim. I did it in the park so I could enjoy the sunshine. I was surprised at how much was going on!

M1: Really? Not just some old people sitting on benches?

F2: No, not at all. A politician was there, giving a speech about saving the park. And there were reporters and cameras and police everywhere.

F1: Well, the "workplace" is easy—that's the park. What are those kinds of work?

F2: You mean the occupation categories from the vocabulary list? I didn't look them up yet.

M1: Here, look at the list. I think you saw communications, and government, and law enforcement, and news media, and photography. . .

F1: What about public service?

F2: You mean the politician? Yes, I guess so.

M1: That's good, Ilse. That's a lot.

F2: Oh, that's not all! There were lots of other people working in the park!

Picture Springboard: *Finish the conversation.*

F2: What place did you go to, Mari?

F1: Well, you know I'm awfully busy, so I really didn't have time to go anywhere special. . .

M1: Yes, but you always manage to do your assignments, Mari. I'm sure you found a way to do it.

F1: You're right, Tim. I did it on the bus on my way to work.

M1: On the bus? What did you see there?

F1: _____

F2: _____

F1: _____

YOUR OCCUPATION (pp. 150–151)

Conversation Springboard: *What's happening?*

M1: This should be a good lesson for the three of us since we all have jobs.

F1: That's true, Hector. What do you do?

M1: Well, I was an auto mechanic for years, Martine. Now I work in the special order department at the auto assembly plant.

F2: You work third shift, don't you, Hector?

M1: That's right. I go to work after class, work all night, and go to bed when the sun comes up!

F1: Doesn't that bother you? Staying up all night and sleeping in the daytime?

M1: Nope. I've always liked working at night.

F2: It sounds like you really enjoy your work, Hector.

M1: Yes, I do, Fatima. I really do. Don't you enjoy your job?

F2: Well, yes, in a way. I work as a hospital aide at City Hospital, and I do enjoy the contact with patients, but. . .

F1: I thought you were a doctor, Fatima.

F2: Yes, I am, and that's the problem. I was a doctor in my country, but I have to pass the English examinations for certification to practice medicine in this country, and that's really hard.

M1: Ah, I see. You're working as a hospital aide to get experience using all that medical vocabulary in English.

F2: That's right. And working with patients has really improved my English. The words patients use to tell how they're feeling aren't in any medical textbook.

F1: Like "feeling queasy," or "throwing up."

M1: Or being "under the weather" or "down in the dumps."

F2: Exactly. That's why I'm taking this conversation class.

F1: Good luck, Fatima! Pass that exam and we can all be your patients!

Picture Springboard: *Finish the conversation.*

M1: How about you, Martine? Do you like your job?

F1: Oh, I love it, Hector! It's part time, and that's perfect for me.

F2: What is your job, Martine? Tell us about it.

F1: _____

M1: _____

F1: _____

THE RIGHT JOB FOR YOU (pp. 152–153)

Conversation Springboard: *What's the process?*

F1: That was an interesting survey, Phong. Our ideal jobs are really different, aren't they?

M1: They sure are, Zelda. That's probably because *we're* pretty different.

F1: Yes, that's true. Let's see, now we have to report our partner's responses to another pair. Hey, Marcos, do you two want to do the reporting with us?

M2: Sure, Zelda. We're ready, right, Samara?

F2: Right. You guys go first, Phong.

M1: OK. The first question was "Which are more important to you in a job?" Then a lot of choices: "friendly co-workers," "a good supervisor," "good pay," etc. Zelda couldn't decide on that one.

F1: No, wait! That's not right, Phong! They're all important to me! We don't have to choose just one answer to that question. It says "Which are more important?" "Are" means more than one. And I care about all those things.

F2: Me, too, Zelda. That was my answer to the first question, too.

M2: How did Phong answer that question, Zelda?

F1: "Good pay" and "chance for advancement."

M1: Of course. That's what's more important. Sure, the other things are nice to have, but you have to admit, if the pay is bad and there's no chance for advancement, it's not a good job!

M2: I agree!

F1: I don't.

F2: Me, neither!

Picture Springboard: *Finish the conversation.*

M1: It's true, our company has had some pretty tough competition and some pretty heavy losses this past year. . .

F1: If anyone can pull our company out of this slump, it's you, John!

M1: Well, I look at this as a challenge for us all—an opportunity to show what our company can do! We're a team. With a little cooperation and our best efforts, we can be winners again!

M2: You know you can count on us, John. So, what's your plan?

M1: _____

F1: _____

M1: _____

LOOKING FOR A JOB (pp. 154–155)

Conversation Springboard: *What happened?*

F1: Did you ever find a job from a newspaper ad, Miki?

F2: No, Celia. Actually, I've never had a job.

F1: Really? Never? Not any kind of job?

F2: That's right. In my country, students study all the time. I never had time for a job. I was always too busy studying.

F1: And you're a good student, too, Miki. What about you, Luis? Have you ever found a job from a newspaper ad?

M1: Oh, sure, Celia. Newspaper ads, employment agencies, help wanted signs, word of mouth—you name it. I've tried them all.

F1: Sounds like you've had a lot of different jobs, Luis.

M1: That's true. I started working when I was a kid. I've lived in different places, and now I have four children, so I've been working for quite a while. But I've been lucky. I've always been able to find a job with no experience required.

F2: You must have a lot of experience by now!

M1: Yes, I guess I have. I've worked in restaurants and road construction and landscaping, and driving a taxi, and cleaning offices, and delivering pizzas. . . I even worked in a cemetery digging graves once!

F2: Oh, no! Why did you want to do that?

M1: I got that job by mistake. My English wasn't very good, and I thought the job was going to be landscaping.

F1: That must have been quite a surprise.

M1: Oh, yes. That's why I'm studying English. I don't want to make a mistake like that again!

Picture Springboard: *Finish the conversation.*

M1: Hi. I wonder if I could speak with the manager?

M2: Well, I'm the owner. Can I help you?

M1: I hope so. My name's Luis Rivera, and I saw your Help Wanted sign in the window.

M2: _____

M1: _____

M2: _____

Conversation Springboard: *What's next?*

F1: Um. . . Excuse me. . .

F2: Yes? What is it?

F1: Um. . . You asked me to fill in this form. . .

F2: The job application, yes. Is there a problem?

F1: Well, um, I'm not sure what to put here. . .

F2: What's that? Job experience? Just list the jobs you've had before.

F1: Um, yes, well. . .

F2: What did you say? Could you speak up, please?

F1: Yes. Sorry. I wonder if that means. . . well, does that mean any kind of work?

F2: Yes, any job you've ever had.

F1: Thank you. Um. . .

F2: Yes? Something else?

F1: No, no. . . I was just wondering whether. . . Well, could that maybe include volunteer work?

F2: You mean like the Red Cross? That kind of thing?

F1: Sort of. Like, helping out at home, maybe?

Picture Springboard: *Finish the conversation.*

F1: Hello, Mr. Rivera. Come right in. I'm Grace Chang. Here, have a seat.

M1: Thank you.

F1: I see from your application that you have a lot of job experience, Mr. Rivera.

M1: Well, I've had a number of different jobs over the years.

F1: Yes, and you have excellent references. Tell me, Mr. Rivera, what is particularly attractive to you about this job?

M1: _____

F1: _____

M1: _____

Conversation Springboard: *What's your opinion?*

F1: Do you think your new job will work out, Takeshi?

M1: I hope so, Izumi. It pays well. And it seems to have a good benefits package.

F1: What benefits are there?

M1: Well, it has really good group health insurance, with complete medical and hospitalization coverage.

F1: So, if we have another baby, that will be covered?

M1: Right. They even have family leave. And we can go to any doctor or any hospital we want!

F1: Is there dental coverage? I know Hiroshi's teeth are going to need braces.

M1: Yes, there's a dental plan. And eye coverage, too. Michiyo can get a new pair of glasses free every year.

F1: Oh, wonderful. Health care is so expensive in this country. I'm glad we won't have to worry about it! What about vacation time for you, Takeshi?

M1: Well, I'll get two weeks of paid vacation every year, plus eleven paid holidays. And six paid sick days.

F1: Well, you won't need those. You never get sick.

M1: I hope not, but it's good to have them, anyway. There's life insurance, too, and a retirement plan.

F1: Oh, Takeshi, it does sound wonderful! We'll be well taken care of.

M1: It looks that way, Izumi. I just hope I like the job now.

F1: You will, don't worry. It sounds perfect!

Picture Springboard: *Finish the conversation.*

F2: If that's all clear, Mr. Suzuki, and you understand this employment contract, then you just need to sign the agreement right here, at the bottom.

M1: Actually, I do have one question.

F2: Well, now's the time to ask. I'll do my best to answer. What's your question, Mr. Suzuki?

M1: _____

F2: _____

M1: _____

UNIT 9: LIFE AT WORK

Conversation Springboard: *What's next?*

M1: Good morning. I'm Tom Rogers. You must be Angela Soulas, our new data entry clerk.

F1: Yes, I am. I'm pleased to meet you, Mr. Rogers.

M1: Oh, just call me Tom—everyone does.

F1: OK. And most people call me Angie.

M1: Well, Angie, this is it—the R & D Data Entry Department. Welcome to the group. You'll get acquainted with everyone here pretty quickly. This is Ellen Grant, Viv Russell, Amy Wang, Dan Long, and Bob Fellows back at the copy machine. Everyone, this is Angie Soulas.

Group: Hi, Angie. Welcome. Glad to have you.

F1: Hi.

M1: Amy will show you how to handle the data entry you'll be working on, and Viv will show you how to handle our complicated copy machine.

M2: That copier has a mind of its own.

F2: That copier works just fine if you treat it right!

M2: Only for you, Viv!

F2: Hmph!

M1: And here's your desk, Angie. I'll leave you in Amy's capable hands now. If there's anything that's unclear or that you're confused about, don't be embarrassed to ask. Amy knows everything about the data programs we use.

F1: Thanks, Mr. Rogers. . . Oh, sorry. . . Tom. Looks like I'll be just fine.

Picture Springboard: *Finish the conversation.*

F1: *(to herself)* Let's see, how did Viv say to start this copier? I think she said you have to restart it each time. . . She explained it so fast that I don't remember what she said. Impatient people make me nervous. I'm always afraid I'll make an error. . . Hmm. . . Maybe it's this green button. . . Yes, I think this must be it. . . *(Copier jams.)* Oh, no!

F2: What are you doing there! Oh. . .

F1: _____

F2: _____

F1: _____

INSTRUCTIONS AT WORK (pp. 164–165)

Conversation Springboard: *What's happening?*

M1: Aha! Roman and Liz, hard at work! How are you two doing with those building modifications?

M2: Not so well, Andrew. This new software isn't very friendly. Right now it's just giving us a bunch of garbage.

F1: You've worked with it, Andrew. What do you think could be wrong? Could you give us a hand?

M1: I'd like to, but I'm on my way to a big meeting, and I'll be tied up for the rest of the day. Here's the software manual. I'm sure you won't have any serious problems.

F1: We've already got serious problems.

M1: Oh, it's probably just something minor. Double check the instructions in the manual again. And remember, these modifications have to be done today!

F1: Right. Have a good meeting, Andrew.

M2: Yes, have fun.

M1: You, too. See you tomorrow.

F1: Well, that's great. "Check the manual," he says.

M2: We'll be here all night at this rate, while he's out on the golf course.

F1: The golf course! I thought he had a big meeting.

M2: That's where they have their big meetings—on the golf course!

Picture Springboard: *Finish the conversation.*

(waitress and customers in restaurant)

M1: I'll have the taco special—and does that come with chips and salsa?

F1: It comes with rice and beans, but I can bring you some chips and salsa if you'd like. . .

F2: Excuse me. Would you change my salad dressing to Italian, please? I think I ordered ranch—or was it French?

M2: Miss? I'd like to order an appetizer. . .

M1: Hold it, everybody! We're going to confuse this poor waitress. Let's try this one at a time! You first, Lucy.

F2: OK, Jim. Sorry. . .

F2: _____

F1: _____

M2: _____

DOING A GOOD JOB (pp. 166–167)

Conversation Springboard: *What's your opinion?*

F1: These are beautiful strawberries, Mr. Garcia. I'll have to buy some for my mom.

M1: Yes, they *are* nice, Katie. Have you seen Melanie this morning?

F1: No, I haven't.

M1: Hmph!

F2: Oh, hi, Mr. Garcia. Hi, Katie.

F1: Hi, Melanie.

M1: Hmph. Let's get these strawberries ready and out front. They're our big produce special today, and everybody's going to want them.

F2: OK, OK, don't worry—we'll have them out there in plenty of time. Right, Katie. . .

M1: Hmm. Well, get to work now, and I want to talk with you later, Melanie. Stop by my office on your break.

F2: What's bothering him? The man is such a grouch!

F1: Well, he's the manager, Melanie. And you're late again.

F2: Oh, great! You're on my case, too! You sound like I'm late every day.

F1: Well, you *are* late a lot.

F2: Mmm. . . beautiful strawberries, aren't they! *(eats one)* Delicious, too! I didn't have time for breakfast, but these will do just fine. Have some, Katie.

F1: We shouldn't be eating them, Melanie. They're for the customers.

F2: Oh, Katie, you're too good. Mmm. . . These *are* good!

Picture Springboard: *Finish the conversation.*

F1: Here's your change, ma'am, and your receipt. Have a nice day.

F2: Oh, dear, what's she doing to my groceries?!

F1: I beg your pardon. . .

F2: The bag is tearing!

F3: What?

F1: _____

F2: _____

F3: _____

INJURIES AT WORK (pp. 168–169)

Conversation Springboard: *What happened?*

F1: Hi, Henry. How're you feeling?

M1: Oh, hi, Jane. I've been better. Where am I?

F1: You're in the hospital.

M1: What happened? How'd I get here? Who are you?

F2: I'm Dr. Latham. You don't remember anything?

M1: No. The last I remember, I was in the lab, working with the XF2 compound. Did I faint? Oh, my head hurts!

F1: No, Henry, you didn't faint. The beaker exploded!

M1: An explosion? That's impossible! We took every precaution.

F1: Well, something went wrong, that's for sure. Those chemicals are highly combustible—you know that. And the fumes are poisonous.

M1: Oh, boy. So, what's my condition, Doctor? Am I going to be all right?

F2: Well, you have a concussion from the explosion, and there's some damage to your lungs from the fumes, but you're going to be OK. You're a lucky man!

M1: Lucky. . . Is everybody else OK? What about the experiment?

F1: Everybody else is fine. And don't worry about the lab, Henry.

F2: That's right. You need to get some rest now. You can talk again later.

Picture Springboard: *Finish the conversation.*

F1: OK, now, Mrs. Delaney. I'm just going to lift you out of the bed and help you into the wheelchair.

F2: I'm pretty heavy for a little thing like you to lift. . .

F1: Oh, don't worry, I do this all the time. Ready now? Lift! Oh! Oh, no!

F2: _____

F1: _____

F2: _____

DEDUCTIONS FROM PAY (pp. 170–171)

Conversation Springboard: *What's the process?*

M1: Oh, a Class Survey. OK, let's start with Bill and Dorina. Did either of you ever have Medicare tax or Social Security contributions deducted from your income?

M2: Sure!

F1: Of course. Everybody does.

M2: Right. You don't have any choice about those deductions. They're required.

M1: For part-time work, too?

F1: I think so.

F2: Well, nobody ever deducts those from my pay when I baby-sit.

M1: And when I mow lawns for people, they pay me in cash. They never deduct anything.

F1: I think they're supposed to, or you're supposed to, or something. . .

F2: Do you know, Bill?

M2: No, I'm not sure about that, either. But we could find out.

F2: Really? How?

M2: There's a toll-free number to call with tax questions. It's listed in the phone directory.

F1: Or we could just ask the teacher. He'll know.

M1: I'm not sure I want to find out. . .

Picture Springboard: *Finish the conversation.*

F1: Oh, Rosa, I got my first paycheck, but something's wrong! I don't understand what happened. Can you help me?

F2: I'll try, Paula. What doesn't seem right?

F1: Well, my earnings say $320, but they've only paid me $211.90. It has to be a mistake!

F2: May I see it? Hmm. . . It looks OK to me, Paula.

F1: But, that's impossible! It's so little money!

F2: _____

F1: _____

F2: _____

SPENDING MONEY (pp. 172–173)

Conversation Springboard: *What's your opinion?*

F1: What a perfect day!

M1: Mmm. . . and great chicken!

F1: Well, chicken was on sale this week.

M1: That's my wife, always economizing.

F1: I just don't like to waste money. And there's something special about simple pleasures. A picnic

in the country, blue sky, sunshine, Tony chasing butterflies. . . Tony, don't go too far!

M2: OK, Mama.

M1: I'm glad you're a sensible woman, Lupita.

F1: Thanks, Roberto. That reminds me—I'm really worried about Costas.

M1: The guy at your office? What did he do now?

F1: Well, he has a new girlfriend, and you know how extravagant he is, always splurging on something.

M1: Oh, yes, I remember—only the best for Costas. So, what's he doing to impress his new girlfriend?

F1: Well, he bought a new car—one of those fancy sports cars—and he's been taking her out to expensive nightclubs and restaurants. Costas and I make the same amount of money, and I know if you and I were spending money that way, we'd go broke pretty fast.

M1: Well, don't worry too much, Lupita. There's nothing you can do about it. Costas is just going to have to learn the hard way.

F1: Yes, I guess you're right. I'm glad you're not like that, Roberto. Want some more chicken?

Picture Springboard: *Finish the conversation.*

M3: Wait a minute. . . What's this? Oh, no! I don't believe it!

F1: What's the matter, Costas?

M3: A repossession notice! They want to repossess my new car! What will Kiki say? We're supposed to go dancing tonight! They can't do that!

F1: _____

M3: _____

F1: _____

PAYING TAXES (pp. 174–175)

Conversation Springboard: *What's next?*

M1: What's the matter, Nick?

M2: I'm pretty worried, Mattiew. I just got a letter yesterday saying that my taxes are being audited!

M1: Do you have any idea why?

M2: No, not at all! I don't think I made any errors in computing. . .

M1: Generally, when they audit somebody's taxes, it's because they found something unusual.

M2: I can't think of anything unusual about mine. I didn't have any unusual income; I took a standard deduction; I don't have any dependents or exemptions or tax credits; and I filed my return on time.

M1: What bad luck!

M2: That's for sure. I don't know much about tax audits, but I do know the taxpayer always loses!

M1: That's why I have an accountant do my taxes, Nick. I was audited once when I moved from one state to another. The auditor said I owed money—and, of course, a late penalty, too!

M2: Oh, boy! Maybe I should talk to your accountant. Is he any good?

M1: It's a she, Linda Ross, and yes, I think she's a good tax accountant. She might be able to help you. Here's her number. Good luck!

Picture Springboard: *Finish the conversation.*

F1: You look really happy, Mai.

F2: Oh, I am, Diana! I just got my tax refund check!

F1: Refund? What's that?

F2: They withheld too much from my income last year, and now they're giving it back to me.

F1: Oh, dear, I don't understand these tax forms at all. What's a W-2? or a 1040EZ? or a Standard Deduction? I mean, I haven't even filed yet! What do I have to do? Can you and Mina help me?

F2: Oh, Mina knows a lot more about it than I do.

F3: _____

F1: _____

F3: _____

LEAVING A JOB (pp. 176–177)

Conversation Springboard: *What's your opinion?*

M1: Hmm. . . I like the questions for this Partner Interview, Ruth. They look interesting.

F1: I think so, too, Kien. Let me ask you first. "Have you ever left a job? Why or why not?"

M1: Yes, I've left jobs for a lot of reasons—low pay, career change, seasonal layoffs, poor working conditions, moving to another city. . .

F1: That *is* a lot of reasons, Kien. "Would you keep a bad job if you really needed the money?"

M1: Well, I did that once. It was just after our first child was born. My wife and I didn't have any money to pay the doctor or buy clothes for the baby. The job I had then was washing dishes in a restaurant—long hours, very low pay; my boss was *always* in a bad mood, and she even once accused me of stealing from her! I wanted to leave that job so badly, but I stayed.

F1: Are you sorry you stayed?

M1: No, I've never regretted staying, Ruth. We needed the money, and I didn't speak much English then.

F1: Would you do it again?

M1: I hope I never have to!

F1: I hope not, too, Kien. What about the last two questions: "What makes a job good?" and "What makes a job bad?"

M1: Those are easy questions for me, Ruth. If you like a job, it's good. If you don't, it's bad.

Picture Springboard: *Finish the conversation.*

M1: We'll be sorry to lose you, Teresa. I'm really going to miss you. You're a beautiful woman, you know. . .

F1: Well, Bob, I'm sorry, too. There are a lot of things I like about this job, but I simply can't continue working here.

M1: Why not, Teresa? Everybody loves you! And you know how I feel. Why do you insist on leaving?

F1: Well, Bob, if you really want to know, I'll tell you. You know I'm a married woman, and you know I'm not interested in having a personal relationship with you, but you keep making improper advances. I've asked you to stop, but you don't. I'm really tired of it, so I'm leaving!

M1: _____

F1: _____

M1: _____

UNIT 10: IN THE NEWS
CLASS NEWS (pp. 180–181)

Conversation Springboard: *What happened?*

F1: Question One: Who has had the best week? How has your week been, Van?

M1: Terrible! I don't want to talk about it. I'm sure everybody else's week has been better than mine!

M2: No, mine's been terrible, too.

F1: I bet it hasn't been as bad as mine!

F2: Or mine. It sounds as though we've all had a bad week.

M2: Maybe we should start with Question Two instead: Who has had the worst week?

F1: Good idea. My car was stolen on Monday. The police found it Wednesday, but it was a mess. I'm not sure I can even get it repaired!

F2: Oh, that's too bad, Mayra!

M2: It is too bad, but my week was still worse.

F1: Really? What happened to you, Norm?

M2: My wife left me.

F1, F2, M1: Oh, dear, how awful! I'm really sorry. That's terrible, Norm!

F1: But maybe she'll come back.

M2: I doubt it.

F2: I guess my week hasn't been so bad after all. I've just had too much work to do.

M2: What about you, Van? You said your week was too terrible to talk about. Do you still feel that way?

M1: I'm afraid so.

F1: Hey, what's happening? It looks like two immigration officers are outside our classroom door. I wonder what's wrong.

M1: Uh-oh. Time to say goodbye.

F2: Goodbye? Where are you going, Van?

M1: Sorry, Emi, you'll have to read about it in the news. So long, guys!

F1, F2, M2: Oh, no! Oh, Van! What on earth. . .

Picture Springboard: *Finish the conversation.*

F1: OK, who has some personal news for the next class newsletter?

F2, M1, M2: I do. I have some. Me, too!

F1: I have some, too. This is going to be a good newsletter! Who wants to take notes?

F2: I can't. I'm right-handed, and look at my arm! That's my news.

M1: I'll do it. I need the practice. OK, Yana, you first. Tell us about your arm. What happened?

F2: _____

F1: _____

M1: _____

M2: _____

Conversation Springboard: *What's your opinion?*

(telephone conversation)

F1: Good evening. I'm calling from WKGB radio. I'd like to speak with the lady of the house, if I may.

M1: That's my mom. Sorry, she's busy right now.

F1: Is your father at home now?

M1: Yes, but he's busy, too. Can I take a message?

F1: We're conducting a survey of people's news preferences at WKGB. May I ask, are you an adult member of the household?

M1: Well, I'm in high school.

F1: And would you be willing to answer a few questions regarding your family's news preferences?

M1: Well, yes, I guess so.

F1: Fine. Does anyone in the household watch news on television?

M1: Yes, that's what my parents are doing right now.

F1: Oh, fine. And does anyone read a daily newspaper?

M1: Yes, my dad does, every day.

F1: Does anyone read a weekly newsmagazine?

M1: My mom does.

F1: And what is *your* personal preference for news?

M1: I get sports news on-line on my computer. That's what I was doing when you called.

F1: I'm sorry I interrupted you. Just one more question. Does anyone in the household listen to WKGB radio news?

M1: Oh, yeah. My dad sets his radio alarm so that he wakes up to the six o'clock news every morning. I guess you could say our family likes to keep up on the news.

F1: That's for sure! Thanks for your cooperation.

Picture Springboard: *Finish the conversation.*

F1: Congratulations, Governor. This is a big victory for you.

F2: Can you tell us how you're feeling right now?

M1: Wonderful!

F2: Do you have anything you'd like to say to our television viewers at this time?

M1: _____

F1: _____

M1: _____

Conversation Springboard: *What happened?*

F1: What about this last question, "Who has experienced a natural disaster?"

F2: I have. When I was a little girl, a terrible hurricane struck The Dominican Republic. It was just awful! The roof blew off our house. And my cousin's whole house was blown away.

F1: Oh, no!

F2: I still have nightmares about the howling wind. I really thought we were all going to die. A lot of people did die.

M1: That's how I felt when my town in Japan was destroyed by an earthquake, Celia. It was so terrifying! Buildings collapsed everywhere. The whole block where we lived was nothing but rubble!

M2: How did you escape, Yukio?

M1: We were just lucky, Will. My sister and I were at home, and we rushed outside as soon as the ground started shaking. Our house collapsed behind us.

F2: How terrible! Where did you go? What did you do?

M1: Well, the International Red Cross helped us—they gave all the people blankets and food. And then our parents sent us away to stay with our uncle.

F1: What about you, Will?

M2: I've never experienced a natural disaster, Connie, and I hope I never do.

F1: Me, too. Watching them on the news and listening to Celia and Yukio tell about them is bad enough!

Picture Springboard: *Finish the conversation.*

M1: Here you go, Miss. You want to hand me the cat first?

F1: She's afraid of the water! She won't let go. . .

M1: OK, I've got her. . . Let me give you a hand now.

F1: Oh, thank you!

M1: I thought we evacuated everybody last night. Another ten minutes and the water will be over the top of that roof! How come you're still here?

F1: _____

M1: _____

F1: _____

Conversation Springboard: *What's the process?*

M1: These Vocabulary Challenges are really hard for me. I can never think of vocabulary fast.

F1: Neither can I, Kuo Hsiu. And especially this one. I don't know any sports well.

M1: Well, I know a lot of sports vocabulary in Mandarin and Cantonese, but I don't know much in English.

F1: I guess it's all up to you then, Manny. What sport do you know well?

M2: Oh, baseball, I guess. A lot of the words are similar in Spanish.

M1: Good. I do know a few words for baseball.

F1: OK, I'll be the recorder. At least I can spell pretty well. What are some words?

M1: Bat, ball, glove, base. And what do they call the one who throws the ball?

M2: The pitcher. And the catcher catches. The ones hitting the ball are the batters. The other players are first baseman, second baseman, third baseman. . .

F1: And fourth baseman? There are four bases, aren't there?

M2: Yes, but the fourth base is called home plate. That's where the catcher stands and the batters bat.

M1: Aren't the players who chase the ball called outfielders?

M2: Yes. But there's one other player we haven't mentioned who plays in closer, between second and third base. That one's the short stop.

F1: Short stop, OK. What about the ones who wave their arms and say, "You're out!"
M2: Those aren't players, Irini. They're the umpires.
M1: Yeah, they control the game. And the ones who run up to the umpires and shout at them? Who are they?
M2: Those are the managers.
Teacher: All right, class, time's up. Let's have the reports.

Picture Springboard: *Finish the conversation.*

M1: And now for a recap of today's international sports events.
F1: The Ukrainians are still leading in the world amateur mixed-pairs figure skating competition.
M1: In Sweden, at the track and field games, Mexico won a gold medal in the pole vault.
F1: There was big news in the soccer finals today, and surprises in two other events. Tell us about them, Greg.

M1: _____

F1: _____

M1: _____

ENTERTAINMENT NEWS (pp. 188–189)
Conversation Springboard: *What's your opinion?*

M1: Where in the newspaper would entertainment be listed?
M2: Sometimes there's an "entertainment" section. Check the "contents" on the front page.
F1: This paper has movies on one page and sports in another section. . .
F2: And an "upcoming events" section with other kinds of entertainment. Oh, look at this one! The Boston Fine Arts Chamber Music Trio is performing music of Bach and Mozart on violin, viola, and cello tonight at 8:00. Doesn't that sound wonderful?
M1: Well, I'm not too fond of classical music, Florence. This one sounds better to me: Cochise County Fair and Rodeo, Saturday and Sunday. I love county fairs and rodeos. How about it?
F1: Hmm. . . maybe. What do you guys think of this one? Open-air art show—"Art in the Park"—featuring crafts and paintings by well-known area artists. Maybe I could find something nice to buy there.
M2: Oh, wait! Listen to this; this is definitely the best! Grand opening! Karchner Caverns opens to the public after ten years of preparation! Caves never seen before! Now that's really a big event!
F2: I still like the chamber music concert best.
F1: And I like the "Art in the Park."
M1: I guess I'm the only one who wants to see the rodeo and county fair, huh?
M2: And the rest of you don't seem very interested in the caverns.
F2: I wonder if the other groups are doing any better than we are. . .

Picture Springboard: *Finish the conversation.*

M1: OK, kids. Where would you like to go for Suzie's birthday? How about a country music show?
M2: Nah. . . Wow! Look at this, Dad. Mario the Magnificent! I saw him on TV. He's a really famous magician. He does amazing tricks. And we could see him in person!
M1: How does that sound to you, Suzie? It's your birthday. Would you like to go see Mario the Magnificent?

F1: _____

M2: _____

M1: _____

CRIME IN THE NEWS (pp. 190–191)
Conversation Springboard: *What's your opinion?*

M1: Hi. I wonder if you two would mind answering a question for me.
F1: That depends. What's it for?
M1: My class is doing a school survey on capital punishment.
F1: The death penalty, huh? OK, what's the question?
M1: Do you approve of capital punishment?
F1: Well, that depends.
M1: You mean you're not sure? You can say, "yes," "no," or "not sure."
F1: No, I'm sure. It depends on how bad the crime is. If somebody does something really terrible, then, yes, I do approve of capital punishment.
M1: OK, thanks. You say "yes."
F1: Yes, I approve in certain cases.
F2: Well, I don't agree with her. I don't think killing another person is ever OK.
M1: So your answer is "no."
F2: That's right. I'm against it.
M1: OK. Thank you both. I appreciate your comments.
F2: No problem.
F1: Good luck with your survey.

Picture Springboard: *Finish the conversation.*

M1: . . . Now, Mrs. Moya, I'm going to ask you to look around this courtroom very carefully and tell me if you see that man here today.
F1: Yes, I do. It's him—that man right over there, sitting at that table.
M1: Are you sure of that, Mrs. Moya?
F1: Oh, yes, very sure. It was in the daytime, and I was only a few feet away.
M1: Thank you. Now, Mrs. Moya, would you tell the jury exactly what you saw that day?

F1: _____

M1: _____

F1: _____

Conversation Springboard: *What's your opinion?*

F1: Who's your personal hero, Jack?

M1: My father was always my personal hero, Jeanine.

F1: That's great, Jack! What did you admire about him?

M1: Well, he wasn't famous, and he wasn't especially big, or rich, or powerful, but he was something a lot more important than those things to me.

F1: In what ways?

M1: He was my ideal of what a father should be—of what a man should be. He worked hard, he believed in himself, he believed in me. He always knew what was important in life. He never made excuses, he seldom complained, and he never backed down from something he believed was right.

F1: He sounds like a wonderful man, Jack. I can see why he's your hero.

M2: Who's your personal hero, Jeanine?

F1: Oh, I've had a lot of personal heroes, Andy. Right now the one I admire the most is Mother Teresa. Her life was so remarkable! It really inspires me. She was just a tiny nun from Albania who wanted to help the poor, and she started over 500 missions in more than 100 countries!

M1: Yes, Mother Teresa was an extraordinary person. What about you, Andy? Who's your personal hero?

M2: I don't think I have one. I just don't think that way. Yes, there are lots of good people who do great things, but I just don't think of any of them as my own personal hero.

Picture Springboard: *Finish the conversation.*

F1: This is the Lincoln Memorial, Johnny.

M1: And that big statue is Abraham Lincoln, isn't it?

F1: Yes, it is. Now look at the penny. What do you see?

M1: The face on the penny looks like the face on the statue.

F1: That's right, honey. What do you know about Abraham Lincoln?

M1: _____

F1: _____

M1: _____

Conversation Springboard: *What's the process?*

M1: Rosa and Sungjoon, would you be our recorders for this Class Brainstorm? Just write all the ideas on the board.

M2: OK. Write everything?

M1: Yes, all the ideas. You write all the local problems and issues on the left side, Sungjoon. And, Rosa, you can write all the good news on the right side.

F1: OK, I'm ready.

M1: Now, let's brainstorm everybody. What are some local problems and issues? Any ideas?

F2: How about car theft? A lot of people have their cars stolen.

M2: Graffiti. Gangs!

F1: Overcrowded schools!

F2: Pollution.

M1: Any more? No? Well, what about good news?

F2: Hmm. . . That's harder to think of. . .

M1: Why is that? There are good things about our community, aren't there?

M2: Yes, but it's easier to think of bad things. . .

M1: Well, how about this—the Thunder Mountain Scuba Club is cleaning up Parker Lake to make it safer for swimmers.

F1: That's a good one. I'm putting it down.

F2: How about the new job the city just created— "Neighborhood Officer"—to enforce the illegal dumping laws?

M2: And the 100 new computers that the employees at Micro Technology donated to our school district?

F2: And the after-school city art program—the kids are painting over graffiti and making beautiful murals.

F1: I've seen some of them. They're great! You know, once we get started, it's not so hard to think of good news.

M2: Yes, that's a relief!

Picture Springboard: *Finish the conversation.*

F1: What a beautiful day!

M1: It sure is, Daria.

F1: The forest always smells so clean and fresh. I love to be able to get out and hike like this, away from all the noise and pollution of the city. . .

M1: Oh, my! Unbelievable!

F1: What's that truck doing, Mike?

M1: _____

F1: _____

M1: _____

Conversation Springboard: *What's your opinion?*

M1: Now we have to list current world problems. That should be easy.

F1: It's true. There are so many. Where do we start?

M2: Anywhere, I guess. How about famine and overpopulation and war. . .

F2: And terrorists and refugees and starvation. . .

M1: And natural disasters! So many people have died this year from floods and earthquakes. . .

F1: And that awful volcanic eruption that destroyed half of an island. . .

F2: And those two airplane crashes that killed so many people. . .

M1: And that big oil spill that destroyed hundreds of miles of coastline, wiping out all kinds of fish and wildlife. . .

M2: And don't forget disease—all the people dying of AIDS, and the cholera epidemic, and what's the name of that new virus?

F1: Oh, this is really depressing! I don't like doing this. It makes me think that the world is in really bad shape!

M1: Well, it is, Jill. Face it, our world is in big trouble!

F2: Oh, Wally, you're such a pessimist.

M2: I don't think so, Kris. I think he's a realist.

M1: Right! We've got two choices: We can either hide our heads in the sand like ostriches, or we can face the problems and do something about them!

Picture Springboard: *Finish the conversation.*

F1: . . . And so at this time the fighting continues. . . In health news tonight, researchers announced today a major breakthrough in a different kind of fight—the battle against the deadly AIDS virus. Mark Britton has the story for us.

M1: Here at the HIV Research Institute in Chicago, an exciting discovery was announced today by AIDS researchers Paul Moreno and Libby Poe. Dr. Poe, can you tell us about this new discovery?

F2 *(Dr. Poe)*: _____

M1 *(M. Britton)*: _____

M2 *(Dr. Moreno)*: _____

POLITICS AND GOVERNMENT IN THE NEWS (pp. 198–199)

Conversation Springboard: *What's your opinion?*

F1: It's hard to believe that this is our last Find Someone Who activity.

F2: I know. The semester has gone by so fast. Do you think my English sounds better than it did at the start of the semester?

F1: Much better, Young Hee. What about mine?

F2: Oh, your English always sounded good to me, Ivana.

F1: Really? Thanks, Young Hee.

M1: Hey, you guys. This is supposed to be a Find Someone Who about politics.

F1: Well, I'm not very interested in politics, Cesar.

F2: Me, neither.

M1: You mean you don't vote?

F1: Well, where I live now, I'm not eligible to vote.

M1: Oh. How about you, Young Hee? Are you interested in politics?

F2: Sometimes, Cesar. . . when there's an issue I care about. I participated in a protest against nuclear weapons once.

M1: That sounds interesting. What happened? Did you get arrested?

F2: No, it was a big protest. The police couldn't arrest everyone, so they ended up not arresting anybody.

F1: Why are you so interested in politics, Cesar?

M1: Well, I think you have to be, Ivana. All of us do. Other people are interested, you know. And if we don't pay attention, and we don't care, then we'll just be stuck with whatever those other people want. And that's not good enough for me.

F2: Maybe you should go into politics, Cesar. I'd vote for you!

F1: Me, too, Cesar. You really should!

Picture Springboard: *Finish the conversation.*

F1: This is Channel 5 reporting live from campaign headquarters, where the winning candidate, Louis Robinson, is about to make his victory speech. . .

M1: Thank you, thank you! My wife and I want to thank you all for your support. Tonight we celebrate *your* victory! And tonight I pledge to you that I will keep each and every one of the campaign promises I have made! *Every* one! And what are those promises? You tell me!

F2 *(woman in crowd)*: _____

_____

M2 *(man in crowd)*: _____

_____

GRAMMAR FOR CONVERSATION CONTENTS

UNIT 1: SOCIAL COMMUNICATION
Word Families (*socialize-society-sociable-sociably*)
Verb Tenses (*do-does–did–will do–have done–has done*)
  (*am/is/are doing-was–were doing–will be doing–has/have been doing*)
Modal - *Would*
It + To Be.
im-/in-/un-
Irregular Verbs (*do–did–done*)

UNIT 2: PERSONAL LIFE
Word Families (*believe-belief-believable-believably*)
Irregular Verbs (*bring-brought-brought*)
dis-/in-/ir-/un-
Used to, Would
Adjectives + Adverbs (*much-more-most*)
Ago
Tell us what, why, how old
Set Verb Phrases

UNIT 3: FAMILY LIFE
Word Families (*agree-agreement-agreeable-agreeably*)
dis-/mis-/in-/un-
Time Clauses (*Before/After/When*)
Irregular Verbs (*grow-grew-grown*)
Passive Voice (*How are they treated? Where were you born?*)
Real Conditionals (*If divorce is not acceptable*)
Unreal Conditionals (*If she were my daughter*)
Modal Auxiliaries (*Should/Would*)
Each/Each other/Every/Everyone/All
Reflexives (*myself, ourselves*)
-ing Nouns (*Who does the cooking?*)
Set Phrases with Prepositions (*idea of, cope with, special about*)

UNIT 4: COMMUNITY AND CONSUMER LIFE
Word Families (*serve-service-serviceable-serviceably*)
Modal Auxiliary: Can (*What can you buy there?*)
Time Clauses (*As you open the door*)
Which one/ones
Noun-Noun (sales tax, credit card)
Passive Voice (*Will he be suspended? Where is it being held?*)
Method of/advantage of/disadvantage of + -ing
Conditionals (*I'm not sure whether/if*)

UNIT 5: STAYING HEALTHY
Word Families (*fill-filling-full-fully*)
Irregular Verbs (*bite-bit-bitten*)
anti-/non-

Passive Voice (*He was stung by a bee. Who should be treated first?*)
Everyone/Someone/No one/Not anyone/Anyone

UNIT 6: HOUSING
Word Families (*decorate-decoration-decorative-decoratively*)
Passive/Active Tenses (*The yard is being fenced./They are fencing the yard.*)
Passive/Active Modals (*The house might be sold./They might sell the house.*)
A person who/groups which/questions that

UNIT 7: TRANSPORTATION AND TRAVEL
Word Families (*commute-commuter-commuting*)
Advantage of taking/disadvantage of commuting/ reason for carpooling
It takes a long time to get there
Time Clauses (*before/when/after he fails the test*)
Do you think/Do you know/I don't know/Could you tell me
The first time (that) you drove
re- [again]

UNIT 8: FINDING A JOB
Word Families (*apply-application-applied*)
-ment, -tion
To be willing + Infinitive
Passive Voice (*What training is required?*)
Noun Clauses (*An advantage is that*)
Modals (*What could/would/should he do?*)
-al

UNIT 9: LIFE AT WORK
Word Families (*stress-stress-stressful-stressfully*)
dis-, im-, in-, ir-, un-
It's confusing/I'm confused
-ful [with]/*-less* [without]
-able, -ent, -eous, -ible, -ic, -ical, -ious, -ive, -ous, -tious, -y)
-sion, -tion
How to, when to, where to, which to, what to, whether to

UNIT 10: IN THE NEWS
Word Families (*compete-competition-competitive-competitively*)
Word Families (*newscast, newspaper*)
The fireman who rescued them
The reporter interviewing people
Passive Voice (*Who will be affected? The boy was shot.*)

GRAMMAR FOR CONVERSATION

UNIT 1

WORD FAMILIES

Verb	Noun	Adjective	Adverb
apologize	apology	apologetic	apologetically
communicate	communication	communicative/ communicable	communicatively
consider	consideration	considerate	considerately
converse	conversation	conversational	conversationally
educate	education/educator	educated/educational	educationally
qualify	qualification	qualified	
socialize	social/society	sociable	sociably
sympathize	sympathy	sympathetic	sympathetically

COMPARISON OF VERB TENSES

Tense	Question					Time Phrase
Present:	What	do does	(I/you/we/they) (he/she/it)	do		every day?
Past:	What	did	(I/you/he/she) (it/we/you/they)	do		yesterday?
Future:	What	will	(it/we/you/they)	do		tomorrow?
Present Perfect:	What	have has	(I/you/we/they) (he/she/it)	done		this week?

Tense & Affirmative Statement

Tense		
Present:	(I/You/We/You/They) (He/She/It)	begin. begins.
Past:	(I/You/He/She) (It/We/You/They)	began.
Future:	(I/You/He/She) (It/We/You/They)	will begin.
Present Perfect:	(I/You/We/You/They) (He/She/It)	have has begun.

Negative Statement

(I/You/We/You/They) (He/She/It)	don't finish. doesn't
(I/You/He/She) (It/We/You/They)	didn't finish.
(I/You/He/She) (It/We/You/They)	won't finish.
(I/You/We/You/They) (He/She/It)	haven't finished. hasn't

COMPARISON OF PROGRESSIVE TENSES

Tense	Question				Time Phrase
Present Progressive:	What	am / are / is	I (you/we/you/they) (he/she/it)	doing	now?
Past Progressive:	What (you/we...ey)	was / were	(I/he/she/it)	doing	at 4:00 A.M. today?
Future Progressive:	What	will	(I/you/he/she) (it/we/you/they)	be doing	at this time tomorrow?
Present Perfect Progressive:	What	have / has	(I/you/we/they) (he/she/it)	been doing	all day?

Tense	Affirmative Statement		
Present Progressive:	I (You/We/They) (He/She/It)	am / are / is	eating.
Past Progressive:	(He/She/It) (You/We/You/They)	was / were	sleeping.
Future Progressive:	(I/You/He/She) (It/We/You/They)	will be	eating.
Present Perfect Progressive:	(I/You/We/You/They) (He/She/It)	have been / has been	sleeping.

Tense	Negative Statement		
Present Progressive:	I (You/We/They) (He/She/It)	am not / aren't / isn't	eating.
Past Progressive:	(He/She/It) (You/We/You/They)	wasn't / weren't	sleeping.
Future Progressive:	(I/You/He/She) (It/We/You/They)	won't be	eating.
Present Perfect Progressive:	(I/You/We/You/They) (He/She/It)	haven't been / has been	sleeping.

MODALS (*Would*/Future Possibility/Probability/Intention)

What **would you do** in each of these situations?
Would you pick up a hitchhiker?
Would you help a stranger in distress?
Would you give work to someone who knocks at your door?
Would you contribute to a charity by telephone?
Would you help a classmate with English homework?
Would you give money to a friend in need?
Maybe I would.

INFINITIVES with *It*

It's nice **to see** you again.
It's useful **to speak** English.
When **is it** bad manners **to be** late?
When **is it** polite **to share**?
It **was** rude **to whisper.**
It was nice **to meet** you.
Why **was it** inconsiderate **to double park?**

NEGATIVE PREFIXES (*im-/in-/un-*)

Negative Adjective	Opposite
impatient	patient
impolite	polite
inconsiderate	considerate
uncomfortable	comfortable
unhappy	happy

PRINCIPAL PARTS OF IRREGULAR VERBS

Simple	Present Participle	Past	Past Participle
buy	buying	bought	bought
do	doing	did	done
give	giving	gave	given
go	going	went	gone
have	having	had	had
know	knowing	knew	known
make	making	made	made
meet	meeting	met	met
say	saying	said	said
see	seeing	saw	seen
send	sending	sent	sent
speak	speaking	spoke	spoken
think	thinking	thought	thought
write	writing	wrote	written

UNIT 2

WORD FAMILIES

Verb	Noun	Adjective	Adverb
	ambition	ambitious	ambitiously
believe	belief/believer	believable	believably
	curiosity	curious	curiously
dream	dream/dreamer	dreamlike	dreamily
fantasize	fantasy	fantastic	fantastically
flirt	flirtation/flirt	flirtatious	flirtatiously
imagine	imagination	imaginary/imaginable	instructively/
instruct	instruction/instructor	instructive/instructional	instructionally
succeed	success	successful	successfully
taste	taste	tasty/tasteful	tastily/tastefully
	tradition	traditional	traditionally

IRREGULAR VERB FORMS

Simple	Present Participle	Past	Past Participle
bring	bringing	brought	brought
choose	choosing	chose	chosen
come	coming	came	come
draw	drawing	drew	drawn
drink	drinking	drank	drunk
eat	eating	ate	eaten
feed	feeding	fed	fed
feel	feeling	felt	felt
fight	fighting	fought	fought
fit	fitting	fit	fit
forget	forgetting	forgot	forgotten
get	getting	got	gotten/got
lend	lending	lent	lent
put	putting	put	put
read	reading	read	read
swing	swinging	swung	swung
take	taking	took	taken
tell	telling	told	told
wake	waking	woke	waked/woken

NEGATIVE PREFIXES (*dis-*, *in-*, *ir-*, *un-*)

Negative Adjective	Opposite
disloyal	loyal
disorganized	organized
insensitive	sensitive
insincere	sincere
irresponsible	responsible
unprepared	prepared
unrealistic	realistic
unreliable	reliable
unshaven	shaven
untidy	tidy
unusual	usual

HABITUAL PAST with Past Tense, *Used to*, or *Would*

Past Tense:	In my childhood, I My brother	loved played	to play with dolls. ball all the time.
Used to:	In my childhood, I My brother	used to love used to play	to play with dolls. ball all the time.
Would:	In my childhood, I My brother	would play with would play	dolls all the time. ball all the time.

DEGREES OF ADJECTIVES & ADVERBS

Positive	Comparative	Superlative
Adjectives	**Adjectives**	**Adjectives**
Does he have **much** fun?	His roommate has **more** fun.	Who has **the most fun** of all?
Did you have a **good** day?	She had a **better** day **than** I.	Who had **the best** day of all?
Did you have a **bad** day?	He had a **worse** day **than** I.	Who had **the worst** day?
Did you have a **big** breakfast?	She had a **bigger** breakfast.	Who had **the biggest** breakfast?
Is the food **appetizing**?	This food is **more appetizing**.	Which food is **the most appetizing**?
Adverbs	**Adverbs**	**Adverbs**
Did you go to bed **late**?	She went to bed **later than** I.	He went to bed **the latest**.
Did she get up **early**?	I got up **earlier than** she did.	He got up **the earliest of all**.
Do you talk **quietly**?	She talks **more quietly**.	He talks **the most quietly**.
Do you work **frantically**?	She works **more frantically**.	He works **the most frantically**.

AGO

Where **were you one month ago**?	I **was** here **one month ago**.
Where **were you five years ago**?	I **was** in Mexico **five years ago**.
What **were you** doing **five minutes ago**?	I **was** telling a story **five minutes ago**.
What childhood dreams **did** you **have years ago**?	I **dreamed** of being a movie star **years ago**.

IMBEDDED QUESTIONS (*What, Why, How old*)

Question				Imbedded Question		
What	**did it look**	like?		Tell us what	**it looked**	like.
What	**did you do**	with it?		Tell us what	**you did**	with it.
Why	**was it**	important to you?		Tell us why	**it was**	important to you.
How old	**were you**	then?		Tell us how old	**you were**	then.

IMBEDDED QUESTIONS (*Who*)

Question			Imbedded Question		
Who likes	to travel?		Find someone	**who likes**	to travel.
Who enjoys	meeting people?		Find someone	**who enjoys**	meeting people.
Who has had	an unusual experience?		Find someone	**who has had**	an unusual experience.

SET VERB PHRASES
Verb + gerund/Verb + preposition + gerund

What subjects do you	enjoy studying	the most?
What do you	dream of accomplishing	in the future?
What do you	plan on doing	next year?

Verb + infinitive

What subjects do you	like to study	the most?
What do you	hope to accomplish	in the future?
What do you	plan to do	next year?

UNIT 3

WORD FAMILIES

Verb	Noun	Adjective	Adverb
accept	acceptance	acceptable	acceptably
agree	agreement	agreeable	agreeably
attract	attraction	attractive	attractively
commit	commitment/commital	commited/commitable	
cooperate	cooperation	cooperative	cooperatively
die	death	dead/deadly	
disagree	disagreement	disagreeable	disagreeably
disobey	disobedience	disobedient	disobediently
encourage	encouragement	encouraging	encouragingly
obey	obedience	obedient	obediently
rebel	rebellion/rebel	rebellious	rebelliously
romance	romance/romantic	romantic	romantically
	similarity	similar	similarly

NEGATIVE PREFIXES (dis-)

Negative Adjective	Opposite
disagreeable	agreeable
dishonest	honest
disobedient	obedient
disorderly	orderly
disrespectable	respectable

(in-/mis-/un-)

Negative Adjective	Opposite
misbehaved	behaved
incompatible	compatible
unacceptable	acceptable
undisciplined	disciplined
unsupervised	supervised

TIME CLAUSES (Before/After/When)

Before:	Describe this couple's life **before their baby was born.** **Before their baby was born,** their life was simpler.
After:	How did their life change **after the baby was born?** **After the baby was born,** they didn't get much sleep.
When:	What happens to elderly parents **when their children move far away?**
When	**their children move far away,** elderly parents are lonely.

IRREGULAR VERB FORMS

Simple	Present Participle	Past	Past Participle
bear	bearing	bore	born/borne
cut	cutting	cut	cut
drive	driving	drove	driven
fall	falling	fell	fallen
grow	growing	grew	grown
leave	leaving	left	left
pay	paying	paid	paid
spend	spending	spent	spent
wear	wearing	wore	worn

PASSIVE VOICE (Present and Past)

Question

How **are** elderly people **treated** in your culture?

Where **were** you born?

Affirmative Statements

They are **treated** with respect.

I **was born** in a hospital.

Negative Statements

They **are not treated** badly.

I **was not born** at home.

REAL CONDITIONALS (Present)

If children **are** disobedient, what **should** parents **do**?
If divorce **is** not acceptable in your country, what **do** incompatible married couples **do**?
If your grandparents **are lonely**, what **do** you **do**?

UNREAL CONDITIONALS

Question

How **would** you **feel if** she **were** your daughter?
What **would** you **do if** you **were** her teacher?

Answer

If I **were** her parent, I **would feel** worried.
If I **were** her teacher, I **would try** to help her.

MODAL AUXILIARIES: *Should/Would*

Question

Should parents **limit** their children's TV watching?
Would you **limit** it?

Should these parents **punish** their children?
Would you **punish** them?

UNREAL CONDITIONALS

Short Answer (Affirmative/Negative)

Yes, they **should**.

Yes, I **would**.

No, they **shouldn't**.

No, I **wouldn't**.

PRONOUNS: *Each, Each other, Every, Everyone, All*

Each:	How did they solve **each** problem?
	Each one of us needs to tell a story.
Each other:	Which family members resemble **each other**?
	How do they feel about **each other**?
Every:	**Every** family has problems.
	Every member of our group comes from a large family.
Everyone:	Give **everyone** a name.
	Everyone was a baby once.
All:	What are good names for **all** the members of these families?
	What are **all** the different relationships in this family tree?

REFLEXIVE PRONOUNS

I hurt **myself**.
What did **you** do **to yourself**?
What does **he** think **of himself**?
What did **she** say **about herself**?
Can **a computer** think **for itself**?
We did all the work **ourselves**.
Did **you** buy something **for yourselves**?
Many people don't like to live **by themselves**.

GERUNDS (*-ing* Verbs as Nouns)

In your family, who does the **cooking?**
Who does the **cleaning?**
Is **shopping** fun?
Parenting isn't always easy.
Learning new things is always important.

SET PHRASES WITH PREPOSITIONS
Noun + preposition

What is your	**idea of**	a romantic first date?
What are the	**causes of**	this divorce?
Whom do you have the closest	**relationship with**	in your family?

Verb + preposition

Who knows what they	**are arguing about?**	
How can they	**cope with**	their problems?
What does the young woman's family	**think of**	her boyfriend?

Adjective + preposition

What ages are most	**common for**	men and women to get married?
What is	**special about**	your family?

UNIT 4

WORD FAMILIES

Verb	Noun	Adjective	Adverb
advise	advice/advisor	advisable	advisedly
electrify	electricity	electric/electrical	electrically
fashion	fashion	fashionable	fashionably
refund	refund	refundable	
serve	service	serviceable	serviceably
style	style	stylish	stylishly

MODAL AUXILIARIES (Ability/Availability/Allowability)

Question	Answer
What **can** you **buy** there?	You can buy all kinds of things there.
How **can** these people **pay** for their purchases?	They can pay with cash or credit card.
What **can** we **do** there?	We can do many things.
What **can be done** about this difficulty?	Nothing can be done about it.
Where **can** the public **go** for recreational reading?	Anyone can go to the public library.
Where **can** students **register** for courses?	They can register in this office.

TIME CLAUSES: *As*

As he was opening the door, he smelled gas.
I'll draw a map **as** you describe the route.

PRONOUNS: *One, Ones*

Question		Answer
Which ones	have you seen?	I've seen all **the best ones.**
Which ones	are for credit?	**The ones** on this campus are for credit.
Which one	is non-credit?	**This one** is.
Which ones	have an admission fee?	**The ones** at the stadium do.

NOUN-NOUN COMBINATIONS

She's placing a **telephone order.**
This item has a **sales tax.**
Do you have a **charge account?**
I'll charge it to my **credit card.**
Our telephone service has **call waiting.**
My husband wears a **hearing aid.**

PASSIVE VOICE (Present/Present Progressive/Future/Present Perfect)

Present:	Baseball games **are** usually **played** in a stadium.
	Where **is** the merchandise **displayed?**
Present Progressive:	What **is being done** about each problem?
	Where **is** the outdoor concert **being held?**
Future:	When **will** this package **be delivered?**
	The boy **will** probably **be suspended.**
Present Perfect:	Your flight **has been delayed** for an hour.
	Have you ever **been lost** in a new city?

GERUNDS (after *Method of/Advantage of/Disadvantage of*)

What **is** the most efficient **method of sending** mail?
What **are** the **advantages of recycling?**
What **are** the **disadvantages of heating** with electricity?

CONDITIONALS: *Whether/If*
Whether

I must decide **whether I should place** him
   in a bilingual program.
I must decide **whether to place** him in a
   bilingual program **or not.**
I'm not sure **whether I should go** to the
   concert or **stay** home.

If

I must decide **if I should place** him in a
   bilingual program **or not.**

I'm not sure **if I should go** to the
   concert or **stay** home.

WORD FAMILIES

Verb	Noun	Adjective	Adverb
abuse	abuse	abused	
addict	addiction/addict	addictive/addicted	
fill	filling	full	fully
immunize	immunity/immunization	immune	
infect	infection	infectious	
injure	injury	injurious	injuriously
irritate	irritation/irritant	irritating/irritated	irritatingly/irritatedly
	nutrition/nutrient	nutritious	nutritiously
	physique/physician	physical	physically
prevent	prevention	preventive	preventively
treat	treatment/treat	treatable	
warn	warning	warned/warning	warningly

IRREGULAR VERB FORMS

Simple	Present Participle	Past	Past Participle
bite	biting	bit	bitten
find	finding	found	found
sting	stinging	stung	stung
swell	swelling	swelled	swelled/swollen

NEGATIVE PREFIXES (*anti-*, *non-*)

Negative Adjective	Opposite
anti-inflammatory	inflammatory
nonprescription drug	prescription drug
nonrefillable	refillable
nontraditional	traditional

PASSIVE VOICE (*To be* + past participle)

Present:	How **are** health problems **treated** in your country? What **are** household chemicals **used** for?
Present Progressive:	They **are being bitten** by a swarm of bugs. Everyone **is being warned** about the poison ivy.
Past:	The man **was stung** by a bee. He **was poisoned** by spoiled food.
Past Progressive:	He **was being admitted** to the hospital. She **was being abused**.
Future:	She **will be referred** to a specialist. He **will be taken** to the Emergency Room.
Present Perfect:	Someone **has been** seriously **injured**. The bottle **has been opened** before.
Modal: *should*	Who **should be treated** first? That cut **should be covered** with a bandage.
Modal: *can*	Back pain **can be relieved** with acupuncture. This medicine **can be taken** orally.

PRONOUNS: *Everyone, Someone, No one, Not anyone, Anyone*

Everyone works or goes to school.
Someone has to do the cooking.
No one is home to shop or prepare meals.
There **isn't anyone** here to make supper.
Can **anyone** get home earlier?

UNIT 6

WORD FAMILIES

Verb	Noun	Adjective	Adverb
afford		affordable	affordably
collect	collection/collector	collective	collectively
	convenience	convenient	conveniently
decorate	decoration/decorator	decorative	decoratively
distrust	distrust/distrustfulness	distrustful	distrustfully
maintain	maintenance	maintained	
notify	notification	notifiable	
organize	organization/organizer	organizational	organizationally
rehabilitate	rehabilitation	rehabilitated	
renovate	renovation	renovated	
rent	rent/renter	rental/rentable	
vandalize	vandalism/vandal	vandalized	

PASSIVE & ACTIVE VOICE (Comparison of Tenses)

Passive

Present:	Everyone	**is satisfied**	with this solution.
Present Progressive:	The yard	**is being fenced.**	
Past:	Their house	**was insured**	against fire and theft.
Past Progressive:	Their house	**was being remodeled.**	
Future:	His telephone service	**will be discontinued.**	
Present Perfect:	The roof	**has been damaged**	by the storm.

Active

Present:	This solution	**satisfies**	everyone.
Present Progressive:	They	**are fencing**	the yard.
Past:	They	**insured**	their house and belongings.
Past Progressive:	They	**were remodeling**	their house.
Future:	The phone company	**will discontinue**	his telephone service.
Present Perfect:	The storm	**has damaged**	the roof.

246

PASSIVE & ACTIVE (Comparison of Modal Auxiliaries)
Passive

Can:	Most utility problems	**can be avoided**	with this solution.
Could:	This room	**could be painted**	easily.
May:	Some utilities	**may be cut off**	for non-payment.
Might:	The house	**might be sold**	by next week.
Should:	That neighborhood	**should be improved.**	
Must:	The bank says our house	**must be insured.**	

PASSIVE & ACTIVE (Comparison of Modal Auxiliaries)
Active

Can:	People	**can avoid**	most utility problems.
Could:	Someone	**could paint**	this room easily.
May:	Some utility companies	**may cut off**	service for non-payment.
Might:	They	**might sell**	the house by next week.
Should:	Someone	**should improve**	that neighborhood.
Must:	The bank says we	**must insure**	our house.

ADJECTIVE CLAUSES (*Who/Which/That* as subjects)

Who:	Describe a person	**who**	is a good neighbor.
Which:	Are there groups	**which**	are improving your community?
That:	Write questions	**that**	are important to ask.

UNIT 7

WORD FAMILIES

Verb	Noun	Adjective	Adverb
collide	collision	colliding	
commute	commute/commuter	commuting	
experience	experience	experienced/experiential	
intoxicate	intoxication	intoxicated/intoxicating	
negotiate	negotiation/negotiator	negotiable	
renew	renewal	renewed/renewable	
restrict	restriction	restrictive/restricted	

Advantages of/Disadvantages of/Reasons for + gerund

What are the	**advantages of taking**	a bus or a train to work?
What are some	**disadvantages of commuting**	a long distance to work?
What are some good	**reasons for carpooling?**	

It takes + infinitive
Question

How much time	**does it take to renew**	your license?
How long	**did it take to drive**	to work today?
How many hours	**will it take to get**	there?

Answer

It takes	a long time!
It took	twenty minutes.
It will take	three hours.

TIME CLAUSES (*Before/After/When*)

Before:	What does the man do **before he takes the driving test?** **Before he takes the driving test,** he practices driving.
After:	What does he do **after he fails the test?** **After he fails the test,** he practices some more.
When:	What happened **when he went through the security check?** **When he went through the security check,** the alarm went off.

QUESTIONS & IMBEDDED QUESTIONS (Comparison of Word Order)
Question

Where	is the nearest gas station?	
How much	is the fare?	
How much	is the toll?	
How fast	is he driving?	
What bus	does she take?	
Where	did I leave	my suitcase?
When	will the train arrive?	
What	should they do?	

Imbedded Question

Do you know	where the nearest gas station is?	
Do you know	how much the fare is?	
I don't know	how much the toll is.	
We can't tell	how fast he is driving.	
I don't know	what bus she takes.	
I'm not sure	where I left	my suitcase.
Could you tell me	when the train will arrive?	
What do you think	they should do?	

CLAUSES with Optional *That*

Adjective Clauses:	When was the first time (**that**) you drove? Choose a car (**that**) you would like to buy. When was the last time (**that**) you traveled by train?
Noun Clauses:	Did you notice (**that**) your car is losing its exhaust pipe? You remember (**that**) you left your suitcase on the carousel. Do you think (**that**) the plane will arrive on time?

PREFIX: *re-* (again)
Verb

do	**re**do
take	**re**take
tell	**re**tell
test	**re**test
think	**re**think

UNIT 8

WORD FAMILIES

Verb	Noun	Adjective	Adverb
analyze	analyst	analytical	analytically
apply	application/applicant	applied	
manage	management/manager	manageable	
employ	employment/employer	employable/employed	

NOUN SUFFIXES: *-ment, -tion*

advertise**ment**	applic**ation**	hospitaliz**ation**
bereave**ment**	avi**ation**	occup**ation**
depart**ment**	certific**ation**	posi**tion**
dismember**ment**	communic**ation**	presenta**tion**
employ**ment**	compensa**tion**	qualifica**tion**
enforce**ment**	competi**tion**	recommenda**tion**
entertain**ment**	construc**tion**	repeti**tion**
govern**ment**	coopera**tion**	transporta**tion**
manage**ment**	educa**tion**	
require**ment**		

To be willing + INFINITIVE

Question

How much time **are you willing to spend** in job training?
What hours **are you willing to work?**

Are you willing to travel outside the country?

Answer

I'm willing to spend as much as I need to.

I'm willing to work any hours except third shift.
Yes, **I am.**

PASSIVE VOICE

Question

What training **is required** for the job?
What experience **is needed?**
Have you ever **been self-employed?**

Answer

On-the-job training **is provided.**
No experience **is needed.**
No, **I haven't.** I've always **been employed** by one company.

NOUN CLAUSES: *To be + that*

One good thing about my job	**is**	that it's close to home.
Another advantage	**is**	that it has good benefits.
The only disadvantage	**is**	that the pay is low.
The best thing about it	**is**	that I have a good boss.

MODALS: *Could/Should/Would*

What **could** you **list** as special skills?
What work **would** he **do** in each job?
Which job **should** he **choose?**
Should you **include** all of your work history on a job application?
What **should** you **do** if you cannot arrive on time for an interview?
What **would** he **wear** for each job?
What **would** be the advantages of each job?
What **would** the disadvantages **be?**

ADJECTIVE SUFFIX (*-al*)

manual
medical
mental
physical
technical

UNIT 9

WORD FAMILIES

Verb	Noun	Adjective	Adverb
advance	advance/advancement	advanced/advancing	
demonstrate	demonstration	demonstrable	demonstrably
	eagerness	eager	eagerly
economize	economy	economical/economic	economically
	enthusiasm	enthusiastic	enthusiastically
explode	explosion/explosive	explosive	explosively
	extravagance	extravagant	extravagantly
	prudence	prudent	prudently
resign	resignation	resigned	resignedly
	sense	sensible	sensibly
stress	stress	stressful	stressfully
waste	waste	wasteful	wastefully

NEGATIVE PREFIXES (*dis-/im-/-in/-ir/un-*)

Negative Adjective	Opposite
discourteous	courteous
impatient	patient
inflammable	flammable
irresponsible	responsible
uncertain	certain
unclear	clear
uncomfortable	comfortable
unfamiliar	familiar

ADJECTIVE SUFFIXES (*-ed /-ing*)

(*-ing*) Active

The instructions are	**confusing.**	
The illustration is	**puzzling.**	
This is	**interesting**	work.
I made an	**embarrassing**	mistake.

(*-ed*) Passive

I'm	**confused**	by the instructions.
I'm	**puzzled**	by the illustration.
I'm	**interested**	in this work.
I was	**embarrassed**	by my mistake.

ADJECTIVE SUFFIXES (*-ful/-less*)

-ful (with)   *-less* (without)

care**ful**	care**less**
thought**ful**	thought**less**
	sense**less**
waste**ful**	

ADJECTIVE SUFFIXES (-able/-ent/-eous/-ible/-ic/-ive/-ous/-tious/-y)

-able	-ent	-eous	-ible	-ic/-ical
flammable comfortable	dependent	courteous	combustible responsible sensible	energetic economical

-ious	-ive	-ous	-tious	-y
industrious	cooperative explosive	dangerous hazardous poisonous	conscientious	hasty sloppy worthy

NOUN SUFFIXES (-sion/-tion)

-sion	-tion
confusion evasion explosion	deduction demonstration exemption explanation illustration instruction promotion repetition resignation

QUESTIONS & IMBEDDED QUESTIONS (Question words + Infinitive)

How do you switch Where can I find When should I start Which should I do What should I do Should I spend	a phone call to another extension? the office supplies? the machine? first? about my problem at work? my tax refund?

I don't know **how to switch** a phone call to another extension.
Can you tell me **where to find** the office supplies?
I'm not sure **when to start** the machine.
I don't know **which** step **to do** first.
I don't know **what to do** about my problem at work.
I haven't decided **whether to spend or to save** my tax refund.

UNIT 10

WORD FAMILIES

Verb	Noun	Adjective	Adverb
assassinate	assassination/assassin	assassinated	
brave	bravery	brave	bravely
compete	competition/competitor	competitive	competitively
	courage	courageous	courageously
defend	defense/defendant	defensive	defensively
devastate	devastation	devastating	devastatingly
elect	election/electorate	elected/elective	
entertain	entertainment/entertainer	entertaining	entertainingly
	heroism/hero	heroic	heroically
	magic/magician	magical	magically
	patriotism/patriot	patriotic	patriotically
	politics/politician	political	politically
separate	separation	separate	separately
	victory/victor	victorious	victoriously

WORD FAMILIES: Compound Nouns

news
newscast
newscaster
newsmagazine
news media
newsperson
newspaper
newsroom

ADJECTIVE CLAUSES: *Who*

That's the fireman **who rescued a whole family from a terrible fire.**
The newscaster interviewed a twelve-year-old girl **who has AIDS.**
This is the fifteen-year-old boy **who defended the elderly woman from an attacker.**
On today's news I saw the woman astronaut **who was chosen to be the captain of a space shuttle mission.**
The first witness is the woman **who saw the crime.**

REDUCING ADJECTIVE CLAUSES

Adjective Clause	Reduced
She was the news reporter **who was interviewing people at the scene.**	She was the news reporter **interviewing people at the scene.**
There are several local events **which are coming soon.**	There are several local events **coming soon.**
The fireman **who was burned in the fire** has recovered now.	The fireman **burned in the fire** has recovered now.
The young woman **who is looking at her hand** is engaged.	The young woman **looking at her hand** is engaged.
The sports event **which is on TV right now** is a championship game.	The sports event **on TV right now** is a championship game.
The toxic waste **which was dumped here last month** has been cleaned up.	The toxic waste **dumped here last month** has been cleaned up.

PASSIVE VOICE: (Present/Present Progressive/Past/Future/Present Perfect/*Can*)

Present:	What heroes **are pictured** on money? What martyrs **are admired** in your culture?
Present Progressive:	For what heroic acts **are** these people **being honored?** What natural disaster **is being shown** on each TV screen?
Past:	The boy **was shot** in the arm. The fireman **was** badly **burned.**
Future:	The winning team **will be honored** at a banquet. How many people **will be affected?**
Present Perfect:	What discoveries **have been reported** in the news recently? A woman **has been chosen** to be the captain of the mission.
Can (modal):	Which natural disasters **can be forecast?** Where **can** toxic waste **be dumped** legally?

AFRICA

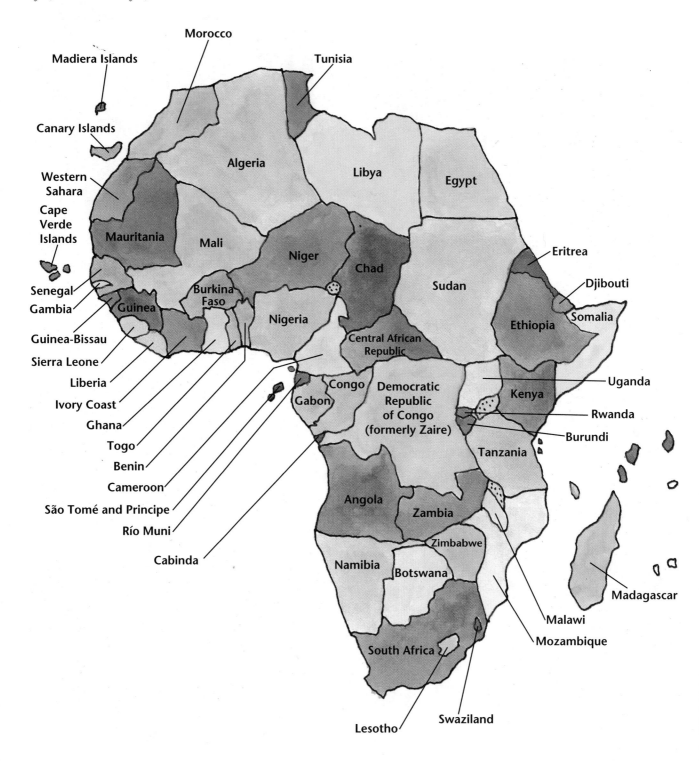

Morocco

Madiera Islands

Tunisia

Canary Islands

Algeria

Libya

Egypt

Western Sahara

Cape Verde Islands

Mauritania

Mali

Niger

Chad

Eritrea

Djibouti

Senegal

Gambia

Guinea

Burkina Faso

Sudan

Somalia

Ethiopia

Guinea-Bissau

Nigeria

Sierra Leone

Central African Republic

Liberia

Congo

Uganda

Ivory Coast

Gabon

Democratic Republic of Congo (formerly Zaire)

Kenya

Ghana

Rwanda

Togo

Burundi

Benin

Tanzania

Cameroon

São Tomé and Principe

Río Muni

Angola

Zambia

Cabinda

Zimbabwe

Madagascar

Namibia

Botswana

Malawi

Mozambique

South Africa

Lesotho

Swaziland

ASIA AND AUSTRALIA

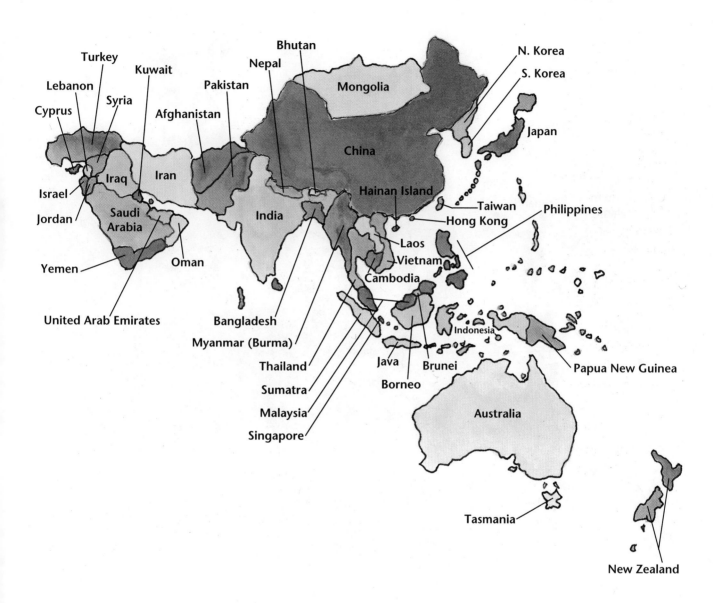

EUROPE

NORTH AMERICA, CENTRAL AMERICA, AND SOUTH AMERICA

UNITED STATES OF AMERICA (U.S.A.) AND CANADA

Alaska

Yukon Territory

Northwest Territories

British Columbia

Alberta

Saskatchewan

Manitoba

Ontario

Quebec

Newfoundland

Nova Scotia

New Brunswick

Washington

Oregon

Montana

North Dakota

Minnesota

Michigan

Vermont

Maine

Idaho

Wyoming

South Dakota

Wisconsin

New Hampshire

Massachusetts

New York

Rhode Island

Connecticut

California

Nevada

Utah

Nebraska

Iowa

Illinois

Indiana

Ohio

Pennsylvania

New Jersey

Delaware

Maryland

West Virginia

Arizona

Colorado

Kansas

Missouri

Kentucky

Tennessee

Virginia

New Mexico

Oklahoma

Arkansas

North Carolina

South Carolina

Texas

Georgia

Louisiana

Mississippi

Alabama

Florida

Hawaii

SPEECH EVALUATION FORM

Speaker's Name: _____

Date: _____

Speech Topic: _____

	Needs Work	Satisfactory
Organization	_____	_____
Pronunciation	_____	_____
Vocabulary	_____	_____
Eye Contact	_____	_____
Visual Aids	_____	_____

Best Part of Speech: _____

Recommendations:_____

Evaluator's Name: _____

AUDIENCE EVALUATION FORM

Speaker's Name: _____

Date: _____

Speech Topic: _____

	Needs Work	Satisfactory
Attentiveness	_____	_____
Quietness	_____	_____
Eye Contact	_____	_____
Appropriateness of Questions	_____	_____
Form of Questions	_____	_____
Number of Questions	_____	_____
Responsiveness	_____	_____

Recommendations: _____

_____

Evaluator's Name: _____

ACTIVITIES GUIDE

All of the activities in **A CONVERSATION BOOK 2**, Third Edition, as in earlier editions, are student-centered. In this edition, there are many new activities that have been structured to utilize information gaps or opinion gaps. Many activities are task-based, and all are designed to require real communication. The activities fall into three major groups: Class Activities, Group Activities, and Partner Activities. We are including here abbreviated suggestions for teaching all types of activities in the student text. For more specific suggestions for individual activities, consult the Teacher's Edition.

CLASS ACTIVITIES

Working as a whole class fosters an atmosphere of cohesion and safety. For the introduction of the lesson, it assures that all students have access to the information for the activities ahead. Other class activities take advantage of the large group for multiple opinions and experiences, especially in community activities. Any of these activities can be done in groups, if you prefer. If you are doing so, use groups of 10 to 15 students to allow for multiple input.

Class Discussion

OBJECTIVE: *To discuss individual questions as a whole class; to have students learn to understand and respect different opinions and viewpoints.*
Discuss these questions with your class. Does everyone agree?

- Ask the questions and call on different students to answer. Involve as many students as possible in the discussion. Write new vocabulary on the board as the situation allows. If there are students from different cultures, use the information to draw conclusions and teach students about different ways of life. To help structure discussions and teach note-taking skills, write a brief heading for each question on the board. Encourage students to do the same in the Activities section of their notebooks.
- Under each heading, list information you gather from the discussions.
- Review your notes and ask the students to review theirs. Together as a class at the end of the discussion, draw conclusions from the notes .

Class Game: Guess Who/What

OBJECTIVE: *To give students practice guessing through clues and prior knowledge. (This activity can be modified to be a Total Physical Response activity.)*
On a slip of paper, write. . . Make a pile. Pick a paper. Read it to the class. (Guess who wrote it!) (Ask for the answer. Whoever answers correctly picks the next paper.)

- Hand out slips of paper.
- Tell the class to write. . .
- Have students fold their slips of paper and make a pile on your desk.
- Open the first one. Read it. Guess who wrote it. (Or ask for the response.)
- Either have that student choose the next slip of paper or call on another student to choose.
- Continue as long as time and/or interest allows.

Class Survey

OBJECTIVE: *To encourage students to voice opinions and preferences, to compare their preferences with those of classmates, and to check accuracy in listening and recording answers.*
With your class, review this list of. . . Add one more. . . Interview your classmates. Report your findings to the class.

- Model the questions; have students repeat; check pronunciation. Together as a class, add one more item. Be sure students understand all the vocabulary and the objective of the activity before the activity begins.
- Have students check off their own answers in the appropriate column.
- Instruct students to circulate and ask their classmates the questions.
- Have students report their results to the class. While students are working, copy the chart on the board.
- Fill in the columns on the chart. Have students draw conclusions about the survey.
- Point out new words and have students write them in the Vocabulary section of their notebooks.

Community Activity

OBJECTIVE: *To broaden students' horizons through discovering the uses of English outside the classroom.*

Instructions will vary.

- Review the task before you ask students to work independently. These tasks can be intimidating at first; students who perform well in class may still worry about using their English outside the classroom.
- To help prepare students, role-play expected outcomes. If possible, the first time out, travel as a class to give the students confidence.
- After the assignment is completed, review in class not only the task but what happened— surprises, reactions, feelings, etc.
- Have students keep important community information in the Community sections of their notebooks.
- In an EFL class, if need be, have students do the research in their first language and then translate. Have students use the opportunity to explore where English is used in their own country and culture. This activity will give students an insight into how important the study of English is, even in the midst of their own familiar surroundings! Follow up the lesson with appropriate writing activities from **A WRITING BOOK.**

Find Someone Who

OBJECTIVE: *To encourage students to share personal information with classmates; to have students practice creating and asking yes/no questions*

Add two more items. Then interview your classmates and find someone who . . This activity is similar to the Survey activity, except that in Find Someone Who, students are searching for "Yes" answers.

- Review the vocabulary and create the Yes/No questions with the class before they start the activity. Write the questions on the board.
- Give students the grammar constructions in chunks. Review appropriate grammar from the Appendix.
- Have the class ask the questions by circulating around the class. If the class is very large, break the class into groups of 10 to 15 and have students do the activity within their group.
- When students have completed their work, have them sit in their seats.
- Review the questions and answers. Individual answers should provide interesting springboards for conversation.

School or Community Survey

OBJECTIVE: *To gather specific survey information outside class, report back, and analyze the results.*

Ask three people (in your school) these questions. Fill in the chart. Report their answers to the class. What are the total class results of the poll? (Do you see any trends?)

- Model the questions; have students repeat; check pronunciation. Together as a class, add one more item.
- Be sure students understand all the vocabulary and the objective of the activity. Discuss possible people they can survey and ways to introduce themselves and the survey.
- Rehearse together in class.
- Have students gather their information, either in the school or out in the community.
- Have students report their results, either individually to the class or to a group first, and then in groups to the whole class.
- As a class, review the results. Help students note trends. Take advantage of any conversation topics.

Speech

OBJECTIVE: *To give students practice in organizing thoughts, preparing, and giving speeches.* Instructions will vary.

- Read the instructions aloud.
- Write the outline for a very brief speech on the board. Explain how to write an outline rather than writing out every word.
- Model the speech. Make students aware of the time limit. Have students prepare speeches at home. Help students correct their speeches. Suggest they prepare note cards so they won't be reading the speeches. Help them limit their speech to the time limit.
- Have students practice their speech with you or in small groups. Have the listeners give helpful hints on how to improve the speech. Give some hints yourself. Always phrase feedback in a positive way to encourage students and boost their confidence and self-esteem.
- Assign different students to be evaluators for different speakers.
- Evaluate the speech also. Point out general errors and problems without singling out any students.

Who Else?

OBJECTIVE: *To have students identify with some of the questions; to have students find others who identify with any of the same questions.*

With your class, add more choices. Check all the choices that apply to you. Then find classmates who have checked the same choices. Make a class chart on the board.

- Review the items with the class.
- Check for understanding of the vocabulary and the instructions. Draw a class chart (like the one in the text) on the board that is large enough to include every student's name.
- Elicit more choices. These choices will be added to the students' charts. Encourage new vocabulary.
- Allow students time to check their choices in their charts.
- Have students circulate the room, interviewing their classmates.
- When they have finished the activity, have them return to their seats.
- Have students transfer their information to the class chart on the board. Include your own responses as part of the class.
- In reviewing the activity, encourage common ground in the students. Take advantage of interesting cultural information that may emerge. Have students write new vocabulary words in the Vocabulary section of their notebooks.

GROUP ACTIVITIES

These activities promote cooperation and information exchange, as well as the opportunity to share knowledge and develop understanding in a small group setting. If possible, mix language groups and ability levels. Separate friends. Small groups encourage maximum participation before sharing discoveries with the class. Have students appoint a conversation monitor and a recorder.

Advantages/Disadvantages

OBJECTIVE: *To guide students in making judgments, voicing opinions, and analyzing in a small group.*

In groups of. . . , list the advantages and disadvantages of. . . Share your information with another group. Report the most interesting ideas to the class.

- Explain the issues.
- Divide the class into groups.
- Have each group choose a conversation monitor and a recorder. Have students discuss the issues and fill out their charts. Circulate; help as needed.
- As students are doing the task, draw the chart on the board. Ask groups to report on the results of their discussion. Fill out the chart accordingly.
- Take advantage of any interesting information that arises in the discussion to talk more about the topics.

Conversation Squares

OBJECTIVE: *To have students work cooperatively in groups of three to fill out a chart on various topics and to classify information.*

In groups of three, answer the questions. First write your own answers. Then ask your partners the questions and write their answers. Discuss your differences. Compare your group's answers with another group.

- Have students help create the questions they will ask. Write the questions on the board.
- Construct a chart on the board similar to the one in the text.
- Choose two "partners" to demonstrate. Take the "You" column for yourself.
- Put the names of your partners at the top of the chart as indicated in the text.
- Fill in your column. Ask and answer the questions as you fill out your partner's information.
- Ask others in the class the questions for more practice.
- Divide the class into groups of three and have the groups do the activity.
- When all of the groups have finished, ask different groups individual questions from the conversation squares.
- Write new vocabulary on the board for students to copy in the Vocabulary section of their notebooks.

Cross-Cultural Exchange

OBJECTIVE: *To encourage exchange of information about students' cultures; to compare cultural similarities and differences; to let students voice opinions and confusion about cultures associated with English; to encourage intercultural openness and awareness without judgment.*

In groups of. . . , choose a conversation monitor and a recorder. Discuss these questions. Compare cultures when possible. Have the recorder report the results of your discussion to the class.

- Divide the class into the suggested groups. Have each group appoint a conversation monitor and a recorder. If necessary, remind students about the function of each.
- Either have the conversation monitor ask the questions, or have students take turns asking and answering the questions. Circulate; help as needed.
- Be sure everyone's culture is represented in the discussion.
- Whenever possible, have students teach their group something interesting about their native culture, either how to say something in their native language or an interesting cultural note. This validates students' backgrounds, fosters self-esteem, and is essential in building a humanistic classroom.
- At the end of the group activity, bring the class together. Have the recorders report to the class on the results of the discussions.

Finish the Story

OBJECTIVE: *To have students work cooperatively in groups; to use creativity to complete a story and use new vocabulary.*

In groups of. . . , create an ending for this story. Then tell your ending to another group (or to the class). Answer these questions in your ending (questions will vary).

- Divide the class into the suggested groups.
- Read the instructions together.
- Go over the questions to answer, if applicable.
- Choose a conversation monitor and a recorder for each group.
- Combine groups to share endings if the class is large or if time is short. Otherwise, have each group report to the class.

Group Brainstorm

OBJECTIVE: *To encourage students to think about topics without bounds of "right" or "wrong." To tap into their prior knowledge and build skills from there.*

In groups of. . . , list all. . . Read your list to the class. Write the new words in the Vocabulary section of your notebook.

- Present the topic to be discussed.
- Explain the concept of "brainstorming"—allowing for the free flow of ideas without worrying about being restricted.
- Divide the class into groups.
- Have each group choose a recorder who will be responsible for writing down all the words or ideas.
- Instruct the groups to call out to the recorder words or ideas associated with the topic.
- Remind students to work quietly and not to comment on or judge anything being said.
- When the list is completed, have the recorders read the list to their groups.
- Advise the groups to edit their lists.
- Ask each recorder to read his/her group's list to the class. Make a class list on the board.
- Have students write any new words in the Vocabulary section of their notebooks.
- Keep the list on the board for further reference in the lesson.

Group Decision

OBJECTIVE: *To encourage sharing of preferences and opinions; to have students work cooperatively to reach consensus in situations where group members have differing preferences and opinions.*

In groups of. . . , decide. . . Report your decisions to the class. Explain why you made your decisions.

- Divide the class into groups.
- Read the instructions together.
- Be sure students understand what to do. Explain the concept of "compromise."
- Have each group agree on a decision. Circulate; help as needed.
- When the groups have completed their work, have them report their decisions to the class.

Group Discussion

OBJECTIVE: *To integrate new vocabulary into the context of students' experiences; to have students talk in small groups about an issue and to research answers; to teach them how to listen to other students, take notes, and report findings.*

In groups of. . . , answer these questions. Research any question you are not sure of. Share your information with another group. Report your answers to the class.

- Divide the class into the suggested groups. Have each group appoint a conversation monitor and a recorder. Circulate; help as needed.

- Help students use the information from their discussions to draw conclusions and learn about different ways of doing things and different ways of life.
- To help structure the conversations and teach note-taking skills, write a brief heading for each question on the board. Encourage students to do the same in the Activities section of their notebooks.
- Under each heading, list information you gather from the discussion reports.
- Review your notes and ask the students to review theirs.
- Have the recorders report the results of the discussions to the class.
- Together as a class, draw conclusions from the notes.

Group Problem Posing/Solving

OBJECTIVE: *To guide students in stating a problem; to have them work cooperatively to find a solution and to share solutions with the class.*

In groups of. . . , state each problem. What advice would you give? Report your solutions to the class.

- Divide the class into the suggested groups. Have each group choose a recorder. Instruct the groups to first decide what the problem is and how to state it clearly in one or two sentences.
- Have the recorder write down the problem. Tell the groups to decide on a solution for the problem. Circulate; help as needed.
- Have each recorder state the problem and the solution to the class.
- Have the class decide how to state the problem best and which solutions are workable.

Group Questions

OBJECTIVE: *To have students practice formulating questions; to have them ask and answer questions with another group.*

In groups of. . . , write as many questions as you can about. . . Ask another group your questions. Then answer their questions. (Read your questions to the class. Make a class list on the board. How many different questions did the class have?)

- Divide the class into small groups, each with a conversation monitor.
- Either ask the questions yourself or ask different students to ask the questions and call on various students to answer.
- Be sure all students have the opportunity to participate. Circulate; help as needed.
- As new vocabulary and important grammatical phrases arise, list them on the board.
- Have groups read their questions to the class.
- Create a class list of the questions on the board.
- Have groups ask each other some of the questions.
- When the activity has been completed, point out the new vocabulary to the students. Have them write new words and phrases in the Vocabulary section of their notebooks.

Group Role Play

OBJECTIVE: *To teach students to collaborate and create a scenario based on the conversation topic and act it out; to have them practice both verbal and non-verbal communication.*

In groups of. . ., create a role play. . .Present your role play to the class.

- Read the instructions with the class to be sure everyone understands what to do.
- Create a sample role play with the class. Act it out with volunteers.
- Ask students to write a script for some role plays; other times, have them plan the action without a script and present it extemporaneously for fluency practice.
- Divide the class into the suggested groups. Have each group plan their own role play. Circulate; help as needed.

- Have several groups present their role plays to the class.
- Note on the board any new vocabulary that arises from the role plays.
- Have students copy new words and phrases in the Vocabulary section of their notebooks.
- Discuss any interesting topics that arise during the presentations.

Group Survey

OBJECTIVE: *To have students collaborate first on the answers, then compare their answers with the whole class.*

In groups of four, answer these questions. Choose a recorder to write your answers and report to the class. What experiences do your classmates have in common? Who has a unique experience to tell about?

- Divide the class into groups of four.
- Review the questions with the class; check for understanding.
- Have groups appoint a recorder and a conversation monitor.
- Have the conversation monitor ask the questions and the recorder write the answers.
- Circulate; help where needed.
- Have each group report their answers to the class.
- Draw conclusions, make comparisons. Use the information as a springboard for discussion.

Group Vocabulary Challenge

OBJECTIVE: *To practice in combining brainstorming with discrete vocabulary recall. Cooperation and collaboration are needed to successfully complete the contest.*

In groups of. . ., list. . . Work quickly! Read your list to the class. Which group has the longest list? Make a class list on the board. Copy the new words in the Vocabulary section of your notebook.

- Divide the class into the suggested groups. If applicable, allow students to look at the illustration(s), then close their texts. (Some Challenges use the illustrations in the text, some don't.)
- Instruct students to use a page in the Vocabulary section of their notebook. Have students choose a recorder to write down the words they dictate. Give students a time allotment to complete the task. Use a stopwatch to time the contest! Circulate; help as needed.
- Remind the recorder to number the words as they are written, and to tally the total at the end of the time frame.
- Have the recorders either read the lists or write them on the board.
- Have students write the new words or phrases in the Vocabulary section of their notebooks.

Share Your Story

OBJECTIVE: *To create an awareness that everyone has a story to tell; to have the class share interesting stories and anecdotes about their own lives.*

In groups of. . . , tell about. . . Decide which story to tell the class. (Use these questions as a guide.)

- Divide the class into the suggested groups.
- Read the instructions together; check for understanding.
- If the activity includes guide questions, review the questions.
- Have students think about any experiences they have had concerning the topic.
- Encourage them to make notes before they speak so that they will remember the details.
- Circulate; help as needed.
- Have each group choose one story to tell the class.
- Have the groups help the individual student practice the story before telling the class.

Superlatives

OBJECTIVE: *To have students share and compare personal information; to have students practice creating questions and discover superlatives.*

In groups of. . . , answer these questions. Choose a recorder. Report your answers to the class.

- Divide the class into suggested groups and choose recorders.
- Read the questions together with the class.
- Ask the class what key questions they need to ask in their groups to find the superlatives.
- Write the key questions on the board. Circulate; help the groups as needed.
- Have groups report to the class.
- Decide on superlatives for the whole class.

What do you do if. . . ?

OBJECTIVE: *To have students analyze situations cooperatively and to decide on solutions to everyday dilemmas; to pool their knowledge, come to consensus, and report to the class.*

In groups of. . . , decide what to do in each situation. Share your answers with the class.

- Divide the class into the suggested groups.
- Read the problem(s) together; check for understanding. Have students appoint a recorder who will write down the solution(s) to be read to the class.
- Encourage maximum participation of all group members. Circulate; help as needed.
- Have the recorders read the groups' suggestions to the dilemmas.
- Note any new vocabulary on the board and have students write it in the Vocabulary section of their notebooks.

What do you say? What do you do?

OBJECTIVE: *To allow students the chance to try out new phrases and behavior; to have them decide what to say and what to do in everyday situations with the help of the group.*

In groups of. . . , decide what to say and do in each situation. Compare your decisions with the class.

- Divide the class into the suggested groups.
- Read the situation together; check for understanding.
- Have students work together to decide what they would do in the various situations. More than one solution is acceptable. Circulate; help as needed.
- Have several groups tell the class the results of their discussion.

What's the Story?

OBJECTIVE: *To have students work cooperatively to write a story based on the lesson's topic.*

In groups of. . . , tell a story about one of the scenes. Choose a conversation monitor and a recorder. Everyone in the group should contribute. . . .Edit the story. Tell your story to the class.

- Divide students into the suggested groups. Have students read the directions and look at the illustration, if applicable.
- Have each group select a conversation monitor and a recorder.
- Encourage students to help each other. Try to have even the reluctant or shy students participate by contributing sentences. Circulate; help as needed.
- After the stories are written, have all groups listen to their recorder read the story, make changes and corrections, and edit their story. Have each group decide whether their recorder will read the story or whether each student will read his or her sentence in turn.
- Photocopy the stories and distribute them in class the next day for students to read. Decide on categories: Which was the funniest? the saddest? the longest? the shortest? Which used the most new vocabulary words? Etc.

PARTNER ACTIVITIES

Partner activities are important because they foster face-to-face communication, one on one. Each student should get to talk 50 percent of the time and should maximize the opportunity to hold solid conversations.

Dialog Journal

OBJECTIVE: *To let students practice expressing feelings and experiences and sharing these thoughts with a partner; to have the partner respond in conversation and/or in writing.*

Write a journal entry about. . . Read your journal entry to a partner. Write a response to your partner's entry.

- Explain the task and encourage freedom of expression.
- Tell students they are going to write a dialog journal entry, then give it to a partner. The partner will respond in writing, so students have to leave space in their entry for their partner's response.
- Be sure one section of the students' notebook is labeled Dialog Journal.
- Have students do their Dialog Journal writing in class or at home.
- Have them exchange entries with a partner.
- Have the partner respond to the written selection in writing, setting up a "dialog journal." Or collect the journals and construct a dialog journal with each student. Respond with encouragement and positive feedback to their writing.

Draw with a Partner

OBJECTIVE: *To have students practice listening to a partner and follow directions; to discuss their drawings; to allow students to express their artistic creativity and to express their thoughts and feelings without words.*

Instructions will vary. Draw. . . Explain your drawing to your partner.

- Explain the tasks to the class. Check for understanding. Provide a model of what is expected. Sometimes, the worse your own art is, the better. Students will be less reluctant to share theirs if yours isn't very good.
- Divide the class into pairs, and have partners do the activity.
- Circulate; help as needed. At the same time, scout students who may be particularly skilled in drawing and will be able to share a useful drawing, either on the board, on a transparency, or on photocopies. Have several pairs report to the class on what they drew. Note new vocabulary words for students to copy into the Vocabulary section of their notebooks.

Partner Activity: *Dear Aunt Betty*

OBJECTIVE: *To have students practice analyzing personal situations and to either ask for or give advice.*

With a partner, read and discuss this letter. Together, write a response from Aunt Betty, giving advice to. . . Read your letter to the class.

- Read the problem letter together. Check for understanding.
- Divide the class into pairs.
- Have partners discuss the problem and figure out solutions. Circulate; help as needed.
- Have each pair read their solution to Aunt Betty's column.

With a partner, write to Aunt Betty, asking for advice about a. . . problem. Exchange the letter with another pair. Respond to their letter. Read their letter and your response to the class.

- Divide the class into pairs.
- Have partners decide what problem to write to Aunt Betty about and compose their letter.

- Combine pairs into groups of four.
- Have groups exchange letters and write a response. When groups have completed their task, ask several groups to read the letters to Aunt Betty and Aunt Betty's responses.

Partner Game: *"What do you remember?"*

OBJECTIVE: *To have students practice observation skills and remembering details.*

Look at (one of) the scene(s) with your partner. Remember as much as you can. Close your books. Describe the scene with your partner. List everything you can remember. Open your books and look at the scene. What did you forget?

- Discuss strategies for students to remember the details of the illustrations. Then have students close their texts.
- Divide the class into pairs.
- When all pairs have completed the activity, have them open their books and compare their lists with the illustration.
- Have several groups report their results to the class. Take notes on the board. Which pair had the longest list?

Partner Interview

OBJECTIVE: *To give students practice asking and answering, listening to and restating answers about a partner's experiences, and restating their partner's responses to other students.*

Ask a partner these questions. Then report your partner's responses to another pair of students (or to the class).

- If necessary, practice the interview questions with the students. Be sure they understand the questions and the vocabulary. Supply additional words as needed.
- Divide the class into pairs.
- Have students interview their partners. Circulate; help as needed.
- After the students conduct their interviews, have them report their partners' answers and responses to another pair.
- On the board, write new vocabulary generated from the interviews. Have students copy the new words in the Vocabulary section of their notebooks. Use the students' responses to the questions in the interviews for further discussions that may be of interest to the class.

Partner Questions

OBJECTIVE: *To give students practice formulating questions; to have them answer the questions formed; to work cooperatively with another pair with practice asking and answering.*

Write. . . questions. Ask another pair your questions. Present your questions and answers to the class.

- Explain the task.
- If necessary, do some practice question formations with the class. Divide the class into pairs.
- Allow a sufficient time frame for pairs to form their questions.
- If the activity calls for a role play, have students create a role play. Or, combine pairs into groups of four.
- Have groups ask and answer their questions. Circulate; help as needed.
- If applicable, have several pairs present their role plays to the class.

Partner Role Play

OBJECTIVE: *To have students practice and present one-on-one conversations: telephone calls, interviews, and interactions in everyday situations.*

With a partner, choose a situation. Create a role play. Present your role play to the class/to another pair.

- Divide the class into pairs.
- Generate the vocabulary needed. Leave the vocabulary on the board as a reference.
- Have students write "scripts" for their role plays. Explain that correct grammar and usage are important in formal business telephone conversations and interviews. Alternatively, have students do a more extemporaneous role play by discussing what they will say and presenting it without a script.
- Have students practice reading their "scripts" with the "read and look up" technique. (Scan the line; remember it as accurately as possible; SAY the line, don't read it. This technique helps with appropriate eye contact and body language required in English.)
- Call on several pairs to present their role plays to the class.

Partner Vocabulary Challenge

OBJECTIVE: *To have students practice combining brainstorming with discrete vocabulary recall between partners.*

With a partner, list. . . Compare your list with another pair. Combine lists. Read your combined list to the class. Which group has the longest list?

- Divide the class into pairs.
- Instruct students to use a page in the Vocabulary section of their notebooks.
- Give students a time allotment to complete the task. Circulate; help as needed.
- Remind students to number the words as they are written, and to tally the total at the end of the time frame.
- Have pairs combine their list with another pair.
- Ask groups of four to read their combined lists or write them on the board. Determine which group had the longest list. Have students add the new words and phrases to the Vocabulary section of their notebooks.

Write with a Partner

OBJECTIVE: *To have students work cooperatively to complete a written task and compare results with another pair.*

Instructions will vary.

- Explain the task to the class.
- Divide the class into pairs and have the pairs complete the task.
- Combine pairs into groups of four.
- Have groups work together to compare notes. Have groups report to the class on the results of their discussion.

ALPHABETICAL WORD LIST TO PICTURE DICTIONARY

credit risk, 172
credit union, 170
crib, 50
crime in the news, 190
crime watch, 124
criminal, 190
crisis, 20
crisp, 26
critical condition, 96
crunchy, 26
crush, 166
cultural, 34
culture, 34
curb, 130
curiosity, 32
curious, 32
current, 112
current event, 182
custom, 34
customized, 108
customs, 142
customs declaration form, 142
cut class, 52
cut in line, 14
cut off, 112

D

daily, 24
daily commute, 128
damage, 116
damaged, 78
dangerous, 32
date, 46
day care, 66
daydream, 38
daydreamer, 38
day surgery, 96
dead, 60
deadline, 174
deadly, 184
deadly weapon, 190
death, 20
debate, 198
debt, 172
decent condition, 114
decision, 58
decline, 16
decorate, 108
dedicated, 192
deductible, 174
deduction, 170
defective, 78
defend, 190
defendant, 190
defense, 190
dehydrate, 90
dehydration, 90
delay, 14
delicate, 118
delicious, 26
delightful, 36

deliver, 50
deliver newspapers, 120
delivery room, 50
democracy, 198
democratic, 198
demonstrate, 164
demonstration, 164
dent, 132
dental coverage, 158
depart, 140
dependency, 102
dependent, 174
dependent coverage, 158
deserve, 10
design, 146
despair, 102
desperation, 102
destination, 140
destroy, 184
destruction, 184
destructive, 56
detention, 80
determination, 38
determined, 28
detour, 128
devastating, 184
diagonal, 64
diagonally, 64
dial tone, 112
dictator, 198
dictatorship, 198
die, 60
die for, 192
diet pills, 88
difference, 24
dilapidated, 122
dilemma, 78
diligent, 166
dining car, 140
direct deposit, 170
directions, 64
director, 156
disagree, 58
disagreement, 58
disciplinary action, 80
discipline, 80
disciplined, 56
discontinue, 112
discount store, 76
discourteous, 166
discuss, 40
discussion, 40
disembarkation card, 142
dishonest, 54
dishw. (dishwasher), 110
disinfect, 100
disinfectant, 100
disloyal, 30
disobedient, 54
disobey, 54
disorderly, 56
disorganized, 24

disposable income, 172
disrepair, 122
disrespect, 54
disrupt, 14
dissatisfaction, 78
dissatisfied, 78
distract, 56
distraction, 56
distressed, 140
distrust, 120
distrustful, 120
divorce, 58
divorce lawyer, 58
dn. pmnt. (down payment), 110
dog bite, 116
doing a good job, 166
dolly, 70
(do not) induce vomiting, 100
Don't worry, 12
door knocker, 120
door-to-door, 120
dosage, 98
dose, 98
double-check, 164
double-park, 14
dramatic, 36
dreadful, 36
dream, 38
dream (n), 38
dreamer, 38
dress code, 80
dressing (bandage), 96
drinking problem, 102
driver education, 130
driver license, 130
driving instructor, 130
driving manual, 130
driving under the influence, 132
drought, 184
drowsiness, 92
drowsy, 92
drug, 98
druggist, 98
drugstore, 98
drunk driving, 132
dry up, 184
dump, 68
dumpsite, 194
durable, 76
dwelling, 116

E

eager, 162
early retirement, 158
earn, 170
earthquake, 184
ease of shopping, 74
economical, 134
economize, 172

economy car, 134
ecstatic, 180
educated, 6
education, 6
educational, 56
efficient, 70
elated, 180
elderly, 60
elec. (electricity), 110
elect, 198
election, 198
elective, 82
electrical storm, 68
electricity, 68
electric wires, 68
electronic mail (e-mail), 70
elegant, 74
elementary school, 64
elementary school teacher, 152
embarkation card, 142
embarrassed, 162
embarrassing, 36
embrace, 180
emergency care, 66
emission, 132
employee contribution, 170
employment, 6
employment agency, 154
employment counselor, 154
empty calories, 88
empty stomach, 98
encourage, 56
encouragement, 56
energetic, 28
energy, 88
engagement, 46
English, 83
entertain, 188
entertainer, 188
entertaining, 188
entertainment, 146
entertainment expenses, 172
entertainment news, 188
enthusiasm, 162
enthusiastic, 162
entry level, 154
envious, 30
environment, 68
erupt, 184
eruption, 184
escape, 184
evacuate, 184
evacuation, 184
event, 10
exact change lane, 138
examining room, 94
excel. (excellent), 110
excessive, 88

haste, 162
hasty, 162
haul, 118
have a baby, 50
Have a nice day., 2
Have you met. . .?, 2
hay fever, 90
hazard, 90
hazardous, 100
headline, 182
head-on collision, 194
headset, 40
health care industry, 146
health care provider, 96
health hazard, 194
health insurance card, 96
health insurance plan, 96
health risk, 88
hearing aid, 72
hearing loss, 60
heart medicine, 98
heart-rending, 36
heartwarming, 36
heat exhaustion, 90
heating pad, 92
heavy equipment
  operator, 152
heavy traffic, 128
Hello./Hi., 2
help out, 124
help wanted sign, 154
hem, 78
herb, 92
herbal tea, 92
heritage, 34
hero, 192
heroic, 192
heroism, 192
high-rise, 106
highway, 138
highway patrol, 138
hijack, 196
hike, 136
hiker, 136
hire, 156
history, 34
hitchhike, 16
hitchhiker, 16
HMO (Health Maintenance
  Organization), 96
home assignment, 52
homecoming, 180
home delivery, 70
homeless, 122
homeless shelter, 66
homeowner, 116
home remedy, 92
home shopping channel,
  74
honest, 54
honeymoon, 46
honor, 192

hope, 38
hope (n), 38
hospitalize, 96
hospital worker, 150
hostage, 196
hot water heater, 112
household chemical, 100
household cleaner, 100
household goods, 118
household poison, 100
housing development, 106
How are you?, 2
ht. (heat), 110
hug, 180
human interest story, 194
humanitarian, 196
human resources, 156
hurricane, 184
hurry, 24
hysterical, 36

I
I believe you've already
  met. . ., 2
icy, 90
identical, 44
identification bracelet, 96
identity, 34
I'd like you to meet. . ., 2
ignite, 168
illegal dumping, 194
illness, 92
illustrate, 164
illustration, 164
imaginary, 32
imagination, 33
imagine, 38
I'm fine, thanks., 2
immigration, 142
immune, 94
immunization, 94
immunize, 94
impatience, 162
impatient, 14
impolite, 14
impractical, 76
impress, 172
improve, 102
improvement, 102
I'm sorry., 12
I'm sorry I'm late., 12
incl. (included), 110
income, 158
income tax, 174
in common, 44
incompatible, 58
incomplete, 78
inconsiderate, 14
incredible, 36
independent, 152
independent study, 40
in distress, 16

indoor sport, 186
industrious, 166
industry, 146
inexperienced, 130
infant, 50
infatuation, 46
infection, 94
infectious disease, 94
inflammable, 168
in-flight call, 72
in-flight meal, 142
influence, 56
inform, 140
informal, 2
information board, 140
information booth, 140
ingest, 100
initiative, 166
injure, 96
injury, 96
in labor, 50
in love, 46
in mourning, 20
inner city, 122
innocent, 190
inoculate, 94
inpatient, 96
inquire, 154
inquisitive, 28
insect, 90
insecticide, 100
insensitive, 30
insert, 92
insincere, 30
inspector, 150
instruct, 40
instruction, 40
instruction manual, 164
instructions at work, 164
instructor, 66
insurance adjustor, 116
insurance coverage, 116
insurance deduction, 170
insurance policy, 158
insurance premium, 158
intentional, 12
interested, 166
interesting, 152
Internal Revenue Service
  (IRS), 174
international competition,
  186
international incident, 196
Internet, 40
interrupt, 14
intersection, 64
interstate, 138
interview, 156
interviewer, 156
in time of need, 20
intimidate, 162
intimidating, 162

intoxicated, 132
intoxication, 132
intramural sport, 80
introduction, 2
introductory offer, 74
introverted, 28
invitation, 16
invite, 16
ironing board, 112
irreconcilable differences,
  58
irresponsible, 30
irritate, 100
irritation, 100
issue, 130
itch, 90
itchy, 90
item number, 74
It's my pleasure to
  introduce. . ., 2
It was nice to meet you., 2

J
jack, 132
jack up, 132
jail, 190
jealous, 30
job application, 156
job lead, 154
job listing, 154
job offer, 156
job opening, 154
job qualification, 154
job reference, 156
job search, 154
jobs in your community,
  146
job training, 152
join, 80
joint custody, 58
judge, 58
juicy, 26
junk, 122
juror, 190
jury, 190
justice, 190

K
keyboard, 70
kidnap, 194
kind, 30
kitch. (kitchen), 110
kitchen cleaner, 100
kneeling bus, 128
knock over, 130
knowledgeable, 162

L
laboratory, 168
labor union, 170
land, 106
landlady, 114